Teaching and Learning Vocabulary

Bringing Research to Practice

Teaching and Learning Vocabulary

Bringing Research to Practice

Edited by

Elfrieda H. Hiebert
University of California, Berkeley

Michael L. Kamil
Stanford University

2005

LAWRENCE ERLBAUM ASSOCIATES, PUBLISHERS
Mahwah, New Jersey   London

Lawrence Erlbaum Associates, Inc., Publishers
10 Industrial Avenue
Mahwah, New Jersey 07430
www.erlbaum.com

Cover design by Kathryn Houghtaling Lacey

Library of Congress Cataloging-in-Publication Data

Teaching and learning vocabulary : bringing research to practice
/ edited by Elfrieda H. Hiebert, Michael L. Kamil
    p. cm.
Includes bibliographical references and index.
ISBN 0-8058-5285-9 (cloth : alk. paper)
ISBN 0-8058-5286-7 (pbk. : alk. Paper)
   1. Vocabulary—Study and teaching. 2. Language Arts.
   I. Hiebert, Elfrieda H.   II. Kamil, Michael L.

LB1574.4 T42 2005
372.61—dc22   2004057708
                                       CIP

Printed in the United States of America
10 9 8 7 6 5 4 3

Dedicated to the memory of our friend and colleague,
Steven A. Stahl (1951–2004)

Contents

Preface

In early 2002, colleagues from the Pacific Resources for Education and Learning (PREL) asked us to facilitate a series of conferences as part of a national leadership initiative on reading/language mastery within the Regional Educational Laboratory system. At that time, the report of the National Reading Panel had been available for 18 months. Discussion on listservs and at conferences about the phonemic awareness and phonics section of the report had been extensive. For the educational leaders within states and districts at whom the national leadership initiative on reading/language mastery was aimed, we reasoned that it was also critical to focus attention on the other three topics of the report—fluency, vocabulary, and comprehension. Consequently, over the next 3 years, PREL held forums for educational leaders that focused on fluency (2002), vocabulary (2003), and comprehension (2004).

The core group of chapters in this volume originated from presentations at the forum on vocabulary that was held in Dallas, Texas on October 1–2, 2003. In designing the conference and this volume, we were particularly interested in addressing those areas that the National Reading Panel had identified as requiring investigation. As the report of the National Reading Panel and the content of chapters in this volume illustrate, vocabulary holds a special place among the five literacy components of reading. First, vocabulary is not a developmental skill or one that can be seen as ever fully mastered. The expansion and elaboration of vocabularies—whether speaking, listening, reading, or writing—can be expected to extend across a lifetime. It is difficult, if not impossible, to separate vocabulary from comprehension.

The chapters cluster around three persistent issues in the learning and teaching of vocabulary: (a) how are words learned and taught as a function of word features, content areas, and developmental levels? (b) how do vocabulary interventions differ for different age groups and content areas? and (c) what words should be emphasized in instruction?

We identified scholars whose programs of research address one or more of these questions. These programs of research have been recognized by national panels and editorial boards of archival journals. Scholars were asked to summarize the findings that have resulted from these programs of work, including studies that may be ongoing, and to describe the implications of these findings for educators who are responsible for implementing state and federal policies in state and district agencies, and for researchers who are beginning programs of work on vocabulary. As will become evident in reading the chapters, many of these scholars are considering the nature of vocabulary learning in relation to the diversity that is present in many current-day classrooms.

There are many people who collaborate in making an endeavor such as this one successful. The authors of the chapters responded with alacrity and graciousness to our deadlines. As a result, this volume is available to educational leaders and researchers in a timely fashion. We would not be publishing this volume without the continued faith of Lane Akers of Lawrence Erlbaum Associates (LEA) in our work and also his ongoing patience. Sara Scudder at LEA has been the most efficient production editor with whom we have had the pleasure of working. Fran Lehr and Laurie Clark Klavins were instrumental in ensuring that Sara and her colleagues at LEA received a carefully edited manuscript. We also recognize the colleagues who have been part of our effort on a day-to-day basis: Alice Folkins, Charles Fisher, and Diana Arya. They have checked and rechecked texts, contacted and re-contacted authors, and coded and recoded materials to ensure accurate author and topic indices. We are thankful for their efforts.

Our colleagues at PREL had the vision for the forum series. They also provided the resources to organize the forum and edit the volume. Their support made it possible for speakers to come to the forum and prepare their chapters for publication. Ron Toma was the director of the Regional Educational Laboratory at PREL who invited us to participate in the project initially. Ludy van Broekhuizen was the associate director of the Regional Educational Laboratory when the project was initiated and, after Ron's retirement, the director who continued to support our efforts. Jan Jenner was the administrator extraordinaire whose efforts have ensured a product of quality. For the hard work and vision of Ron, Ludy, and Jan, we will always be grateful.

Finally, the educational leaders who have attended the forums—many of whom attended all three—have been a compass for us in editing this volume and in designing our research programs. Their questions and eagerness to learn have been the source behind this volume. We are hopeful that many students will benefit from the findings of the research reported in this volume.

—*Elfrieda H. Hiebert*
Michael L. Kamil

Chapter 1

Teaching and Learning Vocabulary

Perspectives and Persistent Issues

Michael L. Kamil
Stanford University

Elfrieda H. Hiebert
University of California, Berkeley

This book addresses the role of vocabulary in reading text. The role of vocabulary and reading is a complex one, as reading researchers have long recognized. In 1925, Whipple described the central role of vocabulary thus: "Growth in reading power means, therefore, continuous enriching and enlarging of the reading vocabulary and increasing clarity of discrimination in appreciation of word values" (p. 76). In 1942, Davis described comprehension as comprised of two skills: word knowledge, or vocabulary, and reasoning.

Words represent complex and, often, multiple meanings. Furthermore, these complex, multiple meanings of words need to be understood in the context of other words in the sentences and paragraphs of texts. Not only are students expected to understand words in texts, but also texts can be expected to introduce them to many new words. The vocabulary of written language is much more extensive and diverse than the vocabulary of oral language (Hayes, Wolfer, & Wolfe, 1996).

One way of illustrating some of the challenges that readers can have with vocabulary is to provide a real-life example from instructional materials. The following words illustrate approximately four or five of every 100 words in the first-grade anthologies of the reading programs that are approved for purchase with state funds in Texas (Texas Education Agency, 1997):

scritch, spittlebug, steeple (Adams et al., 2000)

snowcones, sneezed, spooky (Afflerbach et al., 2000))

saleslady, steered, stump (Farr et al., 2001)

shuns, scampered, sopping (Flood et al., 2001)

scatting, skiddle, succulents (Scholastic, 2000)

These words demonstrate the diversity of vocabulary in a reading program even at the end of Grade 1. Based on the frequency of words within a corpus of 17.25 million words taken from representative kindergarten through college texts (Zeno, Ivens, Millard, & Duvvuri, 1995), each of the words just listed had a frequency of less than three occurrences within a million words of running text. Indeed, most are likely to appear fewer than once in a million words of text. Some of the words such as *sneezed, spooky, saleslady, steered,* and *stump* are likely easy for students to understand once they decode or hear the word pronounced because most children have heard or even spoken these words in conversation. Other words such as *shuns, scatting* (used in this particular text to describe a form of jazz singing), and *scritch* are ones that even high-school students do not know (Dale & O'Rourke, 1981).

The types of vocabulary in texts that are used for instruction is but one of the many problems that need to be addressed in vocabulary research and instruction. Our task, in this introductory chapter, is foreshadowing the themes that run throughout the book. In so doing, the chapter begins by outlining a perspective on vocabulary *learning,* especially as it relates to the reading of text. The second section of the chapter develops a perspective on vocabulary *teaching* as it pertains to reading text. The final section of the chapter presents several persistent issues in the teaching and learning of vocabulary—issues that, if not the direct focus of every chapter in this volume, underlie much of the work of contributors to this volume.

A PERSPECTIVE ON VOCABULARY LEARNING

The National Reading Panel (NICHD, 2000) identified the components of reading as phonemic awareness, phonics, fluency, vocabulary, and comprehension. As the content of the chapters in this book illustrates, vocabulary holds a special place among these components. Vocabulary is not a developmental skill or one that can ever be seen as fully mastered. The expansion and elaboration of vocabularies is something that extends across a lifetime.

A first consideration in delineating the construct of "vocabulary" in research and practice is that individuals have various types of vocabulary that they use for different purposes. Failure to distinguish among the different kinds of vocabulary can lead to confusion and disagreement about both research findings and instructional implications. Generically, vocabulary is the knowledge of meanings of words. What complicates this definition is the fact that words come in at least two forms: oral and print. Knowledge of words also comes in at least two forms, receptive—that which we can understand or recognize—and productive—the vocabulary we use when we write or speak.

Oral vocabulary is the set of words for which we know the meanings when we speak or read orally. Print vocabulary consists of those words for which the meaning is known when we write or read silently. These are important distinctions because the set of words that beginning readers know are mainly oral representations. As they learn to read, print vocabulary comes to play an increasingly larger role in literacy than does the oral vocabulary.

Productive vocabulary is the set of words that an individual can use when writing or speaking. They are words that are well-known, familiar, and used frequently. Conversely, *receptive, or recognition, vocabulary* is that set of words for which an individual can assign meanings when listening or reading. These are words that are often less well known to students and less frequent in use. Individuals may be able assign some sort of meaning to them, even though they may not know the full subtleties of the distinction. Typically, these are also words that individuals do not use spontaneously. However, when individuals encounter these words, they recognize them, even if imperfectly.

In general, recognition or receptive vocabulary is larger than production vocabulary. And, as noted earlier, for beginning readers, oral vocabulary far outstrips print vocabulary. This is one of the determining factors in shaping beginning reading instruction. Beginning reading instruction is typically accomplished by teaching children a set of rules to decode printed words to speech. If the words are present in the child's oral vocabulary, comprehension should occur as the child decodes and monitors the oral representations. However, if the print vocabulary is more complex than the child's oral vocabulary, comprehension will *not* occur. That is, the process of decoding a word to speech does nothing more than change its representation from visual print to oral speech. If it is not in the child's vocabulary, it is simply an unusual collection of speech sounds. The details of this "theory" of vocabulary and reading instruction can be summarized in the following way: *Comprehension is a function of oral language and word recognition*. That is, comprehension of print is a result of the ability to decode and recognize words and oral language knowledge. There are two intermediate steps, though. The first is the link between decoding and oral language.

Decoding to Oral Language

Decoding words to speech requires a background of oral language ability and the knowledge of letter-to-sound correspondences. A reader must translate the print on a page into speech. Once a reader decodes a word, oral language plays the predominant part in comprehension. In fact, Sticht, Beck, Hauke, Kleiman, and James (1974) showed that for younger readers, up to about Grade 3, reading comprehension and oral language comprehension were roughly interchangeable. This relationship implies that the texts that children are given in early reading instruction must be closely tied to their oral language abilities. The vocabulary that young readers are asked to decode cannot be far more complex than that of their oral language. Thus, words such as *shuns* or *scatting* from the Texas-adopted texts cited earlier in this chapter may be decoded eventually but may well be treated as nonsense words by many first graders. Historically—although not currently the pattern in the textbook anthologies, as the previous examples show—beginning readers have been given texts where most of the vocabulary is limited to those words within their oral language. That way, children can devote their attention to the decoding of words that, once figured out, relate to familiar experiences.

The second intermediate step is that oral language ability should lead to oral comprehension. Students need to understand that what they decode should make as much sense as something they would say. This relationship assumes that a host of other factors do not complicate the picture. For example, nonnative speakers of English may not automatically make use of the decoded representations, even if they produce accurate oral representations. For native speakers, the syntactic complexity or the discourse might be complications that prevent comprehension from occurring even after appropriate decoding has taken place.

The foregoing suggests that vocabulary occupies a central place in the scheme of learning to read. Vocabulary serves as the bridge between the word-level processes of phonics and the cognitive processes of comprehension. Once students have become proficient at the decoding task, however, a shift occurs in the vocabulary of text. Texts now become the context for encountering vocabulary that is not within one's oral vocabulary. A preponderance of common and familiar words continues to occur in texts, as running discourse depends on a core group of words. In the Zeno et al. (1995) analysis of 17.25 million words that represented texts used in schools from kindergarten through college, 5,580 words accounted for 80% of the total words (and approximately 90% of the total words in Grades 3 to 9 texts; Carroll, Davies, & Richman, 1971). However, the number of types or unique words that accounted for the other 20% of total words was enormous: 150,000.

These rare words are much more likely to occur in the vocabularies of text than in oral vocabularies. Hayes and his colleagues (Hayes & Ahrens, 1988; Hayes et al., 1996) have considered the commonality and rareness of words in oral and written language. Table 3.1 of Cunningham's chapter in this book presents the data on the numbers of rare words in different kinds of texts ranging from scientific articles to concept books for preschoolers and oral language corpora ranging from television programs to conversations. Common words were defined as those among the 10,000 most common (rather than the words that Zeno et al. [1995] identified as occurring 10 times or more per million-word written corpus). These researchers conclude that speech typically contains far fewer rare words than written language. Even the texts that are considered children's books or literature have more rare words than all oral discourse except for the testimony of expert witnesses.

Presumably, students who are automatic readers recognize the majority of words that are common (i.e., most of the 5,580 most frequent words). The contexts that are provided in paragraphs and sentences can then be used to understand words that occur less frequently but that are critical to the meaning of the discourse. When the number of known words is not sufficient to figure out the meaning of unknown words, comprehension breaks down. Such a scenario can happen with highly proficient readers when they read in highly technical areas for which they may have insufficient background knowledge. Consider the following excerpt:

> If modern techniques such as "optical proximity correction" are applied to compensate for the blurring effects of diffraction, photolithography can create features smaller than the wavelength of light used in projecting the pattern. In this example of optical proximity correction, a complicated pattern used for the mask results in crisp features on the chip. (Hutcheson, 2004, p. 80)

For many readers of this chapter, attending to words that are rare in their written lexicon (i.e., diffraction, photolithography), as well as attending to words with which they are familiar but that appear in a phrase that describes an unfamiliar process (e.g., optical proximity correction), may cause so much attention that overall meaning is compromised.

Once students reach the point where words that are not part of their oral vocabularies become prominent in school texts, numerous issues in the design and/or selection of texts and of instructional activities arise. Hiebert's (chapter 12, this volume) analyses show that, within the typical 1,560-word, fourth-grade text in a reading/language arts program, approximately 4.3 words per every 100 are rare. It is unlikely that all rare words can be taught or even that they should be taught (to ensure that students acquire appropriate context strategies). Texts can thus be seen as both providing opportunities for developing richer vocabularies as well as placing high demands on the vocabulary learning strategies and existing vocabularies of students.

PERSPECTIVES ON VOCABULARY TEACHING

A clear perspective on vocabulary learning is useful. But without a similarly clear perspective on meaningful instruction, students' learning in school will not be optimal. Fortunately for educators, a clear perspective on the components of effective vocabulary instruction is available in the report of the National Reading Panel (NICHD, 2000). The Congressional mandate to the National Reading Panel was to "assess the status of research-based knowledge, including the effectiveness of various approaches to teaching children to read" (p. 1-1). Whereas other researchers have considered aspects of vocabulary teaching (e.g., Kuhn & Stahl, 1998; Swanborn & de Glopper, 1999), the review of the National Reading Panel was a comprehensive analysis of experimental studies that have examined vocabulary instruction.

Using the definitions of Davis (1942) and Whipple (1925), where vocabulary is seen to be an integral part of comprehension, the National Reading Panel defined vocabulary as one of two aspects of comprehension instruction, the other being comprehension strategy instruction. By identifying vocabulary as one of five major components of reading, the National Reading Panel has directed attention to vocabulary instruction. Although some of the research base may not be as extensive or as robust as would be hoped, the report of the National Reading Panel has brought vocabulary into the foreground after a period when little attention was given to vocabulary instruction in classrooms (Scott, Jamieson-Noel, & Asselin, 2003) or in research programs (RAND Reading Study Group, 2002).

Findings of the National Reading Panel

In their synthesis of instructional research on vocabulary, the National Reading Panel (NICHD, 2000) identified 50 studies that met their quality requirements. These 50 studies included a total of 73 samples of students. Of that total, 53 samples (or 73%) were students in Grades 3 to 8. This is not to say that vocabulary instruction is not critical with preschoolers through second graders. In fact, research shows that the vocabularies of preschoolers predict later reading achievement (Hart & Risley, 1995). However, the volume of published studies that met the requirements of the National Reading Panel was simply not sufficient to make substantive conclusions about early levels. Projects such as that of Schwanenflugel et al. (chapter 8, this volume) show what is needed and possible in the design and synthesis of vocabulary programs with preschoolers.

The concluding statement of the National Reading Panel's (NICHD, 2000) synthesis of vocabulary research provides a succinct summary of classrooms where students' vocabularies expand and are elaborated: "Dependence on a single vocabulary instruction method will not result in optimal learning" (p. 4–4). This conclusion is understandable in light of the complexity of what it means to know a word (Beck & McKeown, 1991; Nagy & Scott, 2000). This conclusion also means that educators need to design classrooms experiences that are multi-faceted, if students are to acquire new words and increase the depth of their word knowledge. The design of these environments does not come about, however, by happenstance. The National Reading Panel identified eight specific findings that can provide a scientifically based foundation for the design of rich, multifaceted vocabulary instruction. These conclusions of the National Reading Panel are summarized in Table 1.1.

TABLE 1.1

Summary of the National Reading Panel's Specific Conclusions
about Vocabulary Instruction

1. There is a need for direct instruction of vocabulary items required for a specific text.

2. Repetition and multiple exposure to vocabulary items are important. Students should be given items that will be likely to appear in many contexts.

3. Learning in rich contexts is valuable for vocabulary learning. Vocabulary words should be those that the learner will find useful in many contexts. When vocabulary items are derived from content learning materials, the learner will be better equipped to deal with specific reading matter in content areas.

4. Vocabulary tasks should be restructured as necessary. It is important to be certain that students fully understand what is asked of them in the context of reading, rather than focusing only on the words to be learned. Restructuring seems to be most effective for low-achieving or at-risk students.

5. Vocabulary learning is effective when it entails active engagement in learning tasks.

6. Computer technology can be used effectively to help teach vocabulary.

7. Vocabulary can be acquired through incidental learning. Much of a student's vocabulary will have to be learned in the course of doing things other than explicit vocabulary learning. Repetition, richness of context, and motivation may also add to the efficacy of incidental learning of vocabulary.

8. Dependence on a single vocabulary instruction method will not result in optimal learning. A variety of methods was used effectively with emphasis on multimedia aspects of learning, richness of context in which words are to be learned, and the number of exposures to words that learners receive.

Note.   From National Reading Panel (2000), page 4–4.

As the Panel's conclusions indicate, a critical feature of effective class-rooms is the instruction of specific words. This instruction includes lessons and activities where students apply their vocabulary knowledge and strategies to reading and writing. Discussions are held where teachers and students talk about words, their features, and strategies for understanding unfamiliar words.

Often it has been assumed that the vocabulary of students is too large to be affected by the small number of words that can be taught directly. The research emphatically demonstrates that this is not the case. Direct vocabulary instruction was effective in improving comprehension. This should not be surprising, given the "theory" of vocabulary set forth earlier. Nor should it be surprising in light of the definitions of Davis and of Whipple. It may also be that attention to specific words serves to direct students' attention to features of words that they then generalize in a strategic manner. For example, a text called *The Waterfall* (London, 1999) that is currently part of a leading basal reading program has a number of compound words in addition to its title: *backpack, upstream, rainbow, cookout, bonfire, driftwood*, and *river-smooth*. By directly teaching one or more of these words, it may well be that students' awareness of compound words increases.

As is evident in the Panel's conclusions, the methods for directly and explicitly teaching words are many. In all, the Panel identified 21 methods that have been found to be effective in research projects. Many of these methods emphasize the underlying concept of a word and its connections to other words. Stahl (chapter 5, this volume) illustrates methods such as semantic mapping and Venn diagrams that use graphics. Another method—the keyword method—uses words and illustrations that highlight salient features of meaning. For example, keywords may be words acoustically similar to a salient part of a word as well as connected by meaning (e.g., "hair suit" for *hirsute;* Foil & Alber, 2002). Students are also supported in visualizing or drawing a picture (e.g., a person wearing a suit made of hair) or a picture is made for them (Foil & Alber, 2002). Despite the consistent and extensive research base for this method, the preparation of materials for the keyword method seems to place a heavy burden on instructors. Furthermore, using images or pictures to trigger word associations has limitations in the words that can be learned. For example, it would be difficult to get an acoustic mnemonic for the word *vary* and the family of words that it represents (*variation, variety, varietal*). Consequently, it is not surprising that this technique is not used extensively in classrooms, despite its empirical foundation.

Although direct and explicit guidance on specific words and on word learning strategies are critical, the Panel's conclusions also point to the incidental learning of vocabulary. That is, students acquire vocabulary when it is not explicitly or intentionally taught. Indirect exposure contributes most of the vocabulary learning that occurs with students. Given the size of vocabularies that people attain and the amount of time available for instruction, this finding is not surprising. Research gives us little insight into the precise mechanisms by which this implicit or indirect learning takes place. However, in the Panel's identification of characteristics of effective vocabulary lie possible explanations. Furthermore, although we describe the vocabulary that arises from frequent reading and rich oral language discussions as incidental learning, the creation of such occasions in schools and homes represents intentions on the part of educators and parents. As Graves (2000) noted, students need to know *about* words, not simply acquire new words, if they are to be successful in understanding unfamiliar vocabulary in their reading. The number of words that students will encounter means that priority is given to developing strategies that students can use when they are reading independently and to occasions where they can apply these strategies in their reading and writing, as well as discuss the ways in which the authors they read use words. Underlying these strategies is a curiosity about words—the relationships between words with similar roots, the connotative and denotative meanings of words, the ways in which new words enter language, the idiomatic uses of language, the multiple meanings of individual words, the vocabularies of specialty areas, the connections between English words and Romance or Greek words, and so on.

There has been much discussion about the role of wide reading in incidental learning (see Cunningham, chapter 3, this volume). The National Reading Panel found no experimental studies that confirm this relationship. However, extensive reading may be the means whereby characteristics of effective instruction that the Panel identified can be supported. For example, extensive reading gives students repeated exposure to particular words. Multiple exposures to vocabulary was one of the factors that the Panel confirmed as contributing to vocabulary learning. As Scott's (chapter 4, this volume) review shows, most words are not acquired in a single exposure. Both practice and repeated encounters with words seem to be important for the acquisition of vocabulary. Extensive reading is also one of the means by which students see vocabulary in rich contexts. According to the National Reading Panel, seeing vocabulary in the rich contexts provided by authentic texts rather than in isolation was one of the characteristics of instruction that produced robust vocabulary learning.

The perspective that comes from the Panel's conclusions about classrooms that extend and enrich students' vocabularies is one of *variety* and *richness*. Effective classrooms provide multiple ways for students to learn and interact with words. These ways of learning words and strategies for learning words engage students and motivate them to listen for and look for new words. The contexts in which students see words are rich, such as books that use language inventively, and pertain to many content areas.

The ways of learning words also include technology and multimedia where students can interact with language orally, pictorially, and in writing. What is also clear is that this learning is not a happenstance occurrence. Classrooms where students receive sound word instruction (Scott & Nagy, 2004) are ones where lessons focus their attention on specific words and word-learning strategies, where opportunities to talk about words are many, and where occasions for applying what has been taught with engaging and content-rich texts and with motivating purposes occur with regularity and purpose.

Updates to the National Reading Panel Vocabulary Database

Since the National Reading Panel synthesized their findings, two of the nation's regional laboratories—Pacific Resources for Education and Learning (PREL) and the Laboratory for Student Success (LSS)—have supported the updating of several of the databases on which the National Reading Panel based their findings, including vocabulary instruction (see Kamil & Hiebert, 2004). An additional 13 studies on vocabulary instruction—or an increase of 26% over the original database—were identified through the application of the same search strategies as those used in the National Reading Panel search. Despite this substantial increase in studies, no new findings emerged. There were, however, substantiations of patterns reported in the National Reading Panel. Three of the studies emphasized the positive role that computer-assisted activities can have in the development of vocabulary (Clements & McLoughlin, 1986; Davidson, Elcock, & Noyes, 1996; Heise, Papalewis, & Tanner, 1991). The review also produced continued substantiation for the role that read-aloud events can have in supporting vocabulary development of children, particularly kindergartners (Ewers & Brownson, 1999; Leung, 1992; Robbins & Ehri, 1994). Researchers are using findings such as these to design and implement interventions for preschoolers, as is illustrated in chapter 8 by Schwanenflugel and colleagues (this volume).

There are many other studies of vocabulary that were not included in either the National Reading Panel or the PREL/LSS databases because of the inclusion criteria of those reviews. Many of these studies have relevance for instruction, even though they were not experimental studies of instruction. In the following sections, issues that require additional attention by researchers are raised.

THE TEACHING AND LEARNING OF VOCABULARY: PERSISTENT ISSUES

Four issues are particularly persistent in discussions among vocabulary instruction, as evident in the chapters in this volume: (a) the number of words that should be taught, (b) the particular words that should be taught, (c) the vocabulary learning of two groups of students—English-Language Learners and potentially at-risk students, and (4) the role of independent reading in vocabulary learning. These are not the only issues in vocabulary research and instruction, but these four issues are those that consistently underlie the presentation of issues and solutions by authors in this volume and in broader educational circles. We examine each one in turn.

The Number of Words That Should Be Taught

Researchers' estimates of the size of vocabularies of individuals at the same age level, such as third grade or college, vary by as much as an order of magnitude (Nagy & Anderson, 1984). These variations reflect different definitions of what it means to know a word, as well as types of vocabularies being considered (i.e., the receptive/productive and oral/written dimensions). A more useful perspective, in considering the vocabulary opportunities and tasks that texts present for readers, is to consider the number of different words in the typical texts that students read in schools. Beginning with Thorndike's (1921) effort and continuing through that of Zeno et al. (1995), different research groups have collected and collated the number of words in texts that students might typically read in school. Even these reports of the number of words in school texts leave many questions. For example, what counts as a unique word in a reading vocabulary? In some databases, the possessive of a word is counted as a different unique word from the original word. Nagy and Anderson (1984) used a sample of Carroll, Davies, and Richman's (1971) database, which drew on a corpus of 5 million total words from a sample of Grade 3 through Grade 9 school texts. They clustered unique words into families where knowledge of the root word would support students in determining a related word's meaning when that word was encountered in a text. A related word needed to be semantically transparent to be included in a family. That is, if the meaning of the related word could be inferred with knowledge of the ancestor or original word and the context of text, the word was classified as semantically transparent. According to their definition, words within a family related to the word *know* would include *knowledge, known, knowing, knowledgeable,* but not *know-nothing.* Based on this definition, Nagy and Anderson (1984) estimated that school texts from Grades 3 through 9 contain approximately 88, 5000 distinct word families. For each word that students know, there are approximately two semantically transparent derivatives.

Even if it can be assumed that third graders know approximately 25,000 semantic families (Nagy & Anderson, 1984), the instructional task of promoting the word meanings for the additional 63,500 semantic families that will appear in texts from Grades 3 to 9 is formidable. The instructional task needs to be viewed from the vantage point of what it means to know a word and which vocabulary (i.e., productive–receptive, oral–print) is assessed. Even in teaching a specific group of words, the range of words is sufficiently large that students need to develop a generative stance toward vocabulary. That is, the meanings of specific words need to be taught in ways that support students in understanding how words are connected semantically and morphologically (Graves, Juel, & Graves, 2004).

The Words That Should Be Taught

As the summary of the primary findings of the NRP (NICHD, 2000) indicated, vocabularies are expanded and elaborated in multiple ways. However, whereas the opportunities for learning words may be myriad, the effects of comprehension on vocabulary were found most consistently when at least some words are taught directly. The mandate of the NRP to focus on instructional research meant that the critical question of curriculum or identifying which words are best taught was not addressed. Educators and policymakers are left with the question of identifying which words, from among the thousands of words that students will encounter in their school careers, should be taught directly. Answers to this question are a focus of several authors in this volume, particularly those whose chapters appear in Part III.

Word frequency is one variable that will be proposed. According to Beck and her colleagues (chapter 10, this volume), frequency should be applied by ignoring the most frequent and the least frequent words, concentrating on the middle levels of words. The argument is that the most frequent words are probably already known and that the least frequent words should be taught when they occur in reading.

Importance and utility are clearly factors that should guide the selection of words to be taught. These criteria suggest that only words that are of some use for students—words that they will see and use sufficiently often—should be taught explicitly. However, this criterion should be applied with the frequency criterion in mind. As students are likely to know many high-frequency words, these are not good candidates for the importance criterion.

Instructional potential is another criterion that is clearly related to the selection of words for explicit vocabulary instruction. That is, as suggested by many of the authors of chapters in this volume, vocabulary instruction should make sense in the context of the reading lesson. Words that are related to the selection, the content, or to a thematic unit have instructional potential and should be considered high on the list of candidates for explicit instruction.

There is also an oral component that should be considered. The vocabulary theory presented earlier suggests that younger students have a greater

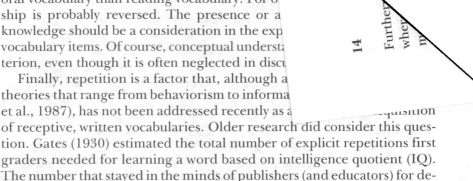

oral vocabulary than reading vocabulary. For o
ship is probably reversed. The presence or a
knowledge should be a consideration in the exp
vocabulary items. Of course, conceptual underst;
terion, even though it is often neglected in disc

Finally, repetition is a factor that, although a
theories that range from behaviorism to informa
et al., 1987), has not been addressed recently as a ....quisition
of receptive, written vocabularies. Older research did consider this question. Gates (1930) estimated the total number of explicit repetitions first
graders needed for learning a word based on intelligence quotient (IQ).
The number that stayed in the minds of publishers (and educators) for decades was the one assigned to the middle IQ group (90–109): 35 repetitions. Students with high IQs (120–129) needed only 20, Gates
hypothesized, whereas students with IQs from 60–69 needed 55 repetitions. As were many of his era, Gates was concerned with IQ as an indicator
of learning ability. Today we no longer accept this one-dimensional view
of learning ability. What is valuable is that Gates and his counterparts saw
the learning of a word to result from numerous repetitions. Except for
very noteworthy occasions (e.g., the first time *turbulence* is experienced on
a plane—and this involves an oral vocabulary), single exposures to words
are unlikely to produce the desired learning.

Although repetitions are important, it is less clear how sufficient exposure to particular words should be accomplished. For example, spacing of
exposure over time is more effective in the learning of most content than
bunching the learning in a single session (Donovan & Radosevich, 1999).
However, evidence for spaced presentations came from studies where instruction was explicit and where words often appeared in lists or singly, not
in texts. How this transfer to the incidental learning that takes place when
students encounter words in, for example, reading self-selected or even assigned texts on their own is unclear.

Addressing the Needs of English-Language Learners and Potentially At-Risk Students

A consistent 40% of a fourth-grade cohort falls into the below-basic category
on the National Assessment of Educational Progress (NAEP; Donahue,
Finnegan, Lutkus, Allen, & Campbell, 2001). This figure has not changed
substantially over the past decade, despite various school reform efforts.
Overly represented among this below-basic group are students whose families qualify for free/reduced-price school lunches. Whereas 24% of students
not eligible for free/reduced-price school lunches had scores in the below-basic category, 55% of those eligible fall into the below-basic category.

more, a substantial percentage of these students live in contexts
e poverty is not the only variable in which their homes differ from the
ainstream culture of schools. The NAEP presents achievement level results on race/ethnicity by five groups: White, Black, Hispanic, Asian/Pacific
Islander, and American Indian/Alaska Native. Of these five groups, the majority of two of these five groups perform at the below-basic level: Black (approximately 60% in 2003) and Hispanic (approximately 56% in 2003).

The practices that are described in this volume, particularly the instructional interventions described in Part II and the curricular plans of
Part III, need to be implemented intentionally and strategically for
groups of students who are consistently failing to attain the high literacy
levels required for full participation in the digital age. However, there
are substantial differences between students within the Hispanic group
who are native Spanish speakers and students who are native speakers of
English. We address the linguistic resources of native Spanish speakers
first and then move to the issue of ameliorating potential vocabulary
gaps that may result from poverty.

Linguistic Resources of Native Spanish Speakers. Understanding the
connections between Romance languages and English is critical for the instruction of all learners. However, with native speakers of Spanish accounting for an increasing percentage of school-age children (U.S. Census, 2001)
and the continued below-basic performances of a majority of Hispanic students (Donahue et al., 2001), this attention is particularly salient.

As chapters in this volume by Calderón et al. (chapter 6) and Carlo et al.
(chapter 7) illustrate, a critical aspect of Spanish that has been left ignored
in the vocabulary programs of textbooks in the United States is the connection between "everyday" words in Spanish and the Latin roots of many academic or literary words in English. With French, Portuguese, Italian, and
Romanian, Spanish is one of a handful of Romance languages that has its
origins in Latin. English has its linguistic roots in the Germanic languages
of the Angles and the Saxons. When the Normans conquered England in
1066, a layer of Latin-based, French words was added to label concepts for
which Anglo-Saxons had Germanic-based words. Coupled with the universal use of Latin words in science, this layer added to a preponderance of
Latin-based words to English. Typically, written discourse, especially that of
academic texts, uses words from the Latin-derived system of English to a
greater degree than does speech. Instead of using Anglo-Saxon-based
words such as *bug, cold, dig, enough,* and *first,* writers of narrative or expository literature are likely to use words such as *insect, frigid, excavate, sufficient,*
and *primary.* As Spanish is an immediate descendant of Latin (rather than a
secondary one, like English), some of the common words in Spanish are
closer to these literary and academic words. A list of 10 common words in

Spanish and their relationship to the literary and academic English words is illustrated in Table 1.2. This may make it easier for ELL students to understand these words if they recognize that they can use their knowledge of Spanish to assist in reading English. All shared cognates in Spanish and English are not of this type where the Spanish word is more literary or academic than the English word. There are also many cases where the shared cognate is a commonly used word (e.g., animal/animal, plant/planta).

TABLE 1.2

10 Common English Words & Their Latin & Spanish Equivalents

English common word	English literary/academic words	Latin root	Spanish common word
brave	Valiant, valid, value, valorous, valor	Valere (to be strong)	valiente
bug	Insect, insecticide, insectivore, insectile	Insectum	insecto
cold	Frigid, Frigid Zones: South & North	Frigus (coldness, frost)	Frío
dig	Cavern(ous), cave, cavity, excavate	Cavus (hollow)	excavar
empty	Vacant, vacate, vacancy	Vacare (to be empty)	vacía
enough	Sufficient, suffice, sufficiency	Sufficiere (to provide)	suficiente
first	Prime, primate, primal, primacy, primary, primarily, primer, primitive, primeval, primogeniture, primordial, primordium; phrases: prima facie, prima donna	Primus (first)	primero
mean	Significance, significant	Significans (meaning)	significar
moon	Lunar, Luna, lunacy, lunatic, lunation, lunarian phrases: lunar month, lunar year	Luna (moon)	luna
sell	Vendor, vender, vend, venal	Venus (sale)	vender
sun	Solar, solstice, solarium	Sol (the sun)	sol
tree	Arbor, arboraceous, arboreal, arboretum	Arbor (tree)	árbol
wash	Lather, lathery, lavender (originally used as a bath perfume), lavatory, lavation, laver, lavish	Lavare (to wash)	lavar

There are also a substantial number of words where both the Spanish and English cognate are unknown by most elementary-level students, especially in the primary grades (e.g., *terrarium/terrario, adaptation/adaptación*). However, in a subject area such as science (Bravo, Hiebert, & Pearson, 2004), the percentage of cognates where the Spanish word is a high-frequency word can account for as much as one third of the critical theme words.

Some native speakers of Spanish who are taught to read in English make these connections (Nagy, Garcia, Durgunoglu, & Hancin-Bhatt, 1993). Many do not. A neglected aspect of instruction has often been the generative nature of the Latin-based cognates. For native speakers of English and speakers of native languages that are not Romance languages, such instruction is essential. For native Spanish speakers (and smaller percentages of children who enter American schools speaking one of the other Romance languages), failing to build on this knowledge base is a missed opportunity.

Although it is erroneous to believe that simple cognate instruction will ameliorate the achievement gap for Hispanic students, a modicum of instructional emphasis on cognates can lead to increased achievement (Jiménez, García, & Pearson, 1995). This instruction, of course, has limits. Nash (1997) produced a compendium of 20,000 cognates in Spanish and English, but many words are ones that elementary-level students are unlikely to have encountered in Spanish, such as the Greek-derived words that are used internationally in science and commerce for new inventions (e.g., bionics). However, Nash estimates that for Spanish and English, cognates account for between 30% and 50% of academic language. As academic language *is* the language of school, this is clearly a resource than should not be overlooked.

Much more scholarship is needed about the literacy learning of nonnative speakers of English. Despite the fact that Spanish speakers make up the overwhelming majority of nonnative English speakers in this country, scholarship needs to be directed to the students who speak one of the other 383 languages reported on the most recent U.S. Census (2001). A panel that extends the efforts of the National Reading Panel to English-Language Learners—the National Literacy Panel for Language Minority Children and Youth, of which several contributors to this volume (August, Beck, Kamil, and Calderón) are a part—is examining this research, although the preliminary reports point to the paucity of the research on ELL.

Students Potentially At Risk.   Research findings that are described in several chapters are those of Hart and Risley (1995, 1999). This research team followed the daily lives of 42 families in which, initially, the children were between 1 and 2 years of age. The amount of language experience before age 3 accounted for all of the correlation between socioeconomic status (SES) and verbal–intellectual competence of children at age 3 and then again at ages 9–10. Prior to age 3, children in welfare families had heard 176 utterances per hour, whereas their peers in working-class and professional families had heard 301 and 487 utterances, respectively, during the same period. All families talked to young children to ensure their needs or safety ("Don't touch the stove."). Where families were different was in what Hart and Risley characterized as extra talk. Extra talk went beyond the everyday business of family life such as questions about books that children had heard or about experiences that the family had shared such as a trip to a store or park. Unlike their counterparts in professional families, the children in welfare families were infrequently asked questions such as "What did you do when we went to Nana's last time?" that required them to describe and elaborate experiences.

The role of texts in the development of rich conversations is likely critical, although researchers such as Hart and Risley do not separate the effects of talk around books from parent conversation. Even professional parents typically do not use words such as *charming* or *knapsack* (words used in a popular read-aloud for young children; Hoban, 1964) or *monumental* and *cellar* (words used in another popular read-aloud for young children; Wells, 1973).

The projects of Dickinson and Tabors (2001), as well as that of Schwanenflugel and colleagues (chapter 8, this volume), illustrate efforts to translate findings such as these into preschool contexts. However, school-age children continue to need to be part of rich classroom talk environments. Snow and her colleagues (Snow, Barnes, Chandler, Goodman, & Hemphill, 2000; Blum-Kulka & Snow, 2002) also demonstrate how opportunities to interact with adults influence the vocabulary of school-age children. According to Snow et al. (2000): "Our findings suggest that ten or twenty minutes a day alone with an adult is more than most children have access to, but that even so little time can make a difference in children's vocabularies and in their reading comprehension skills" (p. 171).

Texts provide an ideal context in which to foster at least some of this rich classroom talk, as Beck et al. describe in chapter 10 in this book. When the design of activities in classrooms will need to be arranged carefully, ameliorating the vocabulary gap may be within the realm of possibility. This suggestion comes from the extensive experiences that language educators have had, such as those in the Army Language School. In the latter context, adults have been able to develop near-native competence in Vietnamese after approximately 1,300 hours of instruction (Walberg, Hase, & Rasher, 1978). Using those numbers as a guide, a child who spends about 10 hours a day in school, in play, and with media in English might gain comparable, although seemingly natural and effortless, experience in 130 days (Walberg et al., 1978, p. 428).

The Kinds and Amounts of Appropriate Independent Reading in Vocabulary Learning

Substantial differences have been documented in the amounts that students of different achievement levels read as part of reading instruction (Biemiller, 1977–1978; Juel, 1990). Furthermore, strong connections have been shown between wide reading, reading achievement, and vocabulary acquisition (Cunningham & Stanovich, 1998). Good and poor readers read for vastly different amounts outside of school. In a study where fourth and fifth graders tracked their out-of-school reading, Anderson, Wilson, and Fielding (1988) found that students at the 98th percentile rank reported 65 minutes daily. Over a year-long period, a student reading for this amount daily would read around 4.4 million words. Declines were sharp after this point. By approximately the 75th percentile, students averaged approximately 12 minutes of reading daily, covering around 884,000 words annually. Students at the 50th percentile read 4.6 words daily, reading 282,000 words annually, whereas students at the 25th percentile read about a minute daily, reading around 60,000 words annually. In a million words of text, students will have been exposed to a core group of 5,580 words 10 times or more—and they will have encountered many more words.

However, such data leave unanswered the question of whether good readers are good because they read more or whether they simply choose to read more because they are good readers. In the National Reading Panel's review of existing data, few well-conducted experimental studies on the effects of independent reading were found. Among the existing studies, most researchers reported small or no gains, or even slightly negative results, in reading achievement as a result of such classroom activity (Carver & Liebert, 1995; Holt & O'Tuel, 1989; Vollands, Topping, & Evans, 1999).

The Panel did not reject the practice but called for more experimental evidence before implementing this as a routine classroom practice. The form that this reading should take and the levels and types of text that should form the focus of this reading remain to be documented in experimental studies. Particular areas in which this research could be particularly illuminating pertain to whether independent reading can be designed and implemented to ensure features of effective vocabulary instruction identified by the Panel and summarized in Table 1.1. For example, can independent reading contexts enhance the active engagement in learning tasks that the Panel found to characterize effective vocabulary learning (#5, Table 1.1)? Does independent reading provide the repeated and multiple exposures to vocabulary (#2, Table 1.1)? Can computer technology be used in ways that improve the efficacy of independent reading (#6, Table 1.1)?

OVERVIEW OF THE VOLUME

As is evident in the scholarship reviewed in this chapter, the relationship between vocabulary and literacy is impossible to separate. To be literate necessitates and supports a rich vocabulary. The work in this volume brings together the work of scholars whose goal it is to have vocabulary experiences that support conceptual learning and comprehension of text. Even during the past two decades when vocabulary research has been limited (RAND Reading Study Group, 2002), these scholars have continued to examine how best to support vocabulary and comprehension. In particular, many of these scholars are considering the nature of vocabulary learning in relation to the diversity that is present in many current-day classrooms.

We have organized this research into three sections that can help the educators who read this book to frame policies and practices. Our intention was to write this for educators who are responsible for educational policy and practice, whether at a regional, state, county, or district level.

Part I develops the rationale. To begin school reform, the rationale for initiating or eliminating instruction and content needs to be understood by participants. Nagy (chapter 2) reviews the rationale for a comprehensive and long-term vocabulary program. Without understanding the manner in which vocabulary develops, it is unlikely that vocabulary will be given either the priority or the kind of attention required to develop the foundational vocabularies children need. The relationship between vocabulary and literacy is a unique one, as we have developed in this chapter. Cunningham (chapter 3) and Scott (chapter 4) describe in detail the manner in which vocabulary is extended through text. Scott's chapter addresses a research literature that has not been considered carefully in the recent creation of school reading programs—the characteristics of texts in which words are (or are not) learned.

Part II addresses the manner in which instruction is implemented. The section begins with Stahl's comprehensive presentation (chapter 5) of how different kinds of words need to be treated and what constitutes the varied, rich methods for knowing words that the National Reading Panel (NICHD, 2000) described. This overview is followed by four chapters that describe specific vocabulary treatments. In each case, the researchers have designed instruction for a specific group of students and tested its effectiveness.

The chapters by Calderón and colleagues (chapter 6) and by Carlo and colleagues (chapter 7) describe a vocabulary treatment with students whose first language is Spanish. This instruction is illustrative of the alternative stance described earlier in the chapter, where knowledge of Spanish is used as a linguistic resource in becoming more adept at reading literary and academic English.

The two subsequent chapters present instructional interventions at two ends of the developmental continuum. Schwanenflugel and colleagues (chapter 8) describe a program that aims to build a foundation for children during their most fertile language learning years—in preschool. Baumann and colleagues (chapter 9) describe the kind of instruction that supports students in the middle grades and beyond. To read the many rare words that occur in different content area texts and in literature, students require strategies and skills in the manner in which affixes affect root word meaning. Readers of these texts also need to make use of context for those rare words that are central to these texts. Baumann et al. describe a program in which knowledge of both semantic families and context are developed.

There was a dilemma about whether Part III should be aligned with the first—the role of curriculum, or what words to teach. We decided to put it at the end because it integrates the issues of learning and of instruction. It is also the area in which the least amount of work has often been done. We believe it to be a good ending point. Without addressing domains of words that we wish students to get good at, selecting the texts that they read and designing lessons around these texts will be difficult. It also indicates the point that has been least studied—and the cutting edge. It is likely the most challenging of issues.

Concluding this volume with the topic of *what words to teach* demonstrates that techniques have been validated (NICHD, 2000) but a substantial amount of research continues to be needed. By the same token, as is evident in the chapters in this book and the report of the National Reading Panel (NICHD, 2000), much is known about the need for strong vocabulary instruction and the features of such instruction. If the goal of higher levels of comprehension is to be achieved, then vocabulary instruction requires intensive and extensive attention.

REFERENCES

Adams, M. J., Bereiter, C., McKeough, A., Case, R., Roit, M., Hirschberg, J., Pressley, M., Carruthers, I., & Treadway, G. H., Jr. (2000). *Open court reading*. Columbus, OH: SRA/McGraw Hill.

Afflerbach, P., Beers, J., Blachowicz, C., Boyd, C. D., Diffily, D., Gaunty-Porter, D., Harris, V., Leu, D., McClanahan, S., Monson, D., Perez, B., Sebesta, S., & Wixson, K. K. (2000). *Scott Foresman reading*. Glenview, IL: Scott Foresman.

Anderson, R. C., Wilson, P. T., & Fielding, L. G. (1988). Growth in reading and how children spend their time outside of school. *Reading Research Quarterly, 23,* 285–303.

Beck, I. L., & McKeown, M. G. (1991). Conditions of vocabulary acquisition. In R. Barr, M. Kamil, P. Mosenthal, & P. D. Pearson (Eds.), *Handbook of reading research,* (Vol. 2, pp. 789–814). New York: Longman.

Biemiller, A. (1977–1978). Relationships between oral reading rates for letters, words, and simple text in the development of reading achievement. *Reading Research Quarterly, 13,* 223–253.

Blum-Kulka, S., & Snow, C.E. (2002). *Talking to adults: the contribution of multiparty discourse to language acquisition.* Mahwah, NJ: Lawrence Erlbaum Associates.

Bravo, M., Hiebert, E. H., & Pearson, P. D. (2004, August 2). *Tapping the linguistic resources of Spanish/English bilinguals: The role of cognates in science.* Paper submitted for presentation at the annual meeting of the American Educational Research Association, Montreal, Quebec.

Carroll, J. B., Davies, P., & Richman, B. (1971). *The American Heritage word frequency book.* Boston: Houghton Mifflin.

Carver, R. P., & Liebert, R. E. (1995). The effect of reading library books in different levels of difficulty on gain in reading ability. *Reading Research Quarterly, 30,* 26–48.

Clements, D. H., & McLoughlin, C. S. (1986). Computer-aided instruction in word identification: How much is enough? *Educational & Psychological Research, 6,* 191–205.

Cunningham, A. E., & Stanovich, K. E. (1998). What reading does for the mind. *American Educator, 22,* 8–15.

Dale, E., & O'Rourke, J. (1981). *Living word vocabulary.* Chicago: World Book/Childcraft International.

Davidson, J., Elcock, J., & Noyes, P. (1996). A preliminary study of the effect of computer-assisted practice on reading attainment. *Journal of Research in Reading, 19,* 102–110.

Davis, F. B. (1942). Two new measures of reading ability. *Journal of Educational Psychology, 33,* 365–372.

Dickinson, D. K., & Tabors, P. O. (Eds.). (2001). *Beginning literacy and language: Young children learning at home and in school.* Baltimore: Brookes.

Donahue, P. L., Finnegan, R. J., Lutkus, A. D., Allen, N. L., & Campbell, J. R. (2001). *The nation's report card for reading: Fourth grade.* Washington, DC: National Center for Education Statistics.

Donovan, J. J., & Radosevich, D. J. (1999). A meta-analytic review of the distribution of practice effect: Now you see it, now you don't. *Journal of Applied Psychology, 84*(5), 795–805.

Ewers, C. A., & Brownson, S. M. (1999). Kindergartners' vocabulary acquisition as a function of active vs. passive storybook reading, prior vocabulary, and working memory. *Reading Psychology, 20,* 11–20.

Farr, R. C., Strickland, D. S., Beck, I. L., Abrahamson, R. F., Ada, A. F., Cullinan, B. E., McKeown, M., Roser, N., Smith, P., Wallis, J., Yokota, Y., & Yopp, H. K. (2001). *Collections: Harcourt reading/language arts program.* Orlando, FL: Harcourt.

Flood, J., Hasbrouck, J. E., Hoffman, J. V., Lapp, D., Medearis, A. S., Paris, S., Stahl, S. Tinajero, J. V., & Wood, K. D. (2001). *McGraw-Hill reading.* New York: McGraw-Hill School Division.

Foil, C. R., & Alber, S. R. (2002). Fun and effective ways to build your students' vocabulary. *Intervention in School and Clinic, 37*(3), 131–139.

Gates, A. I. (1930). *Interest and ability in reading.* New York: Macmillan.

Graves, M. F. (2000). A vocabulary program to complement and bolster a middle-grade comprehension program. In B. M. Taylor, M. F. Graves, & P. van den Broek (Eds.), *Reading for meaning: Fostering comprehension in the middle grades* (pp. 116–135). New York: Teachers College Press; Newark, DE: International Reading Association.

Graves, M. F., Juel, C., & Graves, B. B. (2004). *Teaching reading in the 21st century* (3rd ed.). Boston: Allyn & Bacon.

Hart, B., & Risley, T. (1995). *Meaningful differences in everyday parenting and intellectual development in young American children.* Baltimore: Brookes.

Hart, B., & Risley, T. R. (1999). *The social world of children: Learning to talk*. Baltimore: Brookes.

Hayes, D. P., & Ahrens, M. (1988). Vocabulary simplification for children: A special case of "motherese"? *Journal of Child Language, 15,* 395–410.

Hayes, D. P., Wolfer, L. T., & Wolfe, M. F. (1996). Schoolbook simplification and its relation to the decline in SAT-verbal scores. *American Educational Research Journal, 33,* 489–508.

Heise, B.L., Papalewis, R., & Tanner, D.E. (1991). Building base vocabulary with computer-assisted instruction. *Teacher Education Quarterly, 18*(2), 55–63.

Hoban, R. (1964). *A baby sister for Frances*. New York: HarperCollins.

Holt, S. B., & O'Tuel. F. S. (1989). The effect of sustained silent reading and writing on achievement and attitudes of seventh and eighth grade students reading two years below grade level. *Reading Improvement, 26,* 290–297.

Hutcheson, G. D. (2004, April). The first nanochips. *Scientific American, 290*(4), 76–83.

Jiménez, R. T., García, G. E., & Pearson, P. D. (1995). Three children, two languages and strategic reading: Case studies in bilingual/monolingual reading. *American Educational Research Journal, 32,* 67–97,

Juel, C. (1990). Effects of reading group assignment on reading development in first and second grade. *Journal of Reading Behavior, 22,* 233–254.

Kamil, M. & Hiebert, E. H. (2004). *NRP Plus bibliographies*. Honolulu, HI: Pacific Resources for Education and Learning. Retrieved May 20, 2004, from www.prel.org/programs/rel/nrp.html

Kuhn, M. R., & Stahl, S. A. (1998). Teaching children to learn word meanings from context: A synthesis and some questions. *Journal of Literacy Research, 30*(1), 19–38.

Leung, C. B. (1992). Effects of word-related variables on vocabulary growth through repeated read-aloud events. *National Reading Conference Yearbook, 41,* 491–498.

London, J. (1999). *The waterfall*. New York: Viking Children's Books.

Nagy, W. E., & Anderson, R. C. (1984). How many words are there in printed school English? *Reading Research Quarterly, 19*(3), 304–330.

Nagy, W. E., Garcia, G. E., Durgunoglu, A. Y., & Hancin-Bhatt, B. (1993). Spanish–English bilingual students' use of cognates in English reading. *Journal of Reading Behavior, 25,* 241–259.

Nagy, W. E., & Scott, J. A. (2000). Vocabulary processes. In M. L. Kamil, P. Mosenthal, P. D. Pearson,, & R. Barr (Eds.), *Handbook of reading research* (Vol. 3, pp. 269–284). Mahwah, NJ: Lawrence Erlbaum Associates.

Nash, R. (1997). NTC's dictionary of Spanish cognates: Thematically organized. Lincolnwood, IL: NTC Pub. Group.

National Institute of Child Health and Human Development. (2000). *Report of the National Reading Panel: Teaching children to read: An evidence-based assessment of the scientific research literature on reading and its implications for reading instruction: Reports of the subgroups*. Washington, DC: Author.

RAND Reading Study Group. (2002). *Reading for understanding: Toward an r&d program in reading comprehension*. Santa Monica, CA: RAND. Available online at www.rand.org/publications

Robbins, C., & Ehri, L.C. (1994). Reading storybooks to kindergartners helps them learn new vocabulary words. *Journal of Educational Psychology, 86,* 54–64.

Scholastic (2000). *Literacy place*. New York: Scholastic, Inc.

Scott, J., Jamieson-Noel, D., & Asselin, M. (2003). Vocabulary instruction throughout the day in 23 Canadian upper-elementary classrooms. *Elementary School Journal, 103*(3), 269–286.

Scott, J., & Nagy, W. (2004). Developing word consciousness. In J. F. Baumann & E.J. Kame'enui (Eds.), *Vocabulary instruction: Research to practice* (pp. 218–238). New York: Guilford.

Snow, C., Barnes, W.S., Chandler, J., Goodman, I.F., & Hemphill, L. (2000). *Unfilled expectations: Home and school influences on literacy.* Cambridge, MA: Harvard University Press.

Sticht, T. G., Beck, L. B., Hauke, R. N., Kleiman, G. M., & James, J. H. (1974). *Auding and reading: A developmental model.* Alexandria, VA: Human Resources Research Organization.

Stillings, N., Feinstein, M., Garfield, J., Rissland, E., Rosenbaum, D., Weisler, S., & Baker-Ward, L. (1987). *Cognitive science: An introduction.* Cambridge, MA: MIT Press.

Swanborn, M.S. L., & de Glopper, K. (1999). Incidental word learning while reading: A meta-analysis. *Review of Educational Research, 69,* 261–286.

Texas Education Agency. (1997). *Proclamation of the State Board of Education advertising for bids on textbooks.* Austin, TX: Author.

Thorndike, E. L. (1921). *Teacher's word book.* New York: Teachers College Press.

U.S. Census (2001). *Language use in the United States (2000).* Washington, DC: Author.

Vollands, S. R., Topping, K. J., & Evans, R. M. (1999). Computerized self-assessment of reading comprehension with the Accelerated Reader: Action research. *Research and Writing Quarterly, 15,* 197–211.

Walberg, H. J., Hase, K., & Rasher, S. P. (1978). English mastery as a diminishing function of time. *TESOL Quarterly, 12,* 427–437.

Wells, R. (1973). *Noisy Nora.* New York: Picture Puffins.

Whipple, G. (Ed.) (1925). *The twenty-fourth yearbook of the National Society for the Study of Education: Report of the National Committee on Reading.* Bloomington, IL: Public School Publishing Co.

Zeno, S. M., Ivens, S. H., Millard, R. T., & Duvvuri, R. (1995). *The educator's word frequency guide.* Brewster, NY: Touchstone Applied Science Associates.

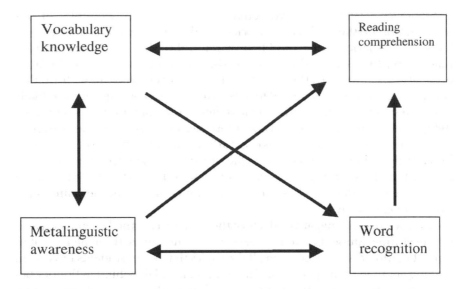

FIG. 2.2.   Some hypothesized causal links between metalinguistic awareness, vocabulary knowledge, word recognition, and reading comprehension.

- Vocabulary knowledge contributes to metalinguistic awareness.
- Metalinguistic awareness contributes to word recognition.
- Vocabulary also may contribute to word recognition.
- Metalinguistic awareness may contribute to reading comprehension through means other than enhancing word recognition.
- Most if not all of these relationships may be reciprocal (hence the two-headed arrows).

To the extent that this picture is valid, vocabulary contributes both directly and indirectly to reading comprehension.

Some evidence indicates, for example, that vocabulary knowledge contributes to phonological awareness. The more words children know, the more likely they are to be analytic in their representation of the sounds of those words. This relationship is supported by several studies (e.g., Fowler, 1991; Gathercole, Hitch, Service, & Martin, 1997; Goswami, 2001; Metsala, 1999; Metsala & Walley, 1998). Phonemic awareness, in turn, has an impact on word recognition (Ehri, Nunes, Willows, Schuster, Yaghoub-Zadeh, & Shanahan, 2001), which ultimately contributes to reading fluency and comprehension.

It also appears that vocabulary may contribute to knowledge about print, and hence to word recognition. Dickinson, McCabe, Anastopoulos,

Peisner-Feinberg, and Poe (2003) examined the emerging literacy knowledge of Head Start children, using an instrument called the Emergent Literacy Profile. This profile primarily reflects knowledge about print, a precursor to word recognition. The researchers were particularly interested in the effects of two independent variables: phonological awareness (as measured by the Early Phonological Awareness profile) and receptive vocabulary (as measured by the PPVT). A key finding of the study is that both vocabulary and phonological awareness made significant independent contributions to the literacy measure. Thus, vocabulary knowledge appears to make a direct contribution to word recognition, above and beyond any effect it may have via phonemic awareness.

Dickinson et al. (2003) report another very interesting finding concerning the relationship of vocabulary knowledge and phonological awareness: For students who had limited phonological awareness, vocabulary was not related to early literacy. For students who had normal phonological awareness, vocabulary was linked to early literacy. Conversely, for students who had small vocabularies, phonological awareness was not related to early literacy. For students with more normal vocabularies, phonological awareness was linked to early literacy.

This may be a bit hard to visualize, so let me say it another way: If students' vocabularies are too small, phonological awareness does not contribute to their knowledge about print. If students' levels of phonological awareness are too low, vocabulary does not contribute to their knowledge about print. In other words, the extent to which phonological awareness contributes to knowledge about print depends on vocabulary and vice versa.

The point is that each of these variables functions as a necessary but not sufficient condition. Students need to have a certain level of vocabulary knowledge for phonological awareness to be of any benefit to them in learning to read, and they need to have a certain level of phonological awareness for vocabulary knowledge to be of any benefit in learning to read. Each element makes a contribution, but it may be a necessary ingredient for the others to function as well.

In a study conducted with colleagues at the University of Washington (Nagy, Berninger, Abbott, Vaughn, & Vermeulen, 2003), we likewise found that for second graders at risk for failure in reading, oral vocabulary made a significant, unique contribution to word recognition, even when orthographic, phonological, and morphological factors had been statistically controlled for. We also found that morphological awareness made a significant, unique contribution to reading comprehension, above and beyond that of vocabulary. These findings and those of Dickinson et al. (2003) thus provide evidence for the two diagonal lines in Fig. 2.2.

It should be noted that the indirect links between vocabulary knowledge and reading comprehension just discussed are also likely to involve reciprocal relationships. In particular, the relationship between vocabulary and morphological awareness is likely to go both ways: Knowing more words gives us more opportunities to become aware of relationships among words that share meaningful parts, and awareness of morphology should facilitate our learning of words that are related to others by prefixation, suffixation, or compounding.

IMPLICATIONS FOR INSTRUCTION

As the preceding discussion was intended to demonstrate, the causal links underlying the vocabulary–comprehension relationship are relatively complex. The instrumentalist, knowledge, aptitude, and access hypotheses each focus on a different aspect of this complexity. The possibility of reciprocal and indirect links between vocabulary knowledge and reading comprehension further complicates the picture. As already noted, these hypotheses are not mutually exclusive. All have at least some plausibility, and in some cases, empirical support.

To the extent that vocabulary instruction is motivated by the causal relationship between vocabulary and reading comprehension, we have to take the complexity of this relationship into account when we think about what constitutes effective vocabulary instruction. In the remainder of this chapter, I briefly sketch some implications of the picture of the vocabulary–comprehension relationship that I outlined.

The Instrumentalist Hypothesis

According to instrumentalist hypothesis, word knowledge contributes directly to reading comprehension; therefore, to improve comprehension, vocabulary should be taught. However, the fact that the instrumentalist hypothesis is only one causal connection in a complex network of causal links also has important implications. Vocabulary interventions are usually carried out with the expectation that a successful intervention will impact comprehension. Despite some successes, however, the impact of vocabulary interventions on standardized measures of reading comprehension has been sporadic, and even when there is an effect, it is generally not sizeable.

The fact that the instrumentalist hypothesis is only one part of a larger, more complex picture should lead us to have more modest expectations about what a vocabulary intervention can produce in terms of gains in comprehension. The expectation that a short-term vocabulary intervention, whatever its quality, will produce large improvements in reading comprehension is simply not realistic.

This is not to say that vocabulary interventions are not worthwhile, or that they should not be expected to impact comprehension positively. But, as I hope the following sections make clearer, the complexity and reciprocal nature of the vocabulary–comprehension connection makes it much more likely that effects of vocabulary instruction will tend to be long-term and cumulative, rather than short-term and dramatic. The remaining hypotheses also tell us more specifically what effective vocabulary instruction should look like.

The Knowledge Hypothesis

The knowledge hypothesis implies that word meanings do not exist in isolation; rather, they are part of larger knowledge structures. As a result, it is not just word knowledge alone, but word knowledge combined with world knowledge that enables improved comprehension. For instruction to affect comprehension, therefore, vocabulary should be taught in conjunction with concepts and content. One of the attributes of effective vocabulary instruction identified by Stahl (1986), and exemplified in the rich vocabulary instruction developed by Beck and her colleagues (e.g., Beck et al., 2002), is making connections between the instructed words and students' prior knowledge and experiences.

The Aptitude Hypothesis

The instructional implications of the aptitude hypothesis vary, depending on the specific version that is used. In the version proposed by Sternberg and Powell (1983), the implication is that students should receive instruction that helps them infer the meanings of new words.

Two recent reviews of research on teaching students to infer the meanings of new words (Fukkink & de Glopper, 1998; Kuhn & Stahl, 1998) have indicated that such instruction, in fact, can help students learn the meanings of new words. An impact on comprehension of such instruction has not been demonstrated (Baumann, Edwards, Boland, Olejnik, & Kame'enui, 2003). I suggest, however, that the implication of the aptitude hypothesis is that strategies for word learning and strategies for comprehension should not be taught separately. Some successful comprehension strategy packages have a component that addresses unknown words—for example, the "clarification" component of reciprocal teaching (Palincsar & Brown, 1984), or the "clunk" component of Collaborative Strategic Reading (Klinger & Vaughn, 1999).

The implication from the metalinguistic hypothesis is that having a large vocabulary and doing well on vocabulary tests is associated with being able to talk and think about language and, in particular, about word meanings. The implication for vocabulary instruction is that such instruction should aim not just at teaching new words, but at helping students learn to talk and think about language. That is, effective vocabulary instruction should promote word consciousness (Graves & Watts-Taffe, 2002; Scott & Nagy, 2004). Likewise, vocabulary instruction, especially for younger children, should aim at increasing children's facility with decontextualized language (McKeown & Beck, 2003), which depends heavily on metalinguistic awareness.

The Access Hypothesis

The instructional implication of the hypothesis is that words (some words, at least) need to be taught thoroughly. McKeown et al. (1985) indicate that students need to encounter a word as many as 12 times before they know it well enough to improve their comprehension. This suggests that for vocabulary instruction to be most effective, it must not only introduce important vocabulary words, but provide ways for students to solidify their understanding of the words by seeing and using them multiple times.

The Reciprocal Hypothesis

What are the instructional implications of a reciprocal relationship between vocabulary knowledge and reading comprehension? One obvious implication is to start some form of vocabulary instruction as early as possible. The causal relationship between vocabulary knowledge and reading comprehension starts early, before children are reading connected text. Thus, the correlation between vocabulary and reading comprehension for fifth graders is not just a matter of how much these students know about the meanings of the words in the text they are tested on. It reflects a long history of mutual facilitation between vocabulary knowledge, reading comprehension, and a variety of other literacy-related abilities. If the goal is to increase children's reading comprehension by teaching them vocabulary, it helps to start working on their vocabularies when they are in preschool.

The overriding implication of the reciprocal hypothesis, however, is the need to develop comprehensive literacy programs. "Balanced" is too weak a word because it implies that there are only two sides to be balanced. But in the cycle of learning that leads to vocabulary and comprehension growth, it is crucial to support students at each point in the cycle. Figure 2.3 illustrates some of the ways to make sure that each part of the cycle is functioning.

Indirect Links Between Vocabulary and Comprehension

I have argued that vocabulary knowledge also may have an indirect impact on reading comprehension through its relationship with morphological

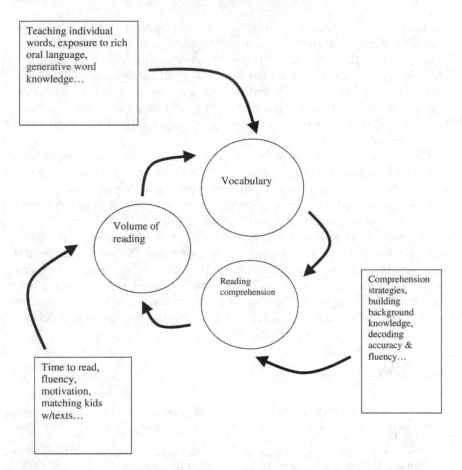

Teaching individual words, exposure to rich oral language, generative word knowledge…

Vocabulary

Volume of reading

Reading comprehension

Comprehension strategies, building background knowledge, decoding accuracy & fluency…

Time to read, fluency, motivation, matching kids w/texts…

FIG. 2.3.   Some instructional implications of a reciprocal model of vocabulary and reading comprehension.

awareness, phonological awareness, and word recognition. One instructional implication of such links is that the impact of vocabulary knowledge on literacy begins very early. Hence there is all the more reason for early attention to vocabulary instruction. The indirect links via morphological awareness also provide evidence for the importance of instruction on prefixes, roots, and suffixes (e.g., Graves, 2004).

CONCLUSION

In this chapter, I have tried to illustrate some of the complexity of the causal links between vocabulary knowledge and reading comprehension. My main purpose has been to argue that this complexity constitutes a powerful rationale for rich and multifaceted vocabulary instruction. Such instruction has to start early and must be kept up over the years, although what constitutes effective instruction changes with grade level. It must increase students' generative word knowledge, as well as their knowledge of individual words. It must include increased exposure to rich oral language as well as wide reading, and it must be part of, and integrated into, a comprehensive literacy curriculum

Effective vocabulary instruction includes components that might look like frills to some: spending valuable instructional time on building word consciousness, helping students to identify morphological and semantic relationships among words, increasing their sensitivity to words with multiple meanings and to contextual variations in meanings.

My intent has been to give some reasons why these things are not frills; they are essential components of effective instruction. No one component is sufficient by itself, but each is important. We still need to figure out exactly how to combine the components in ways that create the most engaging and cognitively challenging instruction for all our students. However, we already know enough to do better than we are often doing, especially for our youngest and our most vulnerable students.

REFERENCES

Anderson, R. C., & Freebody, P. (1981). Vocabulary knowledge. In J. Guthrie (Ed.), *Comprehension and teaching: Research reviews* (pp. 77–117). Newark, DE: International Reading Association.

Anderson, R. C., Wilson, P., & Fielding, L. (1988). Growth in reading and how children spend their time outside of school. *Reading Research Quarterly, 23,* 285–303.

Baumann, J. F., Edwards, E. C., Boland, E. M., Olejnik, S., & Kame'enui, E. J. (2003). Vocabulary tricks: Effects of instruction in morphology and context on fifth-grade students' ability to derive and infer word meanings. *American Educational Research Journal, 40,* 447–494.

Beck, I. L., & McKeown, M. G. (1991). Conditions of vocabulary acquisition. In R. Barr, M. Kamil, P. Mosenthal, & P. D. Pearson (Eds.), *Handbook of reading research,* (Vol. 2, pp. 789–814). New York: Longman.

Beck, I. L., & McKeown, M. G. (2001). Text talk: Capturing the benefits of read-aloud experiences for young children. *The Reading Teacher, 55,* 10–20.

Beck, I. L., McKeown, M. G., & Kucan, L. (2002). *Bringing words to life: Robust vocabulary instruction.* New York: The Guilford Press.

Biemiller, A. (1999). *Language and reading success.* Cambridge, MA: Brookline Books.

Blachowicz, C., & Fisher, P. (2004). Keeping the "fun" in fundamental: Encouraging word awareness and incidental word learning in the classroom through word play. In J. F. Baumann & E. J. Kame'enui (Eds.), *Vocabulary instruction: Research to practice* (pp. 218–237). New York: The Guilford Press.

Dickinson, D., McCabe, A., Anastopoulos, L., Peisner-Feinberg, E., & Poe, M. (2003). The comprehensive language approach to early literacy: The interrelationships among vocabulary, phonological sensitivity, and print knowledge among preschool-aged children. *Journal of Educational Psychology, 95,* 465–481.

Edwards, E. C., Font, G., Baumann, J. F., & Boland, E. (2004). Unlocking word meanings: Strategies and guidelines for teaching morphemic and contextual analysis. In J. F. Baumann & E. J. Kame'enui (Eds.), *Vocabulary instruction: Research to practice* (pp. 159–178). New York: The Guilford Press.

Ehri, L., Nunes, S., Willows, D., Schuster, B., Yaghoub-Zadeh, Z., & Shanahan, T. (2001). Phonemic awareness instruction helps children learn to read: Evidence from the National Reading Panel's meta-analysis. *Reading Research Quarterly, 36,* 250–287.

Foorman, B. R., Seals, L. M., Anthony, J. L., & Pollard-Durodola, S. (2003). A vocabulary enrichment program for 3rd and 4th grade African-American students: Description, implementation, and impact. In B. R. Foorman (Ed.), *Preventing and remediating reading difficulties: Bringing science to scale* (pp. 419–441). Timonium, MD: York Press.

Fowler, A. (1991). How early phonological development might set the stage for phoneme awareness. In S. Brady & D. Shankweiler (Eds.), *Phonological processes in literacy* (pp. 97–117). Hillsdale, NJ: Lawrence Erlbaum Associates.

Fukkink, R. G., & de Glopper, K. (1998). Effects of instruction in deriving word meaning from context: A meta-analysis. *Review of Educational Research, 68,* 450–469.

Gathercole, S., Hitch, G., Service, E., & Martin, A. (1997). Phonological short-term memory and new word learning in children. *Developmental Psychology, 33*(3), 966–979.

Goswami, U. (2001). Early phonological development and the acquisition of literacy. In S. B. Neuman & D. K. Dickinson (Eds.), *Handbook of early literacy research* (pp. 111–125). New York: The Guilford Press.

Graves, M. (2000). A vocabulary program to complement and bolster a middle-grade comprehension program. In B. Taylor, M. Graves, & P. van den Broek (Eds.), *Reading for meaning: Fostering comprehension in the middle grades* (pp. 116–135). Newark, DE: International Reading Association.

Graves, M. (2004). Teaching prefixes: As good as it gets? In J. F. Baumann & E. J. Kame'enui (Eds.), *Vocabulary instruction: Research to practice* (pp. 81–99). New York: The Guilford Press.

Graves, M., & Watts-Taffe, S. (2002). The role of word consciousness in a research-based vocabulary program. In A. Farstrup & S. J. Samuels (Eds.), *What research has to say about reading instruction* (pp. 140–165). Newark, DE: International Reading Association.

Johnson, D., Johnson, B., & Schlichting, K. (2004). Logology: Word and language play. In J. F. Baumann & E. J. Kame'enui (Eds.), *Vocabulary instruction: Research to practice* (pp. 179–200). New York: The Guilford Press.

Klinger, J. K., & Vaughn, S. (1999). Promoting reading comprehension, content learning, and English acquisition through collaborative strategic reading. *The Reading Teacher, 52,* 738–747.

Kuhn, M. R., & Stahl, S. A. (1998). Teaching children to learn word meanings from context: A synthesis and some questions. *Journal of Literacy Research, 30*(1), 119–138.

McKeown, M. G., & Beck, I. L. (2003). Taking advantage of read-alouds to help children make sense of decontextualized language. In A. van Kleeck, S. Stahl, & E.

Bauer (Eds.), *On reading books to children* (pp. 159–176). Mahwah, NJ: Lawrence Erlbaum Associates.

McKeown, M. G., Beck, I. L., Omanson, R. C., & Pople, M. T. (1985). Some effects of the nature and frequency of vocabulary instruction on the knowledge and use of words. *Reading Research Quarterly, 20*, 522–535.

Metsala, J. (1999). Young children's phonological awareness and nonword repetition as a function of vocabulary development. *Journal of Educational Psychology, 91*, 3–19.

Metsala, J., & Walley, A. (1998). Spoken vocabulary growth and the segmental restructuring of lexical representations: Precursors to phonemic awareness and early reading ability. In J. Metsala & L. Ehri (Eds.), *Word recognition in beginning literacy* (pp. 89–120). Mahwah, NJ: Lawrence Erlbaum Associates.

Mezynski, K. (1983). Issues concerning the acquisition of knowledge: Effects of vocabulary training on reading comprehension. *Review of Educational Research, 53*, 253–279.

Nagy, W., Berninger, V., Abbott, R., Vaughan, K., & Vermeulen, K. (2003). Relationship of morphology and other language skills to literacy skills in at-risk second grade readers and at-risk fourth grade writers. *Journal of Educational Psychology, 95*, 730–742.

Nagy, W., & Gentner, D. (1990). Semantic constraints on lexical categories. *Language and Cognitive Processes, 5*, 69–201.

Nagy, W., & Scott, J. (1990). Word schemas: Expectations about the form and meaning of new words. *Cognition and Instruction, 7*, 105–127.

Nagy, W., & Scott, J. (2000). Vocabulary processes. In M. Kamil, P. Mosenthal, P. D. Pearson, & R. Barr (Eds.), *Handbook of reading research* (Vol. 3, pp. 269–284). Mahwah, NJ: Lawrence Erlbaum Associates.

Palincsar, A. S., & Brown, A. L. (1984). Reciprocal teaching of comprehension-fostering and comprehension-monitoring activities. *Cognition and Instruction, 2*, 117–175.

RAND Reading Study Group. (2002). *Reading for understanding: Toward an R&D program in reading comprehension*. Santa Monica, CA: RAND (available online at www.rand.org/publications).

Scott, J. A., & Nagy, W. (2004). Developing word consciousness. In J. F. Baumann & E. J. Kame'enui (Eds.), *Vocabulary instruction: Research to practice* (pp. 201–217). New York: The Guilford Press.

Stahl, S. A. (1986). Three principles of effective vocabulary instruction. *Journal of Reading, 29*, 662–68.

Stahl, S. A., & Fairbanks, M. M. (1986). The effects of vocabulary instruction: A model-based meta-analysis. *Review of Educational Research, 56*, 72–110.

Stanovich, K. E. (1986). Matthew effects in reading: Some consequences of individual differences in the acquisition of literacy. *Reading Research Quarterly, 21*, 360–407.

Sternberg, R. J., & Powell, J. S. (1983). Comprehending verbal comprehension. *American Psychologist, 38*, 873–893.

Swanborn, M. S. L., & de Glopper, K. (1999). Incidental word learning while reading: A meta-analysis. *Review of Educational Research, 69*, 261–285.

Chapter 3

Vocabulary Growth Through Independent Reading and Reading Aloud to Children

Anne E. Cunningham
University of California, Berkeley

A young child sits quietly reading a storybook. The book tells the story of a little boy's adventures on a very snowy day. The child reads, "He pretended he was a mountain-climber. He climbed up a great big tall heaping mountain of snow—and slid all the way down." The child pauses in reading to think about what he just read. He rereads the words "pretended," "mountain-climber," "climbed," "heaping," and "slid." He takes a minute to look at the pictures and consider the meaning of these words before reading on, "He picked up a handful of snow—and another and still another. He packed it round and firm and put the snowball in his pocket for tomorrow. Then he went into his warm house." Again the child stops to consider a few more unfamiliar words: "handful," and "firm," and he notices that he has never seen the word "packed" used in this way before. After deciding that he understands what the little boy is doing, he continues to read.

—From *A Snowy Day* by Ezra Jack Keats

As this child struggles to read the text, he encounters many new words. These are words for which he may or may not know the meaning. Yet in order to comprehend the text, the child is forced to learn the meaning of the unfamiliar words and incorporate them into his lexicon.

The situation described is not unique. Children are constantly learning the meaning of words through their encounters with text. Vocabulary instruction also plays a central role in vocabulary growth in school-age children (e.g., Beck, McKeown, & Kucan, 2002). However, across the life span, most researchers would agree that the *bulk* of vocabulary growth occurs incidentally through exposure to language. This process of vocabulary acquisition occurs via two primary mechanisms: exposure to oral language and to written language. This chapter discusses how exposure to *written* language (i.e., print) contributes to children's vocabulary development.

LEARNING VOCABULARY THROUGH EXPOSURE TO LANGUAGE

The process of learning new words begins in infancy and continues throughout one's adult life. It has been estimated that an 18-month-old child needs to learn an average of 5 new words a day in order to have an average vocabulary of approximately 8,000 words by the time he or she is 6 years old (Senechal & Cornell, 1993). The average student graduating from high school is estimated to know approximately 40,000 words (Nagy & Herman, 1985). In order to increase one's vocabulary from 8,000 to 40,000 in those 12 years, a child needs to learn a total of approximately 32,000 words between 1st grade and 12th grade, which translates to approximately 7 words a day. The research suggests that children typically learn approximately 3,000 words a year (over 8 words a day) between 3rd and 12th grades during the school year (Nagy & Anderson, 1984). On reflection, that seems like a lot of words each year.

These impressive statistics leave us wondering where our children are learning all of these words. Recent research suggests there is a developmental trajectory to vocabulary learning (Biemiller, 2001) and that when instruction exploits the morphophonemic nature of our orthography, children can acquire a multiplicity of word meanings (e.g., magic yields knowledge of magician, magical, magically) through direct and systematic vocabulary instruction (Beck, McKeown, & McCaslin, 1983). However, when we consider that the average program of direct vocabulary instruction covers only a few hundred words and word parts per year, this type of vocabulary development just described seems to be beyond the scope of even the most intensive vocabulary instruction programs (Hiebert, chapter 12, this volume; Nagy & Herman, 1985). Even the most tailored and comprehensive instruction cannot shoulder all of the vocabulary learning that must take place in the school years and beyond. Thus, the argument is made that a substantial amount of vocabulary development occurs through incidental encounters with language (Sternberg, 1987). Not surprisingly, a convergent body of evidence supports this conclusion.

Much of the research investigating the role of incidental learning in vocabulary development has focused on words encountered in the context of reading. For example, Nagy, Herman, and Anderson (1985) attempted to determine the amount of knowledge children acquire about unfamiliar words during natural reading. They asked 57 eighth-grade students to read one of two excerpts (approximately 1,000 words) taken from a junior-high-level text. The students then completed a multiple-choice vocabulary test assessing their knowledge of 15 target words from the passage they read and 15 words from the alternative text. The multiple-choice test was designed to assess the amount or degree of knowledge about a word. Students were also asked to participate in an individual interview aimed at determining partial word knowledge. Results indicated that children made small but statistically reliable gains in word knowledge after reading words in context. Similar patterns have been found by Stahl (1999) and Sternberg & Powell (1983).

McKeown (1985) also investigated the process by which children acquire unfamiliar word meanings through exposure to written language. She argued that various cognitive functions underlie vocabulary learning and, as a result, children of high and low verbal ability experience varying levels of success in the process of acquiring word meaning from context. In order to test this hypothesis, McKeown (1985) assessed the ability of 30 fifth-grade children (15 high vocabulary ability, 15 low vocabulary ability) to derive the meaning of unfamiliar words from context by presenting them with 6 artificial words embedded in multiple sentences with varying levels of contextual support. Indeed, high vocabulary children were more successful in deriving the meaning of an unknown word from text and using the new word in subsequent contexts. In contrast, children of low verbal ability experienced a misunderstanding of the relationship between words and context and demonstrated a semantic interference when considering two contexts simultaneously. McKeown's (1985) work, along with the work of other researchers (e.g., Daneman & Green, 1986; Sternberg & Powell, 1983), demonstrates that there are certain conditions under which reading promotes vocabulary learning.

Nagy, Anderson, and Herman (1987) argued that although it may be true that general verbal ability is associated with the process of successfully deriving the meaning of unfamiliar words, it is unclear to what extent ability affects the volume of learning from context that occurs during *normal* reading. In order to more fully investigate the nature of incidental word learning and the role of ability, Nagy et al. (1987) conducted a study with 352 third-, fifth-, and seventh-grade children with varying levels of cognitive ability. Similar to their previous study (i.e., Nagy et al., 1985), Nagy et al. (1987) investigated the ability to learn unfamiliar word meanings in the context of *natural reading*. Contrary to the work of McKeown (1985) and others, Nagy et al. (1987) found no effects of ability on learning from context. In fact, they explored the interactions of ability and learning from context using several different ability measures including standardized reading comprehension scores, standardized vocabulary scores, measures of decoding skill, and facility with morphology, and found no significant interactions. In addition, they found that children across all age groups made gains in word knowledge from the use of context. They concluded that although it might be true that children of high ability are better able to derive word meaning from context on a general level, in normal reading of real text, as words occur over a wide range of difficulty and familiarity, there is something there for everyone to learn. "If children are given texts they can comprehend, they will gain some knowledge about the meaning of some unfamiliar words" (Nagy et al., 1987, p. 263). In other words, children of all ages and abilities are able to learn words incidentally through encounters with written language. We have found this in our research examining the cognitive correlates of reading volume (e.g., Cunningham & Stanovich, 1997).

Although children of all ages and abilities may be able to learn words through context, there are certain conditions that facilitate the process of incidental word learning. Based on their research program, Anderson and Nagy (1992) provide a summary of their conclusions about the conditions that facilitate word learning. In general, their work has led them to the conclusion that—assuming only one exposure to an unfamiliar word—the overall probability that a child will learn a word while reading is about 1 in 20 (i.e., for every 20 unfamiliar words encountered, a child will learn 1 word). Although this number may seem small, its magnitude is clear when one considers the amount of unfamiliar words read by the average child in a year's time. For example, the average fifth grader reads approximately one million words of text a year and approximately 2% (i.e., 20,000) of those words are "unfamiliar" to the child (Anderson & Freebody, 1983; Anderson & Nagy, 1992). If 1 out of every 20 of those unfamiliar words is incorporated into the child's lexicon, then the average fifth grader learns approximately 1,000 words a year through reading.

However, as mentioned, certain conditions dramatically facilitate the ability to derive word meanings. For example, the difficulty of the text and the child's level of comprehension have a dramatic influence on the likelihood that a child will derive the meaning of an unfamiliar word. In fact, a child is twice as likely to learn an unfamiliar word when reading a narrative text that is matched to his level of comprehension, whereas it is less likely that a child will learn an unfamiliar word when the text is a difficult exposition (Anderson & Nagy, 1992). The ease with which a word is learned from text is also a function of the word's conceptual difficulty (e.g., it may be easier to determine the meaning of the word "participate" than the word "photosynthesis"), the informativeness of the context, the number of times the word is encountered, and the importance of the unknown word for comprehending the surrounding context (Anderson & Nagy, 1992; Nagy & Herman, 1985; Sternberg, 1987; Sternberg & Powell, 1983).

VOCABULARY INSTRUCTION

A large body of research provides overwhelming evidence that a substantial amount of vocabulary development occurs as a result of incidental encounters with language. This is not to suggest, however, that direct instruction of vocabulary does not play an important role. There is great value in the type of conceptual and word-by-word instruction that should take place in classrooms. For example, as pointed out by Anderson & Nagy (1992), there are precise words that children may need to know in order to comprehend particular lessons or subject matter. Waiting for children to encounter the word in natural reading (and hoping that the word is the 1 word in 20 actually learned) is far less efficient than teaching the words through direct and systematic vocabulary instruction. Moreover, the context in which unfamiliar words are embedded can sometimes be uninformative or even misleading, causing children to misinterpret word meanings (Beck et al., 1983). Alternatively, direct vocabulary instruction allows the teacher to control the context in which the word or word parts are introduced, ensures the presentation of the intended definition of the word, and provides control over the number of times the child is exposed to the word (Beck et al., 1983; Nagy & Herman, 1985). Therefore, direct instruction can provide an important foundation for future exposure to words in context (Beck, Perfetti, & McKeown, 1982; Nagy & Herman, 1985).

The work just summarized does, however, suggest the need for a shift in the focus of programs of direct instruction. It indicates that it might be useful to consider programs that provide less intensive coverage of larger numbers of unfamiliar words, coupled with increased opportunities to read and encounter words in a meaningful context (Nagy & Herman, 1985). An alternative method proposed by Anderson & Nagy (1992) would be to develop the "word consciousness" of students by instructing them in the ways that word parts contribute to word meanings. In this approach, children are encouraged to treat an unknown word as an opportunity for problem solving. Children are taught word relationships and families in an attempt to increase their ability to do independent word analysis and derive the meaning of unfamiliar words in text. In other words, the natural redundancies in the English language serve to contribute to vocabulary growth. In this regard, a child who knows the meaning of the word "magic" would be empowered to derive the meaning of the unfamiliar words "magician" and "magical." Other proposed methods of effective vocabulary instruction have also been informed by the research suggesting that a significant amount of word learning occurs incidentally through encounters with words in written text. That is, in order to be effective, programs of vocabulary instruction should simulate the type of word learning that occurs during natural reading (Stahl, 1999) and should focus on words that occur with substantial frequency in written language but are less commonly used in speech (Cunningham & Stanovich, 2003; Hiebert, chapter 12, this volume).

THE CASE FOR WRITTEN LANGUAGE

An important distinction must be made, however, regarding the *quality* of language exposure children receive. One such distinction lies in the comparison between written and oral language. For example, it has been suggested in the literature that the opportunities for incidental vocabulary learning that occur via exposure to language, and specifically between oral and written language, are essentially equivalent. Smith (1989) asserted, "What they read and write may make people smarter, but so will any activity that engages the mind, including interesting conversation" (p. 354). In many ways, this seems to be a reasonable proposition. However, an interesting (and illuminating) body of research comparing the relative frequencies of oral and written language suggests otherwise. These analyses demonstrate that the lexical density of oral language relative to written language is substantially degraded or impoverished, and indicate that text is a particularly effective way of expanding a child's vocabulary compared to "interesting conversation."

Hayes and Ahrens (1988) analyzed the statistical distribution of words in several different categories of oral and written language. They analyzed printed texts including abstracts of scientific articles, newspapers, magazines, adult books, children's books, and preschool books as well as oral language that included the scripts of prime-time adult and children's television shows, educational television, expert witness testimony, and college graduates' conversations with friends and spouses. The words used in these different contexts were ranked according to their frequency of occurrence in the English language. The most common words are lower in number and the most rare numbers are higher in number. For example, the word "the" is ranked 1, the word "it" is ranked 10, the word "know" is ranked 100, and the word "occurrence" is ranked 86,000. For purposes of comparison, the researchers considered a word with a rank lower than 10,000 to be "rare." By this definition, a "rare" word is one that is outside of the vocabulary of a fourth to sixth grader.

In general, Hayes and Ahrens (1988) found that when compared to written language, speech contains far fewer rare or unique words. For example, the text of a child's book uses more rare words than does any kind of oral language except courtroom testimony. Yet, even in the special situation of expert witness testimony, the rarity of words used was substantially lower than those found in the text of popular magazines, newspapers, or abstracts of scientific articles. These observable differences between oral and written language have notable implications for vocabulary development. Namely, a child is far more likely to encounter a word outside of his current vocabulary while reading than while watching television or engaging in interesting conversation with a college-educated adult (Corson, 1995; Hayes & Ahrens, 1988). Table 3.1 provides an illustration of some of the differences observed between the various contexts.

The differences between oral and written language are easily understood and explainable when one considers the different demands and characteristics of the two forms of communication. For example, as Hayes (1988) pointed out, speech and writing normally occur under different time constraints. There are certain time pressures associated with natural conversation that are eliminated when communicating via writing. Speakers must respond quickly and fluently in order to maintain the flow of dialogue or

TABLE 3.1

Selected Statistics for Major Sources of Spoken and Written Language

	Rank of Median Words	Rare Words per 1000
I. Printed texts		
Abstracts of scientific articles	4389	128.0
Newspapers	1690	68.3
Popular Magazines	1399	65.7
Adult books	1058	52.7
Comic books	867	53.5
Children's books	627	30.9
Preschool books	578	16.3
II. Television texts		
Popular prime-time adult shows	490	22.7
Popular prime-time children's shows	543	20.2
Cartoon shows	598	30.8
Mr. Rogers and Sesame Street	413	2.0
III. Adult speech		
Expert witness testimony	1008	28.4
College graduates to friends, spouses	496	17.3

Note. Adapted from Hayes & Ahrens (1988) in Cunningham & Stanovich (1998).

they may be competing for "control of the floor." As a result, speakers must access words very quickly. Access to words in our productive and receptive vocabularies is largely dependent on the word's relative frequency. The less common the word, the longer it takes to retrieve the word from memory (Marshalek, Lohman, & Snow, 1981). Who has not searched their lexicon for the "right" word only to substitute a simpler or more common one to keep the conversation flowing? As a result, conversation relies heavily on the use of common words. By contrast, in writing there is far more time to search one's vocabulary (or thesaurus or dictionary) for the most appropriate, precise, and communicative words. This typically results in the use of rare or less common words in writing.

Baines (1996) provides a clear and compelling example of this type of "lexical pruning" (Stanovich, 2000) that occurs between written language and speech in his comparison of movie scripts and their books of origin. Conducting a simple word analysis of all the words found in both forms (script and text) reveals the general tendency to reduce the complexity of words used in speech. For example, in an analysis of the book *To Kill a Mockingbird,* Baines (1996) illustrates that while the written text of the book uses thirteen "U" words including *up, upstairs, uncrossed, us, upon, unhitched, unpainted, under, use, until, undress, used, and unique,* the script uses fewer, only seven "U" words: *ugly, under, until, up, upstairs, us,* and *used.* This general trend is demonstrated by Baines (1996) for numerous letters in the alphabet across multiple texts and scripts.

Another obvious difference between oral and written language is the amount of contextual information available to the communicants. It is well known that speech is a more contextualized form of communication than writing. Whereas speech often relies on a variety of nonverbal and contextual clues, written communication must use explicit references in order to ensure comprehension. The result is the use of more common words in oral language than in written language. For example, if a child saw a weathervane on top of a barn during a car ride in the country, oral communication might lead to the following interaction: The child points to the object and asks, "What's that on top of there?" The mother looks to where the child is pointing and responds, "That's something farmers use to show the way the wind blows." In fact, the word "weathervane" is not even necessary to respond to the child's question. Alternatively, if the child encountered a picture of a weathervane while reading a storybook, the text below the picture might read, "Atop the dilapidated red barn sat an old-fashioned weathervane used by the farmer to determine the direction of the wind." The latter example includes far more explicit and descriptive words, which are necessary to direct the child's attention to the object being described in text.

Given the apparent differences in lexical richness between oral and written language and the resulting differences in opportunities to encounter new words, it is important to consider the different ways that children are exposed to *written* language. The primary sources of exposure occur via shared and independent reading experiences. The next section focuses on the role of oral reading and independent reading as mechanisms for vocabulary development and growth.

THE CONTRIBUTION OF READING ALOUD
TO VOCABULARY GROWTH

In order for encounters with language to increase a child's vocabulary, the child must be exposed to words that are outside of his or her current lexicon. However, the limits of children's reading abilities often make it difficult to find text that is challenging enough to expand their vocabulary, yet does not exceed the limits of their word recognition and decoding abilities. As a result, novel words are commonly introduced to children via shared reading or "read-alouds." As argued earlier, text provides a different layer of exposure that can support vocabulary growth due to its inherent academic or decontextualized language.

Reading aloud to children, especially preschool and kindergarten age children, has long been viewed as an important aspect of encouraging language and literacy development (Adams, 1990; Baker, Scher, & Mackler, 1997). In fact, it has been argued that reading aloud to children is the most important activity for developing the knowledge that is necessary to succeed in reading (Baker et al., 1997). Early and frequent opportunities to interact with written text and language prior to schooling are thought to aid in the development of skills that serve as the foundation for learning conventional reading and writing. Due to concerns over the increasingly large differences among children in vocabulary and reading comprehension abilities as they begin school, shared storybook reading has become the focus of a large body of empirical research. Specifically, research has sought to answer the following questions: What aspects of shared storybook reading enhance children's language development? Does shared storybook reading lead to vocabulary growth?

The work of several different researchers has suggested that parents and teachers read to children in qualitatively different ways and that these differences may have appreciable influences on the amount of resulting language development (e.g., Beck & McKeown, 2001; Heath, 1983; Ninio, 1980; Snow, 1983). Much of this research was based on the idea that active participation on behalf of the child is necessary for shared book reading to be effective. For example, Whitehust et al. (1988) investigated the effects of a 1-month intervention program designed to optimize parental reading of picture books on the language development of children between 21 and 35 months of age. The researchers divided 30 child–parent dyads into two groups. In the control group, the parents were informed about the merits of reading aloud to children and were instructed to audiotape their regular reading sessions with their child three or four times a week. The other group of parents were given the same instructions, but were also given explicit directions regarding the manner in which they were supposed to read to their child. These parents participated in two 25–30 minute training sessions that instructed them on effective ways to read to their child (e.g., the use of open-ended questions, function/attribute questions, and questions that require verbal responses as opposed to pointing, as well as appropriate ways to respond to children's answers). Following the intervention, children in both groups were assessed using standardized assessments of verbal expressive abilities and vocabulary. Whitehurst et al. (1988) found that children in the experimental group scored significantly higher than children in the control group on measures of expressive (but not receptive) language ability. Furthermore, an analysis of the audio-recorded reading sessions revealed that children in the experimental group had higher mean length of utterance, a higher frequency of phrases, and a lower frequency of single words. The researchers concluded that variations in shared storybook reading can have notable effects on language development.

Other researchers have subsequently sought to examine the specific behaviors or aspects of shared storybook reading that lead to vocabulary development. For example, Senechal & Cornell (1993) investigated whether a single reading of a storybook was sufficient to produce vocabulary growth, and whether participation was necessary in producing that growth. They read a story to 80 four-year-olds and 80 five-year-olds. The passage contained 10 target words known to be unfamiliar to young children. Four different reading conditions were used, representing a continuum of levels of participation on behalf of the children. In some conditions the book was read verbatim, whereas in other groups the vocabulary words were repeated, children were asked questions about the story, or the new vocabulary words introduced were recast. Immediately following the reading and then 1 week later, the children were administered a test designed to assess their expressive and receptive knowledge of the target words. Results indicated that the two age groups were equal in their ability to recognize words immediately following the reading. However, at the 1-week follow-up, the older children remembered more of the vocabulary words. Although the single reading appeared to contribute substantially to receptive vocabulary growth, it was not sufficient in enhancing expressive vocabulary. Interestingly, it was also found that the reading was effective in enhancing receptive vocabulary development regardless of the amount of participation required of the children. In other words, in contrast to Whitehurst et al. (1988), receptive vocabulary learning (not expressive) was robust after a single storybook reading regardless of the level of participation on behalf of the child.

Senechal (1997) made an effort to reconcile the contradictory findings of previous work and to extend our understanding of the effects of book reading behaviors and the role of multiple versus single exposures to storybooks. She investigated the effect of single storybook reading, repeated storybook reading, and questioning (repeated reading and labeling of target items with novel words) on acquisition of expressive and receptive vocabulary in 60 children age 3 and 4. As in the earlier study by Senechal & Cornell (1993), stories contained 10 target words that would be unfamiliar to the children but represented concepts known to the children. Children in the single-reading condition were pretested for receptive knowledge of target words, read the text verbatim, and then were posttested for expressive and receptive knowledge of the target words. In the repeated-reading and questioning condition, the procedure consisted of two sessions. In the first session, children were pretested for their receptive knowledge of the target words, and then read the storybook twice. In the repeated-reading condition, the text was read verbatim, and in the questioning condition, the reader asked "what or where questions" after reading each of the target words. In the questioning condition, if the child did not include the vocabulary word in his or her response, he or she was prompted to do so or the reader labeled the target word. The second repeated-reading and questioning session occurred on the following day. Children were read the story for a third time and then posttested for expressive and receptive vocabulary. Senechal (1997) found that listening to repeated readings of a story facilitated children's expressive and receptive vocabulary growth. In addition, she found that active participation was more helpful in the acquisition of expressive rather than receptive vocabulary.

Taking a fine-grained approach, these studies have sought to clarify which dimensions of book reading are most effective in promoting vocabulary growth. It appears that although a single reading may be sufficient in leading to receptive vocabulary development, multiple exposures are necessary for the development of expressive vocabulary. Moreover, the results collectively indicate that listening may be sufficient in the development of receptive vocabulary, but that active participation in reading is a prerequisite for the development of expressive vocabulary.

Robbins & Ehri (1994) also helped to clarify the role of storybook reading on vocabulary development. Specifically, they sought to determine: (a) whether exposure to target words in the context of shared book reading would, in fact, improve children's knowledge of the words over control words, (b) whether increasing exposure to target words would result in greater learning, and (c) whether children's general vocabulary knowledge would be related to the gains in vocabulary resulting from storybook reading. In order to address these issues, they recruited 38 kindergarten students from a public elementary school. They selected nonreaders (in order to ensure that gains in vocabulary were attributable to hearing the words in a story and not reading the words in print) who were unfamiliar with the experimental texts and scored within one standard deviation below the mean or two standard deviations above the mean on the standardized measure of vocabulary. The children were then divided into three ability groups based on their general vocabulary abilities and were read one of two stories containing 11 target words. The target words occurred one or two times in each story. The story was heard on two occasions and no word meanings were discussed. Children were then given a vocabulary test assessing their knowledge of the 11 target words in the story they heard, as well as their knowledge of the 11 target words in the story they did not hear. Results indicated that children recognized the meanings of significantly more vocabulary words from the story that they were exposed to than the story to which they were not exposed. In addition, they found that gains in vocabulary were greater for children with larger entering vocabularies and that four exposures to words were necessary but not sufficient for higher rates of word learning. This research provided clarification regarding the specific manner in which words are learned through shared storybook reading and provided converging evidence for the general finding that book reading is a potent mechanism in the acquisition of vocabulary.

READING ALOUD TO INDEPENDENT READERS

The research described thus far has investigated the value of shared book reading (i.e., reading aloud to them) for children who were not yet capable of reading independently. However, there is reason to believe that even after acquiring the ability to read independently, children *still* benefit from listening to text read aloud. For example, Elley (1989) examined the effects of teacher-directed storybook reading on vocabulary acquisition in 7- and 8-year-old students. Similar to the studies previously described, children were read a text containing target words and were given pre and posttests of vocabulary knowledge. The frequency of the target word in the text varied, as did the redundancy in the surrounding context and the degree to which the word was depicted by illustrations. Whereas the conditions used in the study of the 7-year-olds required no participation and provided no explanation, the study of the 8-year-old children included varying levels of participation and explanation provided by the teacher. Elley (1989) found that 7- and 8-year-olds showed vocabulary gains of 15% after hearing a story on three different occasions with no required participation or teacher explanation. In addition, 8-year-olds demonstrated gains of 40% when explanation accompanied the story. Overall, word learning was found to be largely a function of word frequency, depiction of the word in illustrations, and redundancy in surrounding context.

One potential limitation of the research described thus far is the fact that all studies report on the vocabulary learning that results from book reading in the context of controlled experiments. Although these experiments address some of the causal hypotheses that are put forth in the literature, they do not inform us as to the incidental growth of vocabulary during read-alouds. Senechal, LeFevre, Hudson, and Lawson (1996) attempted to address this concern by investigating the contribution of assessed book reading to vocabulary knowledge in a more naturalistic manner. The researchers based their work on the assumption that parent and child knowledge of storybooks and children's authors would serve as an index of the *frequency* of shared reading. This assumption was based on the earlier work of other researchers demonstrating that knowledge of book titles and authors is highly indicative of reading volume or engagement in young children and adults (Cunningham & Stanovich, 1990, 1991; Stanovich & Cunningham, 1993; Stanovich & West, 1989). Thus, Senechal et al. (1996) examined whether parent and child knowledge of storybooks was related to children's performance on standardized measures of vocabulary. Interestingly, they found that even after controlling for children's analytic intelligence, parental exposure to adult reading material, and parents' level of education, knowledge of books (or level of print exposure) explained unique and independent variance in children's performance on measures of receptive vocabulary. Moreover, children's knowledge of books was predictive of receptive and expressive vocabulary after controlling for parental print exposure and socioeconomic factors. In other words, convergent results are found both across experimental studies and in more naturalistic circumstances.

The benefits of reading aloud or shared book reading have been found across a wide array of studies that also included special populations. For example, research has demonstrated positive effects of shared reading with children who have limited vocabularies or language delays (Crain-Thoreson, Dale, & Philip, 1999; Hargrave & Senechal, 2000) and among economically disadvantaged children (Dickinson & Smith, 1994; Wasik & Bond, 2001; Whitehurst, Arnold, Epstein, Angell, Smith, & Fischel, 1994).

Collectively, the findings described here help to clarify the role of book reading behaviors and their effect on vocabulary growth. These studies begin to provide an empirical basis for some of the commonsensical suggestions and policy that educators have promoted regarding reading aloud to children. Overall, the results suggest that shared book reading is an important and independent mechanism in the development of vocabulary in young children.

THE CONTRIBUTION OF INDEPENDENT READING
TO VOCABULARY GROWTH

As discussed, the large differences in lexical richness between speech, coupled with individual differences in exposure to literacy, are a major source of variation in vocabulary development. Although a portion of the variability in exposure to text is a result of shared book reading, as children grow and mature into readers, a second mechanism contributes to differential growth in this area. Simply put, some children's vocabularies increase exponentially due to the fact that they read much more than others.

Children display vast differences in their amount of independent reading. Although not a substitute for direct and explicit instruction in reading, independent reading increases reading ability and is a particularly potent mechanism of increasing language skills. We can reliably attribute some of the differences we observe in vocabulary development among school-age children to their level of reading volume.

Stanovich (1986, 1993, 2000; Stanovich & Cunningham, 1992) has emphasized the dramatic differences in the amount of reading individuals choose to engage in and has pointed out that these differences can be observed even within a generally literate society among individuals with similar levels of reading ability and education. As an example. Table 3.2

TABLE 3.2
Variation in Amount of Independent Reading

Percentile	Independent Reading Minutes Per Day	Words Read Per Year
98	65.0	4,358,000
90	21.1	1,823,000
80	14.2	1,146,000
70	9.6	622,000
60	6.5	432,000
50	4.6	282,000
40	3.2	200,000
30	1.3	106,000
20	0.7	21,000
10	0.1	8,000
2	0.0	0

Note. Adapted from Anderson, Wilson, and Fielding (1988) in Cunningham & Stanovich, 1998.

presents the data from a study conducted by Anderson, Wilson, and Fielding (1988) investigating the ways that fifth-grade students spend their time outside of school. Based on daily diaries that the children completed over a period of several months, the investigators estimated the number of minutes per day that children spent engaged in reading and nonreading activities. They found that an average child (i.e., a child whose reading activity placed him or her at the 50th percentile) read only 4.6 minutes per day; however, this is over six times as much as a child at the 20th percentile, who read less than 1 minute daily. In yet another example, the child at the 80th percentile was reading 14.2 minutes daily—over 20 times as much as the child at the 20th percentile. Surely these dramatic differences in exposure to text must result in corresponding differences in vocabulary growth.

Anderson et al. (1988) estimated the children's reading rates and used these, in conjunction with the amount of reading in minutes per day, to extrapolate a figure for the number of words that the children at various percentiles were reading in a year's time. These figures, presented in the far right of Table 3.2, illustrate the enormous differences in word exposure that are generated by children's differential preferences toward reading. For example, the average child at the 90th percentile in reading volume reads almost 2½ million words per year outside of school, over 46 times more words than the child at the 10th percentile, who is exposed to just 51,000 words outside of school during a year's time. Or, to put it another way, the entire year's out-of-school exposure for the child at the 10th percentile amounts to just 8 days reading for the child at the 90th percentile. These differences, combined with the lexical richness of print, act to create large vocabulary differences among children.

EXAMINING THE CONSEQUENCES OF DIFFERENTIAL DEGREES OF READING VOLUME

Although there are clear theoretical reasons to speculate that these differences in reading volume may result in specific cognitive consequences in domains like vocabulary, it is necessary to demonstrate that these effects are genuine. In our research, we have sought empirical evidence for the specific facilitative effects of reading volume—effects that do not simply result from the higher cognitive abilities and skills of the more avid reader. Although there are considerable differences in the amount of reading that children engage in within the classroom (Allington, 1984), it is likely that differences in *out*-of-school reading volume are an even more powerful source of rich-get-richer and poor-get-poorer achievement patterns (Anderson et al., 1988; Stanovich, 1986, 2000). As a research group, we have tried to examine the unique contribution that independent or out-of-school reading makes toward reading ability, aspects of verbal intelligence, and general knowledge about the world. In order to effectively examine the role of reading volume with respect to these cognitive skills, it was necessary to develop a method for assessing reading volume. Therefore, one aspect of our research program involved the development of such a measure. The measure of reading volume designed and pioneered by our research group (Cunningham & Stanovich, 1990; Stanovich & West, 1989) has some notable advantages in investigations of this kind.

In all, we developed two measures of adults' reading volume and one measure of children's reading volume. Briefly, the children's measure, the Title Recognition Test (TRT), requires children to identify the titles of popular children's books from a list of titles. The list includes equal numbers of titles of real children's books and foils or made-up titles. This task is easy to administer to large numbers of children, it does not make significant cognitive demands, and its results are reliable—it is not possible for children to distort their responses toward what they perceive as socially desirable answers. Because the number of wrong answers can be counted against corrected ones, it is possible to remove the effects of guessing from the results (see Cunningham & Stanovich, 1990, 1991; Stanovich & West, 1989 for a full description of these instruments and a discussion of the logic behind them). The adults' measures, named the Author Recognition Test (ART) and Magazine Recognition Test (MRT), have the same task requirements and are described fully in Stanovich and West (1989).

The titles appearing on the various title recognition tests were selected from a sample of book titles generated in pilot investigations by groups of children ranging in age from second grade through high school. In selecting the items that appear on any one version of the TRT, an attempt was made to choose titles that were not prominent parts of classroom reading activities in these particular schools. Because we wanted the TRT to probe out-of-school rather than school-directed reading, an attempt was made to choose titles that were not used in the school curriculum.

Although a score on the TRT is not an absolute measure of children's reading volume and literacy experiences, it does provide us with an index of the *relative* differences in reading volume. This index enables us to investigate the effects that reading volume (rather than general reading comprehension and word decoding ability) has on intelligence, vocabulary, spelling, and children's general knowledge. In short, it enables us to ask: Does reading shape the quality of the lexicon? Does it influence vocabulary growth?

Because it could be argued that an observed relationship between reading volume and vocabulary or general knowledge might be accounted for by a mutual relationship between each of the two variables with a third, more salient variable (e.g., general intellectual ability), our research in this area (Cunningham & Stanovich, 1990, 1991,1997, 2003;

Stanovich & Cunningham, 1992,1993; Stanovich & West, 1989) has relied on the use of a powerful statistical technique known as *hierarchical multiple regression* (see Stanovich and Cunningham, 2004, for a discussion of the methodological uses of this procedure). We have found that, even when performance is statistically equated for reading comprehension and general ability, reading volume is still a very powerful predictor of vocabulary and knowledge differences. Thus, we believe that reading volume is not simply an indirect indicator of ability, it is a separable and independent source of cognitive differences.

READING VOLUME AS A CONTRIBUTOR TO GROWTH IN VERBAL SKILLS

In several studies, we attempted to link children's reading volume to specific cognitive outcomes after controlling for relevant general abilities such as IQ. For example, in a study of fourth-, fifth-, and sixth-grade children (Cunningham & Stanovich, 1991), we examined whether reading volume provides a unique and independent contribution to differences in vocabulary development. We employed multiple measures of vocabulary and controlled for the effects of age and intelligence. We also controlled for the effects of decoding, another specific ability that may be more closely linked to vocabulary acquisition mechanisms. There are numerous reasons to suspect that decoding skill might mediate a relationship between reading volume and a variable like vocabulary size. High levels of decoding skill, which clearly contribute to greater reading volume, might provide relatively complete verbal contexts for the induction of word meanings during reading. Thus, reading volume and vocabulary might be spuriously linked via their connection with decoding ability: Good decoders read a lot and have the best context available for inferring new words. This spurious linkage was controlled by statistically controlling for decoding ability prior to investigating reading volume. But we found that even after accounting for general intelligence and decoding ability, reading volume contributed significantly and independently to vocabulary knowledge in fourth-, fifth-, and sixth-grade children. These findings demonstrate that reading volume, although clearly a consequence of reading ability, is a significant contributor to the development of other aspects of verbal intelligence.

These results were replicated by additional research that utilized even more stringent tests of the contribution of reading volume to verbal skills in a study of college students (Stanovich & Cunningham, 1992). In this study, we removed the contributions of general intelligence and various aspects of reading ability *including* reading comprehension. Because there is substantial reason to believe that avid reading leads to increased reading comprehension, we statistically removed some of the variance that rightfully belonged to reading volume and, therefore, performed a particularly stringent assessment of the relationship between reading volume and cognitive abilities. Even so, it was found that the amount of variation in print exposure or independent reading contributed significantly and substantially to multiple measures of vocabulary knowledge. We maintain that the conservative nature of these analyses only attests to the potency and strength of reading volume.

In another study of nearly 300 college-age students, we found similar results for the influence of reading volume on vocabulary knowledge (Stanovich & Cunningham, 1993). We collected data on the students' general ability (i.e., high school grade point average, performance on an intelligence test, and an SAT-type mathematics test), Nelson-Denny Reading Comprehension, print exposure, and general knowledge (e.g., practical and cultural information). In this study, we also provided evidence that reading volume is an independent contributor to the acquisition of domain knowledge among older students. After the variance associated with general cognitive ability and reading comprehension was partialed out, reading volume accounted for a notable portion of the variance in general knowledge. In fact, not only was print exposure a unique predictor of general knowledge, it was a more robust predictor of general knowledge than the student's general cognitive ability.

This research is particularly meaningful in consideration of recent theories of cognitive development suggesting that domain knowledge and vocabulary are a determinant of information processing efficiency (see Stanovich & Cunningham, 1993). It illustrates the role that environmental factors such as independent reading can play in the growth of basic cognitive variables such as verbal fluency and vocabulary. Although basic cognitive abilities such as intelligence play a role in vocabulary growth and acquisition, these effects are mediated by the active participation in text-related experiences such as independent reading.

Further evidence for the merits of avid reading was provided by a study in which we illustrated the role that reading volume can play in the growth of vocabulary among a high-school-age population. A group of first-grade children who were administered a battery of reading tasks in a previous study (Stanovich, Cunningham, & Feeman, 1984) were followed up as eleventh graders. At the time of the 10-year follow-up, they were administered measures of exposure to print, reading comprehension, vocabulary, and general knowledge (Cunningham & Stanovich, 1997). First-grade reading ability was a strong predictor of all of the eleventh-grade outcomes and remained a significant predictor even when measures of cognitive ability were partialed out. First-grade reading ability (as well as third- and fifth-grade ability) was reliably linked to exposure to print, as assessed in the eleventh grade, even after eleventh-grade reading comprehension ability was partialed out, indicating that the rapid acquisition of reading ability might well help to develop the lifetime habit of reading, irrespective of the ultimate level of reading comprehension ability that the individual attains. Individual differences in exposure to print were found to predict differences in the growth in reading comprehension ability throughout the elementary grades and thereafter.

Hierarchical regressions analogous to those conducted on the data from earlier studies were also conducted on the contemporaneous data. In seven fixed-order, hierarchical multiple regressions, our reading volume measure was entered into the equation after general ability. As in previous studies with college students (e.g., Stanovich & Cunningham, 1992), reading volume in 11th grade accounted for substantial unique variance in both vocabulary measures (37.0% and 15.3%, $p < .001$ and $p < .05$, respectively). Thus, reading volume was consistently found to be a significant predictor of vocabulary knowledge after general ability had been controlled. All of the relationships in this sample of high school students replicated those observed in other studies of college-age students (e.g., Hall, Chiarello, & Edmondson, 1996; Lewellen, Goldinger, Pisoni, & Greene, 1993; Stanovich & Cunningham, 1992, 1993). By conducting a longitudinal study, our analyses have provided us with a glimpse of the past literacy experiences of our first-grade sample and yielded some empirical clues to the cause of their subsequent divergences in verbal abilities and general knowledge.

THE RECIPROCAL EFFECTS OF READING VOLUME

Although the research detailed here allowed us to conclude that reading has positive consequences for the development of various cognitive skills, it is important to point out that the relationship between these skills and reading volume is not a one-way, linear relationship. Instead, there is a reciprocal, bidirectional relationship between reading volume and the development of cognitive skills such as vocabulary and reading comprehension. A child who reads abundantly develops greater reading skills, a larger vocabulary, and more general knowledge about the world. In return, they have increased reading comprehension and, therefore, enjoy more pleasurable reading experiences and are encouraged to read even more. By contrast, a child who rarely reads is slower in the development of reading skills and is exposed to fewer new vocabulary words and less information about the world. As a result, the child struggles more while reading and comprehends less of the text. Not surprisingly, this child derives less enjoyment from reading experiences and is less likely to choose to read in the future. This trajectory was laid out by Stanovich (1986) and has now become the well-known phenomenon entitled the "Matthew Effects" in literacy development. As Stanovich described, these are "educational sequences in which early and efficient acquisition of reading skill yields faster rates of growth in reading achievement and other cognitive skills such as vocabulary—that is, rich-get-richer and poor-get-poorer effects" (Stanovich, 1986, p. 381; Stanovich, 2000; Walberg & Tsai, 1983). Within this model, independent reading and reading aloud to children may explain part of the growing disparities we observe among students in language, literacy, and cognition.

We now appreciate that early success at reading acquisition is one of the keys that unlocks a lifetime of reading habits. The subsequent *exercise* of this habit serves to further develop reading comprehension ability in an interlocking positive feedback logic (Juel, Griffith, & Gough, 1986; Juel, 1988; Snow, Barnes, Chandler, Goodman, & Hemphill, 1991; Stanovich, 1986, 1993). As the young boy struggles to read *A Snowy Day* and comprehend the meaning of the passage, he is building his lexicon through the introduction of new words such as "heaping" and uses of known words such as "*packed* it round and firm." An optimistic account of our research, and of many of the studies described in this chapter, is that reading a lot is efficacious regardless of the level of a child's cognitive and reading ability. We do not have to wait for "prerequisite" abilities to be in place before encouraging independent reading. Even the child with limited reading and comprehension skills will build vocabulary and cognitive structures by being encouraged to read.

CONCLUSIONS

In summary, although vocabulary growth can be explained by a multiplicity of factors including general ability (Sternberg, 1987), home environment and educational background of parents (Hart & Risley, 1995, 1999), and instruction (Beck et al., 2002), there exists an additional avenue to pursue that will promote vocabulary growth: reading volume. In young children who cannot read themselves, reading aloud can provide a level of lexical difficulty that extends beyond everyday conversational language. When the practice of reading aloud from expository and narrative text is consistent and coupled with word analysis and discussion between adult and child(ren), then we can expect vocabulary knowledge to increase. Moreover, these benefits persist beyond the age when children are capable of reading independently. Thus, the practice of reading aloud to children of all ages in texts 2 to 3 years beyond their own reading level should be more widely promoted. Lexical items not typical of everyday conversation are brought to the forefront and, if treated as a point of study, can promote vocabulary growth. Knowing a word's meaning *prior* to reading it in text (and thus not having to guess at its meaning while reading) facilitates comprehension and helps to ensure more positive and enjoyable reading experiences.

Providing structured read-aloud and discussion sessions and extending independent reading experiences outside of school hours would help to encourage vocabulary growth in children. This educational practice would have the benefit of also improving reading comprehension and general knowledge about the world. Although there is no substitute for systematic and explicit instruction in basic reading skills, ancillary experiences such as independent reading can *support* learning to read, as well as reading to learn. One of the cognitive outcomes of reading engagement and volume is a richer lexicon. As we search for empirically based methods for reducing the achievement gap and increasing our students' vocabulary knowledge, the educational practice of promoting opportunities for independent, out-of-school reading should not be overlooked.

REFERENCES

Adams, M. J. (1990). *Beginning to read: Thinking and learning about print.* Cambridge, MA: MIT Press.

Allington, R. L. (1984). Content coverage and contextual reading in reading groups. *Journal of Reading Behavior, 16,* 85–96.

Anderson, R. C., & Freebody, P. (1983). Reading comprehension and the assessment and acquisition of word knowledge. In B. Huston (Ed.), *Advances in reading/language research* (Vol. 2, pp. 231–291). Greenwich, CT: JAI Press.

Anderson, R. C., & Nagy, W. E. (1992, Winter). The vocabulary conundrum. *The American Educator,* 14–18.

Anderson, R. C., Wilson, P. T., & Fielding, L. G. (1988). Growth in reading and how children spend their time outside of school. *Reading Research Quarterly, 23,* 285–303.

Baines, L. (1996). From page to screen: When a novel is interpreted for film, what gets lost in the translation? *Journal of Adolescent and Adult Literacy, 39,* 612–622.

Baker, L., Scher, D., & Mackler, K. (1997). Home and family influences on motivations for reading. *Educational Psychologist, 32*(2), 69–82.

Beck, I. L., & McKeown, M.G. (2001). Text talk: Capturing the benefits of reading-aloud experiences for young children. *The Reading Teacher, 55*(1), 10–20.

Beck, I. L., & McKeown, M. G., & Kucan, L. (2002). *Bringing words to life: Robust vocabulary instruction.* New York: The Guilford Press.

Beck, I. L., McKeown, M. G., & McCaslin, E. (1983). All contexts are not created equal. *Elementary School Journal, 83,* 177–181.

Beck, I. L., Perfetti, C. A., & McKeown, M. G. (1982). Effects of long-term vocabulary instruction on lexical access and reading comprehension. *Journal of Educational Psychology, 74*(4), 506–521.

Biemiller, A. (2001). Teaching vocabulary: Early, direct, and sequential. *The American Educator, 25*(1), 24–28.

Crain-Thoreson, C., Dale, P. S., & Philip, S. (1999). Enhancing linguistic performance: Parents and teachers as book reading partners for children with language delays. *Topics in Early Childhood Special Education, 19*(1), 28–39.

Corson, D. (1995). *Using English words.* Boston: Kluwer Academic.

Cunningham, A. E., & Stanovich, K. E. (1990). Assessing print exposure and orthographic processing skills in children: A quick measure of reading experience. *Journal of Educational Psychology, 82,* 733–740.

Cunningham, A. E., & Stanovich, K. E. (1991). Tracking the unique effects of print exposure in children: Associations with vocabulary, general knowledge, and spelling. *Journal of Educational Psychology, 83*(2), 264–274.

Cunningham, A. E., & Stanovich, K. E. (1997). Early reading acquisition and its relation to reading experience and ability 10 years later. *Developmental Psychology, 33*(6), 934–945.

Cunningham, A. E., & Stanovich, K. E. (1998). What reading does for the mind. *American Educator,* 8–15.

Cunningham, A. E., & Stanovich, K. E. (2003). Reading matters: How reading English influences cognition. In J. Flood, D. Lapp, J. R. Squire, & J. M. Jensen (Eds.), *Handbook of research on teaching the English language arts* (pp. 666–675). Mahwah, NJ: Lawrence Erlbaum Associates.

Daneman, M., & Green, I. (1986). Individual differences in comprehending and producing words in context. *Journal of Memory and Language, 25,* 1–18.

Dickinson, D. K., & Smith, M. W. (1994). Long-term effects of preschool teachers' book reading on low-income children's vocabulary and story comprehension. *Reading Research Quarterly, 29*(2), 105–122.

Elley, W. B. (1989). Vocabulary acquisition from listening to stories. *Reading Research Quarterly, 24*(2), 174–187.

Hall, V. C., Chiarello, K., & Edmondson, B. (1996). Deciding where knowledge comes from depends on where you look. *Journal of Educational Psychology, 88,* 305–313.

Hargrave, A.C., & Senechal, M. (2000). A book reading intervention with preschool children who have limited vocabularies: The benefits of regular reading and dialogic reading. *Early Childhood Research Quarterly, 15*(1), 75–90.

Hart, B., & Risley, T. (1995). *Meaningful differences in the everyday experiences of young American children.* Baltimore, MD: Paul H. Brookes.

Hart, B., & Risley, T. (1999). *The social world of children.* Baltimore, MD: Paul H. Brookes.

Hayes, D. P. (1988). Speaking and writing: Distinct patterns of word choice. *Journal of Memory and Language, 27,* 572–585.

Hayes, D. P., & Ahrens, M. (1988). Vocabulary simplification for children: A special case of "motherese"? *Journal of Child Language, 15,* 395–410.

Heath, S. B. (1983). *Ways with words: Language, life and work in communities and classrooms.* Cambridge, England: Cambridge University Press.

Juel, C. (1988). Learning to read and write: A longitudinal study of fifty-four children from first through fourth grade. *Journal of Educational Psychology, 80,* 437–447.

Juel, C., Griffith, P. L., & Gough, P. B. (1986). Acquisition of literacy: A longitudinal study of children in first and second grade. *Journal of Educational Psychology, 78,* 243–255.

Keats, E. J. (1962). *The snowy day.* New York: Scholastic.

Lewellen, M. J., Goldinger, S., Pisoni, D. B., & Greene, B. (1993). Lexical familiarity and processing efficiency: Individual differences in naming, lexical decision, and semantic categorization. *Journal of Experimental Psychology: General, 122,* 316–330.

Marshalek, B., Lohman, M., & Snow, C. E. (1981). *Trait and process aspects of vocabulary knowledge and verbal ability.* (Technical Report No. 15). Stanford, CA: Stanford University.

McKeown, M. G. (1985). The acquisition of word meaning from context by children of high and low ability. *Reading Reseach Quarterly, 20*(4), 482–495.

Nagy, W. E., & Anderson, R. C. (1984). How many words are there in printed school English? *Reading Research Quarterly, 19,* 304–330.

Nagy, W. E., Anderson, R. C., & Herman, P. A. (1987). Learning word meaning from context during normal reading. *American Educational Research Journal, 24*(2), 237–270.

Nagy, W. E., & Herman, P. A. (1985). Incidental vs. instructional approaches to increasing reading vocabulary. *Educational Perspectives, 23*(1), 16–21.

Nagy, W. E., Herman, P. A., & Anderson, R. C. (1985). Learning words from context. *Reading Research Quarterly, 20*(2), 233–253.

Ninio, A. (1980). Picture book reading in mother–infant dyads belonging to two subgroups in Israel. *Child Development, 51,* 587–590.

Robbins, C., & Ehri, L. C. (1994). Reading storybooks to kindergarteners helps them learn new vocabulary words. *Journal of Educational Psychology, 86*(1), 54–64.

Senechal, M. (1997). The differential effects of storybook reading on preschoolers' acquisition of expressive and receptive vocabulary. *Journal of Child Language, 24,* 123–138.

Senechal, M., & Cornell, E. H. (1993). Vocabulary acquisition through shared reading experiences. *Reading Research Quarterly, 28*(4), 361–374.

Senechal, M., LeFevre, J., Hudson, E., Lawson, E. P. (1996). Knowledge of storybooks as a predictor of young children's vocabulary. *Journal of Educational Psychology, 88*(3), 520–536.

Smith, F. (1989). Overselling literacy. *Phi Delta Kappan, 70*(5), 353–359.

Snow, C. E. (1983). Literacy and language: Relationship during preschool years. *Havard Educational Review, 53,* 165–189.

Snow, C. E., Barnes, W. S., Chandler, J., Goodman, I., & Hemphill, L. (1991). *Unfulfilled expectations: Home and school influences on literacy.* Cambridge, MA: Harvard University Press.

Stahl, S. (1999). *Vocabulary development.* Newton, MA: Brookline Books.

Stanovich, K. E. (1986). Matthew effects in reading: Some consequences for the individual differences in the acquisition of literacy. *Reading Research Quarterly, 21,* 360–407.

Stanovich, K. E. (1993). Does reading make you smarter? Literacy and the development of verbal intelligence. In H. Reese (Ed.), *Advances in child development and behavior, 24,* 133–180. San Diego, CA: Academic Press.

Stanovich, K. E. (2000). *Progress in understanding reading.* New York: The Guilford Press.

Stanovich, K. E., & Cunningham, A. E. (1992). Studying the consequences of literacy within a literate society: The cognitive correlates of print exposure. *Memory and Cognition, 20*(1), 51–68.

Stanovich, K. E., & Cunningham, A. E. (1993). Where does knowledge come from? Associations between print exposure and information acquisition. *Journal of Educational Psychology, 85*(2), 211–229.

Stanovich, K. E., & Cunningham, A. E. (2004). Influences from correlational data: Exploring associations with reading experience. In N. K. Duke & M. H. Mallette (Eds.), *Literacy research methodologies* (pp. 28–45). New York: Guilford Press.

Stanovich, K. E., Cunningham, A. E., & Feeman, D. J. (1984). Intelligence, cognitive skills, and early reading progress. *Reading Research Quarterly, 19,* 278–303.

Stanovich, K.E., & West, R.F. (1989). Exposure to print and orthographic processing. *Reading Research Quarterly, 24,* 402–433.

Sternberg, R. J. (1987). Most vocabulary is learned from context. In M. G. McKeown & M. E. Curtis (Eds.), *The nature of vocabulary acquisition* (pp. 89–105). Hillsdale, NJ: Lawrence Erlbaum Associates.

Sternberg, R. J., & Powell, J. (1983). Comprehending verbal comprehension. *American Psychologist, 38,* 878–893.

Wasik, B. A., & Bond, M. A. (2001). Beyond the pages of a book: Interactive book reading and language development in preschool classrooms. *Journal of Educational Psychology, 93*(2), 243–250.

Walberg, H. J., & Tsai, S. (1983). Matthew effects in education. *American Educational Research Journal, 20,* 359–373.

Whitehurst, G. J., Arnold, D. S., Epstein, J. N., Angell, A. L., Smith, M., & Fischel, J. E. (1994). A picture book reading intervention in day care and home for children from low-income families. *Developmental Psychology, 30*(5), 679–689.

Whitehurst, G. J., Falco, F. L., Lonigan, C. J., Fischel, J. E., DeBaryshe, B. D., Valdez-Menchaca, M. C., & Caulfield, M. (1988). Accelerating language development through picture book reading. *Developmental Psychology, 24*(4), 552–559.

Chapter 4

Creating Opportunities to Acquire New Word Meanings From Text[1]

Judith A. Scott
University of California, Santa Cruz

An accumulation of research indicates that many words are learned incidentally through the independent reading of text, through oral language discussions, and through reading aloud to children (Elley, 1989; Nagy, Anderson, & Herman, 1987; Penno, Wilkinson, & Moore, 2002). Even a single incidental encounter with a word in text can facilitate word learning (Nagy et al., 1987; Schwanenflugel, Stahl, & McFalls, 1997; Swanborn & de Glopper, 1999). However, there is also evidence that children are exposed differentially to infrequent words both in independent reading and in their homes (Hart & Risley, 1995; Stanovich, 1986). Furthermore, recognition is increasing of the importance of informational literacy and students' knowledge of academic language (Duke, 2000; Hirsch, 2003). Every content area has a set of specific concepts and vocabulary. The National Reading Panel Report (NICHD, 2000) calls for an increased focus on vocabulary derived from content area materials. Yet, there appears to be little consensus on how vocabulary should be presented in informational texts and little regard given to factors that might facilitate students' word learning from such texts (Myerson, Ford, Jones, & Ward, 1991).

This chapter provides a review of research regarding word learning through text with a discussion of the implications of this research for teach-

[1]This material is based on work partially supported by the National Science Foundation under Award No. ESI-0242733, in connection with the development of the Seeds of Science/Roots of Reading Program by the Graduate School of Education and Lawrence Hall of Science at the University of California, Berkeley. Any opinions, findings, and conclusions or recommendations expressed in this material are those of the author and do not necessarily reflect the views of the National Science Foundation.

ers, publishers, and researchers. It then directs attention specifically to how this research pertains to the reading, understanding, and learning of new words from informational text. The intent is to spur discussion and interest in maximizing the odds that students, particularly those who depend on schools for exposure to academic language, will be able to read, understand, and learn new words from informational text.

THE COMPLEXITY OF LEARNING NEW WORDS: THE ROLE OF CONTEXT

The process of learning new vocabulary is often perceived as a reductionist activity in which words are learned and tested out of context. In the process of studying vocabulary, researchers often decompose a coherent text to examine a minute element of the text: its individual words. Decades of research indicate that reading comprehension requires more than knowledge of individual words (Beck & McKeown, 1991; Nagy & Scott, 2000). Reading comprehension involves the interplay of the reader, the text, the activity, and the sociocultural context of reading events (RAND Reading Study Group, 2002). In this process, a transaction between the reader and the text must take place in which prior knowledge and the creation of a mental representation of meaning play a central role (Anderson & Pearson, 1984). This does not mean that individual words are unimportant; indeed, words are the central building blocks of communication (Clark, 1993). However, in studying the process of vocabulary acquisition, we need to ensure that we keep the complexity and transactional nature of the process in mind.

One factor that contributes to the complexity of studying word knowledge is the understanding of what it means to know a word. Knowing a word can range from being able to supply a definition to having a vague understanding of its semantic field. Furthermore, for each known word, there are numerous related facets of knowledge that are not captured by a typical definition. Definitions reduce word knowledge to decontextualized features, abstracted from the numerous ways that a word has been used in the past (Landau, 1984). However, a person's knowledge about words is expansive and involves interrelated connections that create networks of knowledge. Such networks of knowledge can be considered word schemas for words (Nagy & Scott, 1990). Nation (1990) identified eight separate facets of knowledge surrounding a word, including knowledge of a word's spoken form, its written form, the way it behaves in sentences, words commonly found near the word, its frequency in oral and written language, its conceptual meaning, how and when it is commonly used, and its association with other words. These different aspects of word knowledge are at least partially independent. Thus, one person may know the definition of a word but not its frequency or how to use it, whereas another may be able to pronounce it but unable to distinguish it from similar words. Words are also polysemous—they often have multiple meanings (i.e., *dinner plate* vs. *home plate*); interrelated—one's knowledge of a given word is not independent from knowledge of other words (i.e., *magma*, *lava*, and *volcano*); and heterogeneous—what it means to know a word depends on the kind of word being learned (i.e., *the* vs. *hypotenuse;* Nagy & Scott, 2000).

Vocabulary researchers have long recognized such multiple dimensions of word knowledge. In addition, accumulated evidence indicates that word meanings are developed incrementally over time (Nagy & Scott, 2000; Schwanenflugel et al., 1997; Stahl, 2003). There appears to be an initial "fast mapping" of new words into general categories or associations, but it takes multiple exposures to a word to build up enough knowledge to be able to use it comfortably (Clark, 1993). As a word is encountered repeatedly over time, information about the word grows and it moves up the continuum toward "known." Dale (1965) proposed four levels of word knowledge ranging from "I never saw it before" to "I know it." More recently, Paribakht and Wesche (1999) added a fifth level: "I can use it in a sentence." This word knowledge may often be subconscious. Adults have been found to have detectable word knowledge about words they claimed not to know (Durso & Shore, 1991). To complicate this further, a person's continuum of word knowledge is unique. For instance, one person may know that *taupe* is a color word, but not be able to pick out a taupe swatch in a paint store. Another may know that a *router* is some kind of tool, but not know how it might be used.

Understanding the transactional process of text comprehension, the complexity of word knowledge, and the incremental process of vocabulary acquisition has implications for understanding how one acquires information about words through the process of reading or hearing text. With this as a backdrop, I pooled information from studies of incidental learning of words from independent reading, studies of incidental learning of words from being read to, and studies on deriving word meanings from text. In the following review, I have organized the studies into those pertaining to "local context"—those having to do with factors within words and within texts—and those pertaining to global factors—those having to do with the purposes and background knowledge of readers. The purpose of this review is to identify factors that might contribute to vocabulary acquisition from text and to suggest generalizations that can be used to maximize opportunities for students to learn new words from context.

Local Context

Local contexts refer to the features of words and to the context created by words and sentences within texts. In considering the local context, there are both within-word factors, such as the morphemes of a word, and the sentences and texts in which a word appears.

Within-Word Factors.   A number of features of a word can influence the attention that readers pay to it as well as the ease with which they remember it. Among those features identified by researchers are: (a) morphology, (b) a word's part of speech, (c) the vividness or concreteness of the word's meaning, and (d) frequency of appearance in written English.

When a person encounters a new word, its morphology is one of the main sources of information available to him or her. Morphemes are the smallest units of meaning, and "because they serve as phonological, orthographic, and semantic/syntactic units, they facilitate both word reading and understanding of words and texts" (Carlisle, 2003, p. 292). Morphemic analysis involves the derivation of a word's meaning by examining and using its morphological structure, such as word roots, prefixes, suffixes, and inflected endings (Edwards, Font, Baumann, & Boland, 2004).

Knowledge of morphology plays a valuable role in word learning from context because of the way in which students can use knowledge of a word's morphological structure to hypothesize the meaning of a new word. If one knows that *botany* relates to the study of plants, and *-phobia* means "fear of," one might hypothesize that *botanophobia* means "fear of plants" (Nagy & Scott, 1990). More than 60% of the words students encounter have a relatively transparent morphological structure (Nagy & Anderson, 1984). Students can be taught to use both morphological analysis and contextual analysis to figure out the meanings of new words (Baumann, Edwards, Font, Tereshinski, Kame'enui, & Olejnik, 2002). Anglin (1993) found that students in all grade levels use some morphological problem solving, with relatively large increases in recognizing derived words between third and fifth grades. The vocabulary knowledge accounted for by derived words represented, on average, 16% of the recognition vocabulary of first graders, increasing to almost 40% by fifth grade (Anglin, 1993).

The ability to figure out a word's meaning by analyzing its component parts has been found to be significantly related to word-reading achievement (Carlisle, 1995, 2003; Champion, 1997), although instruction in morphological and contextual analysis does not necessarily lead to improved reading comprehension (Baumann et al., 2002). Many researchers call for more research in this area, as evidence to date suggests that morphological awareness is an aspect of learning words from context that should not be ignored (Carlisle, 2003).

A second within-word factor is a word's part of speech. It seems intuitively obvious that learning nouns would be easer than learning verbs. Seeing a picture of an aardvark with a brief description of its eating habits may give a reader enough information to know what it is (an animal) even if one does not have extensive background knowledge of African animals. In comparison, illustration of the meaning of the verb *discourage* seems much more difficult. Unfortunately, the research does not seem to support such an intuitively obvious conclusion.

Instead, the ease with which one learns nouns, verbs, adjectives, or adverbs from context seems to vary across studies, is confounded with concreteness of a word, and appears to depend, to a great extent, on the words chosen to represent each category. There seems to be no clear evidence that words in one category are learned more easily than words in another. In some studies, verbs, adjectives, and adverbs were learned more easily than nouns, whereas in others, nouns were learned more frequently.

Schwanenflugel et al. (1997) found that the part-of-speech category positively influenced the gain scores with verbs, adjectives, and adverbs learned more easily than nouns. However, only some nouns in the study referred to distinct objects (i.e., *beacon, sorceress*). The others were either abstract nouns (i.e., *vicinity, tribute*) or mass nouns (i.e., *venom*). Robbins and Ehri (1994) also reported that, although there were too few instances to generalize, verbs and adjectives were learned more easily than nouns in their study. On the other hand, Elley (1989) found part of speech to be a significant factor in the opposite direction during a study of reading aloud to children. Nouns were learned more easily than other parts of speech, with mean gain scores of 24% versus 6%. The various findings regarding part of speech are consistent with Laufer's (1997) analysis of factors that affect word learning in a second language. She concluded that part of speech has no clear effect on learning words from context (Laufer, 1990, 1997). Overall, this factor does not seem to be highly significant when considering vocabulary acquisition from text. The results regarding the type of words learned most easily may depend more on the set of words chosen for a study than on a general factor.

A third feature of a word is its vividness or concreteness. There is substantial evidence that abstract words are harder to understand than words with concrete or vivid imagery (Schwanenflugel, 1991). In addition, Schwanenflugel et al. (1997) found that words' relative concreteness positively influenced students' gain scores in incidental word learning, concluding that individual characteristics of vocabulary words are more important than text features in determining which words are learned. However, Laufer (1990, 1997) claims that no such effect holds for second-language learners because many second-language learners have already developed abstract concepts in their native language, and the addition of a new label for a familiar concept is relatively easy.

If the ability to picture a concept is considered as a measure of concreteness, more studies can be included in this discussion. Elley (1989) found a significant correlation between gain scores and the number of pictorial occurrences, whereas Robbins and Ehri (1994) found no such correlation. Again, this may be due, at least in part, to the words being illustrated. The words pictured in the Elley study were not listed, although he indicated that "a simple count was made" of the number of times a word was pictured. Words in his study included *roadster, dingy, lolling, strewn, debonair, scheming, summoned, spin, outsmarted, redistributed, goner, pizzazz, reform, rapscallion,* and *startling*. The words listed as illustrated in the Robbins and Ehri (1994) study were *irate, survey, toting, abode, decrepit, consume,* and *discard*. At this point, it seems safe to say that the concreteness of words is a factor that needs to be taken into account in research and is worth consideration when publishers and teachers are trying to optimize opportunities to learn words from context.

The fourth factor—that of frequency—is one that has not been well researched in vocabulary learning from context. When word frequency has been considered, the effects of substituting rare words with more common ones has been the focus (e.g., Marks, Doctorow, & Wittrock, 1974; Wittrock, Marks, & Doctorow, 1975). In the past few years, however, levels of word frequency have gained prominence in discussions of vocabulary acquisition.

Several researchers (Beck, McKeown, & Kucan, 2003; Hiebert, chapter 12, this volume; Nation, 2001) make compelling arguments for considering word frequency as a factor in choosing words to be taught explicitly in vocabulary programs. Hiebert (in this volume) has used a corpus of 150,000 words (Zeno, Ivens, Millard, & Duvvuri, 1995) to identify those that occur 10 or more times per million words of text, and she uses this criterion, in part, to develop zones of effective instruction. Beck et al. (2003) identify useful words, or Tier Two words, as those words "likely to appear frequently in a wide variety of texts and in the written and oral language of mature language users" (p. 16), and emphasize instruction on these words. Stahl and Stahl (2004) identify such words as "Goldilocks" words: words that are not too hard or too easy but just right. Although Biemiller (chapter 11, in this volume) discounts the use of printed word frequency in identifying words for instruction, he also expresses the importance of identifying and concentrating instruction on words that are "known at 40% to 80% by median children at a target grade" (p. 241).

The idea behind all of these measures is not that rare words should not be taught, but that it is less efficient to teach rare words than words that occur more commonly in English when developing an overall vocabulary program. This is an interesting point in thinking about word meanings that might be gleaned from texts, although the frequency of words has not been considered in most studies of learning from context.

Although other word-level factors have been studied, there appears to be little evidence that factors such as the length of a word or the number of syllables affect word learning from context (Laufer, 1990, 1997; Robbins &

Ehri, 1994). Baker (1989) did find that younger readers paid more attention to word length and number of syllables than older readers did, but her study focused on the evaluation of nonwords rather than learning from context. In all, word length and number of syllables appear to be less important in determining which words will be learned from context than other factors identified within this chapter.

Word Presentation in Text. There are also factors that influence a word's understanding that have to do with the word's situation or relationship to other words in a text. Among these factors that have been identified in the research literature are: (a) helpfulness of the sentence and text context, (b) density of unknown words, and (c) word repetition.

The contexts in which unknown words are presented in text are not always helpful and, in some cases, can mislead students into making false inferences about word meanings. For instance, one might think that *grudgingly* means "to like or admire" in the sentence: "Every step she takes is so perfect and graceful," Ginny said grudgingly (Beck, McKeown, & Caslin, 1983, p. 178). Beck et al. (1983) identified a continuum of effectiveness of natural contexts for deriving the meanings of words and found some contexts to be so misleading that only 3% of the responses were correct. Negative learning probabilities have been attributed to misleading contexts within the stories read aloud to young children, and lack of contextual support hindered high school students who tried to derive the meaning of rare words in naturally occurring text (Robbins & Ehri, 1994; Schatz & Baldwin, 1986).

Rating of the context's helpfulness in naturally occurring texts had no significant effect in a study by Schwanenflugel et al. (1997), although it was significantly correlated with mean gain in Elley's study (1989). Manipulating the text to increase word learning has had mixed results. Some studies indicate that text revised to be more considerate, or to provide more useful contextual information, can produce significantly higher scores on measures of word learning (Gordon, Schumm, Coffland, & Doucette, 1992; Konopak, 1989). In these studies, fifth-grade through high school students were able to define more words more accurately when sentences were changed to convey more complete and explicit conceptual knowledge, when defining information was placed in close proximity to the unknown word, and when the clarity of connections between unknown words and those surrounding them was increased. Diakidoy (1998), however, reported that increased considerateness or the informativeness of local context did not effect word meaning acquisition from context in her study of sixth-grade students.

It seems plausible that students will learn more when they are given explicit clues to an unknown word in the surrounding context rather than a natural, implicit context. Less skilled readers appear to have greater difficulty accessing word knowledge when the text is less supportive than more able readers. Among 7- and 8-year-olds, less skilled readers had particular difficulty inferring the meaning of novel vocabulary when the definitional information was removed in proximity from the word whose meaning it elucidated (Cain, Oakhill, & Elbro, 2003).

In a secondary analysis of the data collected by Nagy et al. (1987), Diakidoy and Anderson (1991) concluded:

> One thing that is apparent in this study is that factors representing contextual information have contingent rather than independent effects on learning word meanings from context. That is to say, they appear to interact with several other factors, and moreover, the type and nature of these interactions may depend on grade level. (p. 10)

A meta-analysis of 20 experimental studies indicates that grade and skill levels impact word learning from context (Swanborn & de Glopper, 1999), and perhaps factors such as the considerateness or helpfulness of sentences surrounding words impact such a finding.

Density of unknown words is another factor that influences the probability of learning a word. In the meta-analysis conducted by Swanborn and de Glopper (1999), text–target word ratio was the one predictor that explained variance. A high density of unknown words in a text was found to obstruct incidental word learning. If the density of unknown words in a text is 1 word per 150 words, the probability of learning the word is reported to be approximately 30%. However, if the ratio is 1 to 75, the chances of learning the word drop to 14% (Swanborn & de Glopper, 1999).

In early studies of the effect of vocabulary density and difficulty, Anderson and Freebody (1983) replaced content words with more difficult words and concluded that an increase in rare words leads to lower performance, although a large proportion of words needed to be changed in order to see reliable effects. One might conclude from their findings that students can tolerate a high percentage of rare words.

However, a study by Hu & Nation (2000) indicates that, when English is a second language, the majority of adult readers were limited in their comprehension of text when 5% or more of the text contained unfamiliar words. This is similar to the rule-of-thumb of reading educators (e.g., Betts, 1946) that accurate reading of 95%–100% of the words in a text indicates that the text is easy enough to read independently. Nation (2001) suggests that, in developing reading materials for English-language learners, 4% or less of the words should be newly introduced.

For the factor of word repetition, research findings are quite robust. The repetition of a word supports students' understanding of it, whether texts are read aloud to them or are read by students on their own. As McKeown, Beck, Omanson, and Pople (1985) conclude, "For virtually every instructional goal, providing a moderately high number of encounters per word will yield better outcomes than only several encounters" (p. 534).

When words are repeated in stories read aloud to students, several researchers have found mean gains from pre to posttest scores (Elley, 1989; Penno et al., 2002; Robbins & Ehri, 1994). Penno et al. (2002) found a linear effect for three repetitions of stories, with each repetition adding to accuracy in the use of target words. Elley (1989) reported a gain score of 15% when the same story was read three times. A study of 5- and 6-year-old nonreading kindergartners indicates that their recognition vocabularies expanded when they heard stories at least twice with unfamiliar words repeated in the stories (Robbins & Ehri, 1994). Those words repeated four times had a higher probability of being learned than those repeated two times, although some of the words repeated four times had a negative probability. The authors suggest that hearing words four times in stories may be necessary but not sufficient for establishing higher rates of acquisition. When teacher explanations and review were added, word learning was enhanced (Biemiller, 2003; Elley, 1989; Penno et al., 2002).

When words are encountered repeatedly in stories that students read on their own, there is also a greater probability that those words will be learned. Jenkins, Stein, and Wysocki (1984) found significant effects when words were encountered 6 or 10 times in context, but not with only 2 exposures. McKeown et al. (1985) found that a high frequency of exposure (12) resulted in greater learning gains than a low frequency of exposure (4), regardless of instruction type. They also found that it took 12 encounters with a word to reliably improve reading comprehension (McKeown et al., 1985). Although they did not report effects of repetition, Schwanenflugel et al. (1997) found that fourth-grade students gathered information about both unknown words and partially known words while reading texts independently, with similar gains for each.

To summarize, several characteristics of the local context of words have been identified as useful factors in increasing opportunities to learn words from context. Morphology, concreteness, the density of unknown words, the helpfulness of the sentences surrounding unknown words, and word repetition are all factors that appear to significantly influence vocabulary acquisition from text. Part of speech, length of words, and number of syllables do not appear to be significant factors by themselves. The relative frequency of a word is an interesting factor whose influence on word learning from context has yet to be explored.

Global Context

Students come to school with different types of knowledge about words, and some students are advantaged in their opportunities to learn words from context (Hart & Risley, 1995; Scott, 2004). In early grades (K–1), children are learning how to map sounds onto letters, with the expectation that the words that they read will map onto the oral vocabulary that they bring to the task. The system of using letter–sound correspondence to decode for meaning depends on recognizing a word once it is decoded. Thus, the size of one's oral vocabulary influences whether or not a word, once decoded, is known.

By the time children enter kindergarten, a conservative estimate is that native speakers know 4,000 to 5,000 word families, which include each word's inflected forms and regular derived forms. In addition, they know many compound words, proper names, and abbreviations not included in most estimates (Nation & Waring, 1997). Anglin (1993) estimates that 5-year-olds know closer to 10,000 words.

The range, however, among children in their exposure to academic or infrequent vocabulary is substantial. It has been estimated that, by age 4, the average child in an economically disadvantaged home might be exposed to 30 million fewer total words than the average child in an economically advantaged home (Hart & Risley, 1995, 2003). Other researchers have found similar gaps in word knowledge (Chall, Jacobs & Baldwin, 1990; White, Graves & Slater, 1990). Written text contains more complex language and more varied word choices than oral language, so the mismatch between school vocabulary and oral vocabulary can be found from the first texts encountered in school (Hiebert, in press). As students progress through the grades, texts become more complex in discourse style and in the number of words that are rarely encountered in everyday, out-of-school contexts (Cummins, 2000).

Students who are more skilled at reading and are more knowledgeable about word meanings are those most able to learn words from context. Swanborn and de Glopper's (1999) meta-analysis of research studies led to the conclusion that the average probability of learning an unknown word while reading is 15%. Thus, for every 100 unknown words encountered, students appear to gain enough knowledge of about 15 words to enhance their scores on measures of word knowledge. Based on a multilevel regression analysis of the studies, grade and reading level were found to influence the probability of learning a word. Younger students showed a lower probability of learning words incidentally (Grade 4 probability was 8%; Grade 11 probability was 33%), and lower ability readers gained less than high ability readers (low ability average gain was 7%; high ability average gain was 19%).

Thus, as in other aspects of reading, the rich get richer and the poor get poorer (Stanovich, 1986). With a substantial achievement gap in reading comprehension (National Center for Education Statistics, 2003), it is important to look at factors that help *all* students gain knowledge about words from texts. As reading comprehension involves the interplay of factors beyond words and text (RAND Reading Study Group, 2002), we also need to examine global factors found to influence the opportunity to learn word meanings from text: (a) conceptual difficulty, (b) purpose for reading, and (c) importance of world knowledge.

Conceptual Difficulty.   Not all words are equal. Knowing a high-frequency or function word such as *the* is different from knowing the meaning of a word such as *magma*. Graves (1987) points out that words that represent an entirely new concept need a different type of instruction from words that are synonymous for a known concept. Thus, it is relatively easy to teach a word like *superfluous*, for which there exists a close synonym (*unnecessary*). However, when a word is a new or difficult concept, such as *photosynthesis*, conceptual knowledge must be developed.

The idea of an associative network of knowledge is useful in thinking about learning new words. When people learn new word meanings, they are either building a new concept and creating new links (e.g., *photosynthesis*), attaching a new label to a known concept (e.g., gluing *superfluous* onto the concept of *unnecessary*), or expanding the domain of a label (e.g., adding a new meaning of *break* to the associative network). When the word is a new concept, it needs to be anchored and consolidated within the domain of knowledge that is being taught. The word *magma* would not be taught alone but in conjunction with knowledge about volcanoes. In the development of this knowledge, it is important to link what is being learned to familiar words and concepts.

Research indicates that it is harder to learn a word for a new concept incidentally through context than to learn a new word for a known concept (Nagy, 1997; Nagy et al., 1987). In a study of incidental word learning from context during independent reading, conceptual difficulty was found to be the strongest predictor of how easily the words were learned (Nagy et al., 1987). Words for which a new concept needed to be built (e.g., *osmosis*) were rated as conceptually difficult, whereas words that were synonyms for a well-known concept (e.g., *pusillanimous*) were rated as less conceptually complex. Nagy et al. (1987) found little incidental learning from context when words were rated as conceptually complex.

Purpose for reading is a factor that has been shown to be critical in reading comprehension research, but only one group of researchers has looked at this aspect of incidental word learning. In a study of sixth-grade students, Swanborn and de Glopper (2002) found that reading texts for different purposes influences the amount of incidental word learning that occurs. The probability of learning a word incidentally was highest when students read to gain knowledge of the topic (.10) and lowest in a free reading condition (.06). The low-ability group made no significant progress in its knowledge of words, regardless of the reading purpose. The average group made gains only when asked to learn about the topic, and the high-ability group learned significantly more words, with probabilities as high as .27 in both the free reading and the text comprehension conditions.

As world knowledge has frequently been overlooked in studies of vocabulary learning, Nagy (1997) argues cogently for broadening the perspective on acquiring vocabulary knowledge to include both linguistic knowledge (i.e., knowledge about morphemes) and extralinguistic knowledge (i.e., world knowledge). Given current understanding of the reading process (Anderson & Pearson, 1984; RAND Reading Study Group, 2002; Ruddell & Unrau, 2004), it makes sense that inferring the meaning of a word from context

> involves a relationship between the situation model (the reader/listener's model of meaning of the text) and the text model, as well as knowledge of the nature of the possible mapping between the two. These, in turn, draw on the learner's world knowledge, his or her theory of the conceptual domain to which the word belongs and knowledge about the way in which the relevant part of the lexicon is organized. (Nagy, 1997, p. 83)

Studies by Diakidoy (1993, 1998) indicate that a student's familiarity with the topic of a passage has a significant effect on word learning from context; these studies predict more variance as a result of this world knowledge than from measures of local contextual support. Her studies indicate that, although the enrichment of local context may have value, it is less important than the development of rich conceptual knowledge. She found that prior knowledge of the main concepts was most significant in facilitating reading comprehension and in the ability to infer new word meanings. In addition, knowledge of concepts gained gradually over time had a more positive influence on reading comprehension and inferring word meanings from context than passages read immediately prior to the task.

Summary

The complexity of learning words through text is readily apparent, and the factors involved are multifaceted and interrelated. As we have seen, it is unlikely that words that represent new knowledge and are conceptually difficult or complex will be learned incidentally through text. Inferring the meaning of a word from context involves more than accessing linguistic information about a word. It entails mapping the possible meanings for a new word onto an ongoing mental model of the meaning of the text (Nagy, 1997). This construction of meaning is intimately related to the learner's world knowledge. Thus, the more a student knows about a topic, the easier it will be to learn more about that topic from text.

However, the probability that a word will be learned decreases as the proportion of unknown words in a text increases. It seems that a delicate balance must be struck, in which teachers and authors must build background knowledge without overloading the text with unknown words. In addition, considerate local contexts, repetition, and the concreteness of words can enhance the number of words learned incidentally from text (Diakidoy, 1993; Konopak, 1989; Schwanenflugel et al., 1997).

The length of the word and its part of speech have not been found to make a significant difference in word learning from context, although studies are limited in this regard. The effect of frequency is interesting, as words that students have been exposed to in the past may be those words that are learned most easily through context. It does seem that those words that are more frequent in English and have more transparent morphology may be learned more easily than others, if students have the requisite background to take advantage of the morphology or have some previous experience with the words, so that knowledge is being refined and consolidated while students are reading the text. The purpose for reading and the genre of the material may also play important roles in learning through text. The next section looks specifically at informational texts as a genre in which word learning from context is particularly salient.

LEARNING ABOUT WORDS FROM INFORMATIONAL TEXTS

The ability to read and comprehend informational texts is central to success in schools and in life. When students leave school, much of what they read will be for the purpose of gathering information. In a recent study of workplace literacy demands, Craig (2001) found that over 60% of workers surveyed reported that at least 30% of their workday was spent reading for information, equaling approximately 2½ hours in an 8-hour shift.

Textbooks are the dominant form of instructional material for many elementary schools, although they are being supplemented by trade books in many classrooms (Donovan & Smolkin, 2001; Freeman & Person, 1992). However, a large proportion of American students fail to develop adequate skill in reading informational texts (Chall et al., 1990; NICHD, 2000). This could be due, in part, to a lack of exposure to informational texts in lower grades. Research indicates that primary teachers tend to emphasize narrative texts over informational texts, particularly in low SES settings (Donovan & Smolkin, 2001; Duke, 2000).

Differences Between Narrative and Informational Texts

Although there are fuzzy edges to genre distinctions (Lukens, 2003), informational texts are generally distinguished from narrative texts by features such as content, purpose, and structure. Informational books emphasize communication of information based on documented evidence so that a reader may learn something. Although many authors of fictional literature may also hope that the reader will take away a lesson about life, fictional works are largely products of the authors' imagination whose purpose is to entertain (Weaver & Kinstsch, 1991). Structurally, informational texts differ from narratives in the presentation of information rather than the literary elements of plot, setting, character, and theme that characterize fiction (Duke & Kays, 1998; Lukens, 2003).

There is another difference between informational and narrative texts that is often overlooked: the type of words used in the text and how those words are presented. In informational texts, words are often labels for important concepts, and each content area contains its own specialized collection of terms. Thus, words such as *tropical, ecosystem, diversity, climate, canopy, emergents, vegetation, torrential, oxisols, nutrients,* and *organisms* are found on an introductory page of an informational Eyewitness Book about the jungle (Greenaway, 1994). Often, other words, such as *because, furthermore, however, in conclusion, thus,* and *to summarize,* signal structural elements in informational texts. In addition, many of the words used in informational texts are defined either explicitly or implicitly within the text. In comparison, narrative texts tend to emphasize descriptive words related to characterization, setting, and tone. Thus, the words *waterproof, hollow, spacious, comfortable, tunnel, preceding, asparagus, thawed, acquired, slimy, texture,* and *rancid* appear on the first full page of *Mrs. Frisby and the Rats of NIMH* (O'Brien, 1971).

Words can occur in either context, and some forms of nonfiction, such as biography, are written using descriptive words similar to those used in fictional accounts. In narrative texts, it is easy to skip descriptive words or to gain sufficient knowledge to understand the gist of a phrase without sophisticated knowledge of the nuances of a word. However, in informational text, conceptual knowledge is critical, and often the relationship between words is central to overall meaning, rather than a secondary feature of text.

The distinction between the prevalent word types and presentation styles in the two text genres needs to be emphasized in discussions of vocabulary research. These differences may influence word learning from text. This possibility was highlighted in the recent National Reading Panel report (NICHD, 2000), which suggests that a large portion of vocabulary items should be derived from content learning materials as this would both help the reader deal with specific reading material containing content area information and provide the "learner with vocabulary that would be encountered sufficiently often to make the learning effort worthwhile" (chap. 4, p. 26).

However, there are concerns regarding which words to teach and how these words are presented in informational text. Harmon, Hedrick and Fox (2000) report a mismatch between words that teachers rated as central and words highlighted by publishers in social studies textbooks for Grades 4 through 8. In comparing the key word selection in textbooks from seven different publishers, the teachers agreed with publishers' selection only 48% of the time. In addition, in textbooks by six of the seven publishers, over 45% percent of key terms appear only once or twice in each unit.

IMPLICATIONS

Learning words from context is complex but, even so, factors have been identified that may help teachers, publishers, and authors maximize students' opportunities to learn words independently from informational texts. The implications of these findings for each critical group in ensuring students' maximal opportunities—researchers, publishers, and practitioners—are explored next.

Implications for Research

Recent national reports highlighted the need for more vocabulary research (NICHD, 2000; RAND Reading Study Group, 2002). The report of the RAND Reading Study Group (2002), in particular, emphasized the need for research on conditions that optimize learning vocabulary and that consider the interaction of text factors with the reader, activity, and sociocultural context. As is evident in this review, much of the research on learning vocabulary has limited the concept of context to local context, not taking global aspects such as reading purpose or world knowledge into consideration. In these studies, text was seen as a unitary construct. However, the field of reading research has expanded to acknowledge other important factors such as intertextuality and social aspects of language learning (Tierney & Pearson, 1994). This understanding is beginning to be reflected in new studies on learning from context (Diakidoy, 1998; Swanborn & de Glopper, 2002) and should be emphasized in future research.

One particularly distressing gap in our research knowledge concerns school-aged English-language learners. Most of the studies exploring second-language vocabulary acquisition through text involve adult learners (e.g., Hu & Nation, 2000; Huckin & Coady, 1999). Research is needed that explores the relationship between levels of knowledge about English and the factors identified that influence word learning from text. In their review of incidental vocabulary acquisition in a second language, Huckin and Coady (1999) assert that incidental learning requires a basic sight recognition vocabulary of at least 3,000 most frequent word families in English. Does this hold true for English-language learners in the primary grades? How do characteristics of the text, such as density of vocabulary load, repetition of key concepts, and the development of world knowledge, contribute and interact with English-language learners' developing understanding of words in text? Implementation studies concerning best practices for presenting word knowledge to school-aged English-language learners are also important.

The relatively new emphasis on word frequency is promising, as it may link strategies for learning words from context to the idea of learning words incrementally over time. However, the "Goldilocks" words (Stahl & Stahl, 2004) for English-language learners may be different from the "Goldilocks" words for English-only students, and such differences need documentation. Within all studies of vocabulary acquisition from text, the complexity of word knowledge and the transactional nature of learning words from context need to be recognized and explored further.

Implications for Publishers

Basals, textbooks, and tradebooks all contain informational material. In an analysis of the five most widely used basals in K–3 classrooms, Walsh (2003) concludes that none even attempt sustained building of word knowledge. I suggest that this needs to change. Although there is need for further research, this review points to several directions for improvement in the development of informational text. Research indicates that creating more considerate or informative contexts can raise the number of words learned as students read the text (Diakidoy, 1993; Konopak, 1989). In particular, decreasing the density of unknown words while increasing the number of repetitions of key concepts and the strength of contextual support for key concepts could enhance opportunities to learn words from informational texts. These improvements in local context, although not sufficient alone, may help ensure that, in particular, low achieving readers are given the maximum opportunity to learn particular words. For instance, in one textbook used in California, 22 words separate the phrase *elliptical orbit* from a description of a comet's path as *a long thin oval* (Houghton Mifflin Science, 2000, p. B24). It seems that this text could be easily revised to move these pieces of information into proximity.

Because the probability that a word will be learned decreases as the proportion of unknown words in a text increases, it is also important for authors to carefully consider which words are central and which are superfluous in conveying the important information in a unit. For instance, although the phrase "doomed to slow destruction" to describe a comet melting is colorful, it may hinder comprehension by increasing the density of unknown words (Houghton Mifflin Science, 2000, p. B24).

In addition, publishers need to be aware of the importance of developing word knowledge in conjunction with world knowledge through a focus on morphology and the development of a global understanding of concepts. Most textbooks attempt to highlight key vocabulary, but the words highlighted are not necessarily unknown and the selection process for the words seems unsystematic. For instance, *egg* and *adult* are highlighted in a section of the life cycle of an insect, but *cocoon* is not (Houghton Mifflin Science, 2000, p. A74).

Implications for Practice

In recent chapters (Scott & Nagy, 2004; Scott, 2004), Nagy and I identified some principles for effective vocabulary instruction:

- Create multidimensional word schemas with students.
- Help students build connective links in the associative network surrounding the words.
- Create multiple opportunities to see and use concepts.
- Help students develop subtle distinctions between related words that occur in the same semantic field.

These instructional guidelines were developed with all forms of text in mind. They are especially useful in learning from informational text. In light of this review, however, additional principles can be applied to enhancing word learning from informational texts:

- Exploit the link between world knowledge and word knowledge. When students are being asked to learn particular content, there is likely to be a set of new vocabulary words used. The word meanings should be developed in conjunction with the content knowledge, and central, conceptually complex concepts should be taught directly through discussion and experience. Tierney and Pearson (1994) talk about teaching with the text, rather than teaching from it. Words that are being taught need to match the important content of the unit, and teachers need to determine which words are central and unknown, given the background knowledge of their students. The need for multiple exposures to words, along with the development of rich conceptual knowledge, points to the extended use of thematic units in which words are seen in various contexts.
- Exploit the morphology of technical and academic words. Informational texts are rich with terms that are morphologically related. For instance, the words *pollen, pollination, pollinate*, and *pollinated* could be examined to show how they are related both morphologically and semantically. This provides generative knowledge that can be applied to other words.
- Pay attention to useful words that are part of the academic discourse of the discipline. Words like *analyze, hypothesize, dissect*, and *microscope* are all words that are likely to be repeated in a science book. They are also words that may be unknown to disadvantaged students and words that they need to learn to succeed in academic settings. These may be consid-

ered the "Goldilocks" words in science, words of high utility that are just right for building the links and bridges that students need to succeed.

In addition, teachers should increase the amount of time dedicated to studying words, recognizing that learning definitions is not the same as developing word schemas that can enhance students' understanding of the world. In a study of 23 diverse Grade 5–7 classrooms, we found that teachers spent less than 2% of the total school day focused on understanding word meanings in content area instruction (Scott, Jamieson-Noel, & Asselin, 2003). This seems quite low, and I urge teachers to increase the amount of time spent developing word knowledge in conjunction with world knowledge. In addition to a focus on learning specific words, a general focus on word consciousness and generative knowledge about words would enhance opportunities for acquiring new word meanings from text.

• Analyze texts for density of vocabulary load, repetition of key concepts, and helpfulness of the text. Schools and teachers help determine the materials that are set before children. Using the information in this review can help decision makers select materials that maximize opportunities to learn words from context.

A FINAL WORD

Growth in word knowledge is slow, incremental, and requires multiple exposures over time. Much of a student's vocabulary is learned incidentally through multiple exposures to words in multiple contexts (Nagy & Scott, 2000; Stahl, 2003) Through these encounters, students add to their growing network of knowledge about the word. However, not all children learn words from context at an equal rate, nor are all words equally learned from context.

Many children arrive at our doorsteps with little background in the use of academic language or vocabulary. They depend on schools and schooling to become knowledgeable about the words found in an academic discourse. As educators, it is incumbent on us to provide the maximum opportunity for all students to gain access and knowledge about the academic discourse needed to succeed in schools.

There are still many gaps in our research knowledge. However, it seems that a concerted effect on the part of publishers, authors, teachers, and researchers could improve the chances that all students, including those who have been marginalized by texts that are too difficult and inconsiderate, will learn important words. A multifaceted approach is necessary; words are unique, like individual students, and one type of instruction is not adequate. Acquiring both word knowledge and world knowledge is a gradual and cumulative process (Hirsch, 2003). Designing materials intentionally, teaching word knowledge in conjunction with world knowledge, and recognizing those words that are likely to be "picked up" incidentally in texts and those that need more active instruction are necessary steps in closing the language gap.

REFERENCES

Anderson, R. C., & Freebody, P. (1983). *Reading comprehension and the assessment and acquisition of word knowledge* (Tech Report No. 249). Urbana-Champaign: University of Illinois.

Anderson, R. C., & Pearson, P. D. (1984). A schema-theoretic view of basic processes in reading comprehension. In P.D. Pearson, R. Barr, M. Kamil, P. Mosenthal (Eds.), *Handbook of reading research* (Vol I, pp. 255–291). New York: Longman.

Anglin, J. M. (1993). *Vocabulary development: A morphological analysis*. Monographs of the Society of Research in Child Development, Serial No. 238, Vol. 58, No. 10.

Baker, L. (1989). Developmental change in readers' responses to unknown words. *Journal of Reading Behavior, 21*(3), 241–260.

Baumann, J., Edwards, E., Font, G., Tereshinski, C., Kame'enui, E., & Olejnik, S. (2002). Teaching morphemic and contextual analysis to fifth grade students. *Reading Research Quarterly, 37*(2), 150–176.

Beck, I., & McKeown, M. (1991). Conditions of vocabulary acquisition. In R. Barr, M. Kamil, P. Mosenthal, & P. D. Pearson (Eds.), *Handbook of reading research* (Vol. 2, pp. 789–814). New York: Longman.

Beck, I. L., McKeown, M. G., & Caslin, E. S. (1983). Vocabulary development: All contexts are not created equal. *The Elementary School Journal, 83,* 177–181.

Beck, I. L., McKeown, M. G., & Kucan, L. (2003). Taking delight in words: Using oral language to build young children's vocabularies [Electronic version]. *American Educator, 27*(1), 10–13, 16–22, 28–29, 44, 48.

Betts, E. (1946). *Foundations of reading instruction*. New York: American Book.

Biemiller, A. (2003, May). *Using stories to promote vocabulary*. Paper presented at the meeting of the International Reading Association, Orlando, FL.

Cain, K., Oakhill, J., & Elbro, C. (2003). The ability to learn new words from context by school-age children with and without language comprehension difficulties. *Journal of Child Language, 30,* 681–694.

Carlisle, J. F. (1995). Morphological awareness and early reading achievement. In L. B. Feldman (Ed.), *Morphological aspects of language processing* (pp. 189–209). Hillsdale, NJ: Lawrence Erlbaum Associates.

Carlisle, J. F. (2003). Morphology matters in learning to read: A commentary. *Reading Psychology, 24,* 291–322.

Chall, J., Jacobs, V., & Baldwin, L. (1990). *The reading crisis: Why poor children fall behind*. Cambridge, MA: Harvard University Press.

Champion, A. H. (1997). Knowledge of suffixed words in reading and oral language contexts: A comparison of reading disabled and normal readers. *Annals of Dyslexia, 47,* 287–309.

Clark, E. (1993). *The lexicon in acquisition*. Cambridge: Cambridge University Press.

Craig, J. C. (2001). The missing link between school and work: Knowing the demands of the workplace. *English Journal, 91*(2), 46–50.

Cummins, J. (2000). *Language, power, and pedagogy: Bilingual children in the crossfire*. North York, Ontario: Multilingual Matters.

Dale, E. (1965). Vocabulary measurement: Techniques and major findings. *Elementary English, 42,* 82–88.

Diakidoy, I. (1993). *The role of reading comprehension and local context characteristics in word meaning acquisition during reading.* Unpublished doctoral dissertation, University of Illinois at Urbana-Champaign.

Diakidoy, I. (1998). The role of reading comprehension in word meaning acquisition during reading. *European Journal of Psychology of Education, 13*(2), 131–154.

Diakidoy, I., & Anderson, R. C. (1991). *The role of contextual information in word meaning acquisition during normal reading* (Tech Report No. 531). Urbana-Champaign: University of Illinois.

Donovan, C., & Smolkin, L. (2001). Genre and other factors influencing teachers' book selections for science instruction. *Reading Research Quarterly, 36*(4), 412–440.

Duke, N. (2000). 3.6 minutes per day: The scarcity of informational texts in first grade. *Reading Research Quarterly, 35*(2), 202–224.

Duke, N., & Kays, J. (1998). "Can I say 'Once upon a time'?": Kindergarten children developing knowledge of information book language. *Early Childhood Research Quarterly, 13*(2), 295–318.

Durso, F., & Shore, W. (1991). Partial knowledge of word meanings. *Journal of Experimental Psychology: General, 120,* 190–202.

Edwards, E., Font, G., Baumann, J., & Boland, E. (2004). Unlocking word meanings: Strategies and guidelines for teaching morphemic and contextual analysis. In J. Baumann & E. Kame'enui (Eds.), *Vocabulary instruction: Research to practice* (pp.159–176). New York: Guilford.

Elley, W. (1989). Vocabulary acquisition from listening to stories. *Reading Research Quarterly, 24*(2), 174–187.

Freeman, E. B., & Person, D. G. (Eds.). (1992). *Using nonfiction books in the elementary classroom from ants to zeppelins.* Urbana, IL: National Council of Teachers of English.

Gordon, J., Schumm, J. S., Coffland, C., & Doucette, M. (1992). Effects of inconsiderate versus considerate text on elementary students' vocabulary learning. *Reading Psychology, 13,* 157–169.

Graves, M. (1987). The roles of instruction in fostering vocabulary development. In M. McKeown & M. Curtis (Eds.), *The nature of vocabulary acquisition* (pp. 165–184). Hillsdale, NJ: Lawrence Erlbaum Associates.

Greenaway, T. (1994). *Jungle.* Eyewitness Books. London: Dorling Kindersley.

Harmon, J., Hedrick, W., & Fox, E. A. (2000).A content analysis of vocabulary instruction in social studies textbooks for grades 4–8. *The Elementary School Journal, 100*(3), 253–271.

Hart, B., & Risley, T. (1995). *Meaningful differences in the everyday experiences of young American children.* Baltimore, MD: Brookes.

Hart, B., & Risley, T. (2003). The early catastrophe: The 30 million word gap by age 3 [Electronic version]. *American Educator, 27*(1), 4–9.

Hiebert, E. H. (in press). State reform polices and the task for first-grade readers. *Elementary School Journal.*

Hirsch, E. D. (2003). Reading comprehension requires knowledge—of words and the world. *American Educator, 27,* 10–29.

Houghton Mifflin Science (2000). *Discovery Works.* Boston, MA: Houghton Mifflin.

Hu, M., & Nation, I.S.P. (2000). Vocabulary density and reading comprehension. *Reading in a Foreign Language, 13*(1), 403–430.

Huckin, T., & Coady, J. (1999). Incidental vocabulary acquisition in a second language: A review. *Studies in Second Language Acquisition, 21,* 181–193.

Jenkins, J., Stein, M., & Wysocki, K. (1984). Learning vocabulary through reading. *American Educational Research Journal, 21,* 767–787.

Konopak, B. C. (1989). Effects of inconsiderate text on eleventh graders' vocabulary learning. *Reading Psychology, 10*(4), 339–355

Landau, S. I. (1984). *Dictionaries: The art and craft of lexicography.* New York: Charles Scribner's Sons.

Laufer, B. (1990). Why are some words more difficult than others?: Some intralexical factors that affect the learning of words. *International Review of Applied Linguistics in Language Teaching, 28*(4), 293–307.

Laufer, B. (1997). What's in a word that makes it hard or easy; Some intralexical factors that affect the learning of words. In N. Schmitt & M. McCarthy (Eds.), *Vocabulary: Description, acquisition and pedagogy* (pp. 140–155). New York : Cambridge University Press.

Lukens, R. (2003). *A critical handbook of children's literature* (7th ed.). New York: Longman.

Marks, C., Doctorow, M., & Wittrock, M. (1974). Word frequency and reading comprehension. *Journal of Educational Research, 67,* 259–262.

McKeown, M., Beck, I. L., Omanson, R. C., & Pople, M. (1985). Some effects of the nature and frequency of vocabulary instruction on the knowledge and use of words. *Reading Research Quarterly, 20,* 522–535.

Myerson, M., Ford, M., Jones, W. P., & Ward, M. (1991). Science vocabulary knowledge of third and fifth grade students. *Science Education, 74*(4), 419–428.

Nagy, W. (1997). On the role of context in first- and second-language vocabulary learning. In N. Schmitt & M. McCarthy (Eds.), *Vocabulary: Description, acquisition and pedagogy* (pp. 64–83). Cambridge: Cambridge University Press.

Nagy, W., & Anderson, R. C. (1984). How many words are there in printed school English? *Reading Research Quarterly, 19,* 304–330.

Nagy, W., Anderson, R. C., & Herman, P. A. (1987). Learning word meanings from context during normal reading. *American Educational Research Journal, 24*(2), 237–270.

Nagy, W., & Scott, J. (1990). Word schemas: What do people know about words they don't know? *Cognition & Instruction, 7*(2), 105–127.

Nagy, W., & Scott, J. (2000). Vocabulary processing. In M. Kamil, P. Mosenthal, P. D. Pearson, & R. Barr (Eds.), *Handbook of reading research* (Vol. 3, pp. 269–284). Mahwah, NJ: Lawrence Erlbaum Associates.

Nation, I. S. P. (1990). *Teaching and learning vocabulary.* New York: Newbury House.

Nation, I. S. P. (2001). *Learning vocabulary in another language.* Cambridge: Cambridge University Press.

Nation, P., & Waring, R. (1997). Vocabulary size, text coverage and word lists. In N. Schmitt & M. McCarthy (Eds.), *Vocabulary description, acquisition & pedagogy* (pp. 6–19). Cambridge: Cambridge University Press.

National Center for Education Statistics (2003). *The Nation's Report Card: Reading Highlights 2003.* Washington, DC: U.S. Department of Education.

National Institute of Child Health and Human Development. (2000). *Report of the National Reading Panel: Teaching Children to Read.* (NIH Publication No. 00-4754). Washington, DC: U.S. Government Printing Office.

O'Brien, R.C. (1971). *Mrs. Frisby and the Rats of NIHM.* New York: Aladdin/Macmillan.

Paribakht, T. S., & Wesche, M. (1999). Reading and incidental L2 vocabulary acquisition: An introspective study of lexical inferencing. *Studies in Second Language Acquisition, 21*(2), 195–224.

Penno, J. F., Wilkinson, I. A. G., & Moore, D. W. (2002). Vocabulary acquisition from teacher explanation and repeated listening to stories: Do they overcome the Matthew effect? *Journal of Educational Psychology, 94*(1), 23–33.

RAND Reading Study Group. (2002). *Reading for understanding: Toward a research and development program in reading comprehension*. Washington, DC: U.S. Department of Education.

Robbins, C., & Ehri, L. (1994). Reading storybooks to kindergartners helps them learn new vocabulary words. *Journal of Educational Psychology, 86*(1), 54–64.

Ruddell, R. B., & Unrau, N. J. (2004). *Theoretical models and processes of reading* (5th ed.). Newark, DE: International Reading Association.

Schatz, E., & Baldwin, R. (1986). Context clues are unreliable predictors of word meaning. *Reading Research Quarterly, 21,* 439–453.

Schwanenflugel, P. J. (1991). Why are abstract concepts hard to understand? In P. Schwanenflugel (Ed.), *The psychology of word meanings*. Hillsdale, NJ: Lawrence Erlbaum Associates.

Schwanenflugel, P. J., Stahl, S. A., & McFalls, E. L. (1997). Partial word knowledge and vocabulary growth during reading comprehension. *Journal of Literacy Research, 29*(4), 531–553.

Scott, J. A. (2004). Scaffolding vocabulary learning: Ideas for equity in urban settings. In D. Lapp, C. Block, E. Cooper, & J. Flood (Eds.), *Teaching all the children: Strategies for developing literacy in urban settings*. New York: Guilford.

Scott, J., Jamieson-Noel, D., & Asselin, M. (2003). Vocabulary instruction throughout the day in 23 Canadian upper-elementary classrooms. *Elementary School Journal, 103*(3), 269–286.

Scott, J., & Nagy, W. E. (2004). Developing word consciousness. In J. Baumann & E. Kame'enui (Eds.), *Vocabulary instruction: Research to practice* (pp. 201–217). New York: Guilford.

Stahl, S. (2003). How words are learned incrementally over multiple exposures. *American Educator, 27*(1), 18–19.

Stahl, S., & Stahl, K. A. (2004). Word wizards all! Teaching word meanings in preschool and primary education. In J. Baumann & E. Kame'enui (Eds.), *Vocabulary instruction: Research to practice* (pp. 59–78). New York: Guilford.

Stanovich, K. (1986). Matthew effects in reading: Some consequences of individual differences in the acquisition of literacy. *Reading Research Quarterly, 21,* 360–407.

Swanborn, M. S. L., & de Glopper, K. (1999). Incidental word learning while reading: A meta-analysis. *Review of Educational Research, 69*(3), 261–285.

Swanborn, M. S. L., & de Glopper, K. (2002). Impact of reading purpose on incidental word learning from context. *Language Learning, 52*(1), 95–117.

Tierney, R., & Pearson, P. D. (1994). A revisionist perspective on "Learning to learn from text: A framework for improving classroom practice." In R. Ruddell, M. R. Ruddell, & H. Singer (Eds.), *Theoretical models and processes of reading* (pp. 514–519). Newark, DE: International Reading Association.

Walsh, K. (2003). Basal Readers: The lost opportunity to build the knowledge that propels comprehension. *American Educator, 27*(1), 24–27.

Weaver, C. A., & Kinstsch, W. (1991). Expository text. In R. Barr, M. Kamil, P. Mosenthal, & P.D. Pearson (Eds.), *Handbook of reading research* (Vol. 2, pp. 230–245). New York: Longman.

White, T., Graves, M., & Slater, W. (1990). Growth of reading vocabulary in diverse elementary schools: Decoding and world meaning. *Journal of Educational Psychology, 82*(2), 281–290.

Wittrock, M., Marks, C., & Doctorow, M. (1975). Reading generative process. *Journal of Educational Psychology, 67,* 484–489.

Zeno, S., Ivens, S., Millard, R., & Duvvuri, R. (1995). *The educator's word frequency guide.* New York: Touchstone Applied Science Associates.

PART II

INSTRUCTIONS AND INTERVENTIONS THAT ENHANCE VOCABULARY

Chapter 5

Four Problems
With Teaching Word Meanings

(And What to Do to Make Vocabulary an Integral Part of Instruction)

Steven A. Stahl
University of Illinois at Urbana-Champaign

To a large extent, the words we know and use are who we are. Words can define, to the outside world (and maybe even to ourselves), how smart we are (or think we are), what kinds of jobs we do, and what our qualifications for jobs might be. A person for whom *camouflage* or *depravity* or *sultry* falls easily off the lips is likely to be presumed to have a wide-ranging knowledge or at least a high-quality education. A person who can talk about *populism, deficit spending,* and *interest rates* is presumed to know something about economics or politics or both and will be listened to, at least in some circles. Words are not just tokens that one might memorize to impress others. Instead, the words that make up one's vocabulary are part of an integrated network of knowledge. Some of these words might be the "fifty-cent" words that my father used to talk about, and others are words that are simpler but connected.

Vocabulary knowledge *is* knowledge; the knowledge of a word not only implies a definition, but also implies how that word fits into the world. Schemas for even simple concepts such as *fish* may be infinitely expanding, from fish to specific fish, to the anatomy of fish, to broiled fish, to other sea creatures, to scales and gills, *ad infinitum*. The more we know about the concept *fish,* the more words we will bring into our understanding of the concept. And, depending on our interests and our backgrounds, we will bring different words to that understanding. A fishmonger may know more or fewer fish-related words than a marine biologist, but will certainly know different words, some of which make up the jargon used in the business of selling fish. The words we know define who we are.

WHAT DO WE MEAN BY "VOCABULARY"?

The word *vocabulary* itself can be confusing. Sometimes educators talk about a "sight vocabulary" or a set of the most common words in English (e.g., Fry, Fountoukidis, & Polk, 1985). It is certainly important for children to recognize instantly a set of 100 or 300 or more words in print, especially because a small number of words (105, according to Adams, 1990) accounts for 50% of the words children encounter in a typical reading passage. However, in this chapter, I discuss word meanings, and so I use the words *vocabulary* and *word meanings* synonymously. Furthermore, I discuss types of vocabularies other than sight vocabulary, including concept vocabularies, content area vocabularies, and so on. I believe that these different vocabularies have different demands and should be taught in different ways.

FOUR PROBLEMS

One would think that the problem of teaching word meanings is a simple one—just determine what words need to be learned and teach them to children as efficiently as possible. There are, however, four problems with this approach:

1. The sheer number of words that children need to learn so as to understand and use with proficiency both oral and written language.
2. The gap in levels of word knowledge among children.
3. The gap in levels of word knowledge begins even before children enter school.
4. Traditional vocabulary instruction does not teach children word-learning strategies and how to appreciate words.

Let us take a closer look at each of the problems.

The Sheer Number of Words to Be Learned

Achieving thorough vocabulary knowledge is a goal that may never be reached, even by intelligent adults. Even though we, as educated adults, know thousands of words, there are always words that we see or hear that we do not know. A few years ago, as an example, I was reading *Newsweek* and encountered the word *quotidian*. This is a word that I did not know, and I was surprised to see it in a mass-market magazine. Since then, however, I have come across *quotidian* numerous times.

Estimates of how many words are in the English language vary. The *Oxford English Dictionary*, which is the largest compilation of English words—modern, obsolete, and archaic—contains upward of one million words, with new words (such as *McJob* and *JPEG*) constantly being added. English is promiscuous in the way that it adds words and takes words from sources such as other languages, slang, and compounding. Of course, neither children nor adults need to know all of these words, but they are out there to be learned and used.

A more reasonable estimate for the number of words that children need to know is that of Nagy and Anderson (1984), who estimated that the number of different word families found in the books that children read from Grades 1 through 12 is approximately 87,000. Of course, many of these words appear only once and readers may not have to know them to understand what they read. Even so, Nagy and Anderson concluded that an average high school senior knows about 45,000 different words. Forty-five thousand is still a great many words to learn. If it is assumed that a child enters Grade 1 knowing roughly 6,000 different words, the child needs to learn 39,000 additional words or so over the next 12 years. That's about 3,000 new words per year. Three thousand new words a year means that the child must learn roughly 10 new words each *day*. But although this may sound like an impossible goal to achieve, research suggests that the average child *does* learn roughly 3,000 words per year (White, Graves, & Slater, 1990).

This average, however, obscures some important differences. White and his colleagues found a range of growth between 1,000 words for low-achieving children and 5,000 for higher achieving children. This range is important. If one child's vocabulary grows only a fifth as much as another's, the differences between low-achieving and high-achieving children will only grow larger over time.

D'Anna, Zechmiester, and Hall (1991) report even lower estimates of how many words children know and how many words they need to know. Some of these estimates are as low as 5,000 root words over the course of the elementary school years. This would be a more manageable number of words to teach. However, these root words do not include less common but still essential words. Take, for example, a sample from a book I recently read: *bridal, nonchalant, taxidermy,* and *stamina*. None of these words would be on a list of core root words. Children are generally intelligent and inquisitive, making them naturally curious and receptive to learning new and interesting words. Thus, concentrating exclusively on root words, although they are certainly important, would deny children a source of pleasure in the "gift of words," as Scott and Nagy (2004) refer to children's delight in and metacognitive awareness of new and interesting vocabulary.

The Gap in Word Knowledge Among Children

If we accept that children must learn 10 words a day to make normal progress in vocabulary development, we then need to find ways to facilitate this learning. Clearly, 10 words a day is more than can be taught directly. Typically, I have observed teachers directly teaching 10 to 12 words per *week*, but never that many per day, at least not successfully. Although direct teaching of specific words is effective in improving comprehension (National Reading Panel, 2000; Stahl & Fairbanks, 1986), the large number of words that average children must learn cannot be acquired in any way other than from seeing words in context—that is, from wide reading (Stahl, 1991).

Children's books contain a great many rare words—words that often appear only once per book or even once across several million words of text. One group of researchers found a higher density of less frequently used words in an average children's book than in an average television program, or even in the conversation of two college-educated adults (Hayes & Ahrens, 1988). For children who are normally achieving readers, the appearance of rare words poses few difficulties, making the reading of children's books a good source of their word learning. The problem arises with children who have reading problems. Although struggling readers can learn words from children's books, their reading problems mean that they read fewer books and the books that they read are less challenging. As a result, they fall further and further behind their peers in word learning (Stanovich, 1986).

The widening gap in word learning between children who have reading problems and normally achieving children is an important result of reading problems. Because children with reading problems tend to have smaller vocabularies (mainly through a lack of exposure to words in challenging books rather than through differences in abilities), they often have difficulty understanding and participating in class discussions of reading selections that contain challenging words.

The Word-Knowledge Gap Begins Early

The word-learning gap may begin before children enter school. Although children may have sufficient vocabulary to communicate well at home and in their immediate neighborhoods, the "academic" vocabulary they encounter when they start school can be as unfamiliar as a foreign language (Stahl & Nagy, 2004). In a widely cited study, Hart and Risley (1995) found that children from advantaged homes (i.e., children of professionals) had receptive vocabularies as much as five times larger than children from welfare homes (i.e., children in families receiving Aid to Families with Dependent Children). They found that children in welfare homes had fewer words spoken to them, with more words spoken in imperative sentences (e.g., "Turn off the TV.") and fewer in descriptive or elaborative sentences ("Look at the yellow daffodils starting to bloom over by the door."). Their picture is of a widening gap between the well-off and the poor, a gap that threatens to widen over time (Hart & Risley, 1995).

These early differences in vocabulary knowledge can influence children's reading throughout the elementary years—and beyond. Dickinson and Tabors (2001) found that children's word knowledge in preschool still had significant correlations with their comprehension in upper elementary school.

In contrast, Biemiller and Slonim (2001), who examined children's growth in word meanings between Grades 2 and 5, found that children in the bottom quartile learned more words per day (averaging 3 root words) than did children in the upper quartile (averaging 2.3 root words per day). They suggest that children in the lower quartile had more words to learn, so, given the same exposure to words in school, were able to learn more. However, as children in the lowest quartile started so far behind, they knew only as many word meanings by Grade 5 as typical Grade 4 students. Biemiller and Slonim (2001) suggest that, to close this gap, vocabulary instruction should begin earlier.

Traditional Instruction

At issue, then, is not whether to provide instruction, but how best to do so. As others in this book note, vocabulary instruction traditionally has consisted of minimal instruction involving memorization of definitions, instruction that was not very effective. I maintain that, instead, vocabulary instruction should be part of the fabric of the classroom—an integral part of all instruction. Beck, McKeown, & Kucan (2002) and Calderón et al. and Carlo et al. in this book, along with others (see, e.g., Stahl & Nagy, 2004), have provided valuable information about how to do this. All of these approaches view word learning as a part of a knowledge curriculum; that is, as an "instructional conversation" (Saunders & Goldenberg, 1999) in which words are embedded, rather than taught as isolated factoids.

INTEGRATING VOCABULARY LEARNING INTO A KNOWLEDGE CURRICULUM

Programs that make word learning part of an integrated curriculum generally share several common characteristics: (a) frequent reading aloud to children, (b) the use of different methods to teach different kinds of words, (c) point of contact teaching, (d) extensive teaching to ensure that word meanings "stick," (e) teaching complex concepts, and (f) concerted efforts to help children acquire an appreciation of the power of words.

Reading Aloud to Children

We typically view reading to children as an activity for prereaders or primary school children. However, older as well as younger children appear to benefit from read-aloud activities, and older children can learn the meanings of new words as efficiently from hearing stories read to them as they can from reading the stories themselves (Stahl, Richek, & Vandevier, 1991). Reading to older children also can be used as a way of getting them interested in a book so that they will continue reading it on their own.

For reading aloud to be most effective, the books read should be intellectually challenging. Consider the richness of language in a book such as Deborah Wiles' (2001) *Freedom Summer,* a book intended for students in Grades 3 or 4, but challenging enough to be used in the upper grades as well:

> John Henry's skin is the color of browned butter. He smells like pine needles after a good rain. My skin is the color of the pale moths that dance around the porch light at night. John Henry says that I smell like a just-washed sock. "This means war!" I shout. We churn that water into a white hurricane and laugh until our sides hurt. (Wiles, 2001, p. 6)

To deny children such richness of language because they might have difficulties recognizing words would be to do them a terrible injustice. As I said earlier, children's books are "where the words are." Reading aloud may be the only way for some children to experience those words.

This said, listening to stories should never be a passive activity. Children should always be held responsible for what they hear; listening to stories should not be a time to relax. Instead, children should be taught how to listen for a purpose, how to discuss what they heard, to react critically to a reading, and to generate conversations about what they hear. I prefer that active listening be done in groups. But even if tapes are used with individual students (e.g., Chomsky, 1978), children still should be held responsible for what they hear, even if that responsibility is limited to retelling a story to an adult or to answering questions about a reading. Studies have found that having children merely listen to tapes, without assigning them responsibility for what is on the tapes, does not improve achievement (e.g., Haynes & Jenkins, 1986; Leinhardt, Zigmond, & Cooley, 1981).

Different Teaching for Different Words

One of the problems with vocabulary teaching is that it takes a great deal of time. One study, which admittedly attempted to provide the "Cadillac" of vocabulary instruction, devoted about 20 minutes to the teaching of each word (Beck, McKeown, & Caslin, 1983). In most classrooms, of course, teachers allot much less instructional time to teaching words. Even so, given the number of words that must be taught, vocabulary instruction can be time-consuming. Although it may seem to go without saying, it is critical to remember that not all words are the same. As Graves (2000) observed, words are of different types. Consider the following types of words

- Words for which children know synonyms, such as *evil, crimson, speaking,* or *superior;*
- Words that can be explained with definitions, examples, and context, such as *challenge, pedal, harp,* or *betray*; and
- Words that represent complex concepts, such as *liberty, biome,* or *probability.*

Fortunately, each of these different types of words can be taught differently, thus making vocabulary teaching an easier-to-manage and less time-consuming task. The following sections discuss some of these different approaches to teaching different types of words.

Point of Contact Teaching

In teaching a word for which children know synonyms, the focus of the task is to help them relate the word to a synonym so that they can read a passage in which it appears. If, for example, a child seems puzzled when he or she tries to read the word *crimson* in a passage, the teacher can quickly say something such as "*crimson* means *red*" and have the child move on. This brief bit of information may be enough to allow a child to understand what he or she is reading. But although such instruction may help the child understand a specific passage, it probably will not lead to overall improvement in his or her reading comprehension. One study found, in fact, that simply having children memorize synonyms for unfamiliar words in a passage did not affect their comprehension of that passage (for a review, see Stahl, 1998; Stahl & Fairbanks, 1986). Therefore, this instructional approach is best used with words that may be relatively rare (*malefactor* is a good example) or are not particularly important to understanding a passage.

Given the literary language of children's books, even those intended for young children, this "point of contact" teaching is important. Not every "hard" word has to be taught. Choosing which words to teach involves teacher judgment, a process in which good teachers are continually engaged.

Teachers can initiate point of contact teaching (see also, Beck et al., 2002) either before reading a section or during reading a passage or section of text. Such teaching should be quick and used no more than once per page. If it is used more often than that, it becomes disruptive and distracts children from focusing on the flow of the text. Because the purpose of reading is comprehension, such disruptions and distractions should be avoided.

Children also can initiate point of contact instruction. Self-monitoring of comprehension, or becoming aware that something, such as not knowing the meaning of a word, is preventing us from understanding what we read, is a metacognitive ability (Baker & Brown, 1984). Children often do not have this ability and skip or gloss over words that are unfamiliar to them. The awareness that they do not know a word, or that they need to know a word to get the correct meaning from a text, is important. If they become confused or frustrated as they read, children can initiate a point of contact teaching opportunity by giving a signal so that the teacher or a peer can provide the word. This is minimal instruction, and possibly not really instruction at all. It is, however, a way to help children get through a difficult text with little disruption. As with teacher-initiated teaching, it should be done probably no more than once a page, and it should not substitute for more extensive instruction of the type discussed next.

More Extensive Teaching

Point of contact teaching is not adequate for children to learn words in a way that can substantially improve their comprehension or increase their vocabulary. Certainly, some of the words taught this way will "stick," and having even one exposure to a word and its synonym is better than nothing. It is unreasonable, however, to expect too much word learning from such brief exposure. To teach words in a meaningful manner requires instruction that is more extensive, although probably not as extensive as the 20 minutes per word discussed earlier.

In a review of vocabulary instructional studies, Stahl and Fairbanks (1986) found three principles that characterized effective vocabulary instruction:

- Effective vocabulary instruction provides both definitional and contextual information about a word.
- Effective instruction requires that children engage in deep processing of each word, including generating information that ties the new word to already known information.
- Effective instruction involves multiple exposures to each word.

I briefly discuss each of these principles in turn.

Definitional and Contextual Information. Consider the process of placing a call to someone you do not know well enough to call often. You look up the number in the phone book, walk to the phone, dial the number, and, by the time the person you are calling answers, you have forgotten the number. You forget the number because that particular phone number is not meaningful to you. Rather, it is an arbitrary piece of information. We tend to remember meaningful information because we can integrate it with other information, as I discuss later. So it is with the traditional vocabulary instruction that we received in our upper elementary and secondary school years. We remember having to memorize lists of word definitions, with tests over the lists on Fridays. If the test was in the morning, nearly all of the words were out of our heads by lunch. Not only was this memorization boring to most of us, but it also did not lead to appreciable growth in our vocabularies (National Reading Panel, 2000; Stahl, 1998; Stahl & Fairbanks, 1986). Why? Because in this approach to instruction, definitions are treated as arbitrary pieces of information, just as are infrequently called phone numbers.

A word's "meaning" is more than just a definition. Consider the word *swam,* used in its ordinary sense as "moved through water by using one's hands and feet." The word has multiple senses, depending on the context in which it appears, as in:

- Melanie swam toward the wall.
- The five-year-old swam across the kiddy pool on her belly, kicking and splashing and laughing all the way.
- Our team swam strongly, but was not able to win the meet.
- The alligator swam through the swamp toward the girls' dangling feet.
- Dad slowly swam across the pool to get an iced tea from Mom.

The first sentence evokes a fairly typical swimming action. We do not know much about it without any additional context. The second sentence creates a picture of a beginner, the third of a vigorous competition, the fourth of stealth, and the fifth of a leisurely crawl. Each of these is "swam," but each of these is distinctively different. Context can change dramatically the meanings of words, even those as simple and well defined as *swam.*

To learn a new word, we must not only learn how that word relates to other words (the definitional information), but also how the word changes in different contexts. Learning definitional information is more that just learning the definition (and definitions can be difficult to understand), but also learning about:

- *Synonyms*. As discussed earlier, often a synonym is all children need to understand a new word in context.

- *Antonyms*. Encouraging children to think about antonyms for a word requires them to identify the word's crucial aspects. For example, the word *chaos* implies an abyss, a void, or clutter, but its antonym, *order,* narrows the focus to the "clutter" part of the word's meaning.
- *Categories*. Part of definitional knowledge is knowing the category into which a word fits. Being able to classify *vehicle* as a form of transportation, *accountant* as a type of job, or *orca* as a type of whale, which in turn is a mammal, is an important part of building word knowledge.
- *Comparisons to other, similar words*. Comparing words can be a very powerful means of learning new words. Consider the word *debris*. This is a form of "trash," but not all trash is debris. The meaning of *garbage* is actually restricted to discarded organic material, such as apple cores or food scraps. *Debris* means trash that is left over from some sort of accident or catastrophic event, such as an automobile accident or a plane crash (and sometimes from a child's playtime).

Venn diagrams—two overlapping circles, shaded or crosshatched to show relationships between the words in each circle—are a convenient way to illustrate these comparisons. Words such as *helicopter, albatross, penguin, warrior,* and *sparrow,* to pick just a few examples, can be put into a set of interlocking circles. The words I listed pose some ambiguity for comparisons, with a possible set of "birds" or "things that fly" or "military things." Ambiguity, however, can lead to lively discussion, which, in turn, can lead to more word learning.

The basic Venn diagram can be used to make a great many distinctions. For children in the primary grades, distinctions can be made between animals that live in water and animals that live on land (with amphibians in the overlap). For older children, the diagram might be used to make a distinction between "rebellion" and "protest," which might be useful in explaining the American Revolution. One of the reasons that propelled the conflict was that King George viewed the colonists' activities as *rebellion* against the Crown, whose power was to be viewed as absolute. In contrast, the colonists viewed their activities as *protest* against unjust laws. This conflict in values was a critical component in bringing about the revolution.

Semantic maps are basically more elaborate Venn diagrams. To be effective, semantic mapping should be a two-part procedure, beginning with brainstorming. The teacher choses a key word taken from the selection to be read, such as *spider* or *cancer* or *map*. Then students and teacher brainstorm words that relate to this key word. For *map*, they might come up with the words *key, compass, road, scale, border,* and *river*. Such an activity is quite different—and is substantially more meaningful—than the fill-in-the-blank format that is often used for semantic maps. Comparisons between and among words can be part of a discussion about a new word's meaning.

McKeown, Beck, Omanson, and Pople (1985) have an activity called "Silly Questions" that can fit into most vocabulary programs. Because it is short, it can also fit as a "sponge activity" to fill in a space in the classroom day. Silly Questions involves taking two of any set of words and combining them into questions, such as: "Can a hermit be a villain?" "Can an actuary be a accountant?" "Can an accountant be a hermit?" "Can a malefactor be amorous?" "Would a hermit be amorous?" and so on. Some questions are easily answered, others require discussion, and others require some research, but the activity encourages children to think about the meanings of words.

Dictionary Definitions. Although requiring children to write dictionary definitions is likely to generate boredom rather than word learning, a dictionary can be a useful tool, and definitions can and should be taught. Definitions try to preserve the Aristotelian view of meaning. This suggests that words can be categorized by the category (genus) to which the word belongs and how that word differs from other members of the category (differentiae). Thus, to cite two examples, *eider* is "a large sea duck of the northern hemisphere" (genus = duck; differentiae = large, sea, northern hemisphere) and *hagiography* is a "biography that treats its subject with undue reverence" (genus = biography; differentiae = with undue reverence).

Instruction related to dictionary definitions should be simple and direct and involve children in analyzing dictionary definitions in the course of vocabulary instruction. Another way to teach definitions is to use an explanatory dictionary, such as the COBUILD (Cobuild Staff, 2002) dictionary. In this dictionary, the definitions are presented in the form of an explanation. For example, the entry for *fissure* is, "A *fissure* is a deep crack in something, especially in rock or in the ground." Other entries can contain sentences that show how the word is used, along with the explanations. For example, the entry for *plunge* is, "If something or someone *plunges* in a particular direction, especially into water, they fall, rush, or throw themselves in that direction. *At least 50 people died when a bus plunged into a river ... He ran down the steps to the pool terrace and plunged in.*" Although the COBUILD includes examples from American English, it is a British dictionary, and the usages and spellings do differ from those in the United States. This might confuse some children, so caution should be used.

Contextual Knowledge. Just as learning to extend word meaning with dictionaries is critical, children also need to know how that new word fits into different contexts. Adeptness with word use involves examining words in context and, more importantly, generating context.

  • *Generating sentences.* Generating sentences is a useful way for children to learn about word meanings, but the sentences created need to clearly express the meaning of the targeted words. All too often, generating sentences becomes a meaningless time filler, perceived that way by both children and teachers. One way that teachers can avoid this problem is to have three or four children say sentences that contain the targeted word, then have the rest of the class rate how well the sentences express the word's meaning.

• *Scenarios*. Having groups of children make up scenarios that contain a word or, as this activity is time-consuming, a group of words can also be useful in building vocabulary. Scenarios can bring words together, allowing children both to put the words in context and to understand the relationships between words. Scenarios can be in the form of prose, such as stories, or plays that groups of children can act out.

• *Possible Sentences*. Possible Sentences activities allow children to predict both the meanings of the words to be learned and the content of what they are going to read. In Possible Sentences, children are given a set of 10 to 12 words that have been taken from a passage they are about to read. Of these words, about four should be known to the children and the rest unknown. Children are asked to make up sentences, each containing two words from the list that might appear in the passage. The words can (and should) be reused. For a passage on insects, the list of words might include: *antenna, butterfly, abdomen, thorax, grasshopper, wings, jointed, legs, spider, propulsion, feeling, ant.*

Students might come up with sentences such as:

A grasshopper uses its legs for propulsion. (Correct)

A spider is not an insect because it has eight legs. (Correct)

The thorax is the part of the ant that eats. (Incorrect)

A butterfly has pretty wings. (Correct)

Note the emphasis on rich contexts. Having students fill in the blanks on a vocabulary worksheet or generate short, quick sentences both provide contexts to augment definitions and can be included in vocabulary instruction for expediency, but they are not as effective for increasing word knowledge as Possible Sentence activities.

Generating Rich Connections.   The second principle of effective vocabulary instruction is that children need to generate rich connections between the new word and already known information. This involves more than learning a simple association, as in the old-fashioned dictionary memorization activities of our school days. Merely comprehending the word in context, during wide reading alone or with point of contact teaching, leads to more learning, but not as much as does having students process the word deeply, generating connections between the new word and different contexts and prior knowledge of other words.

Consider the following scenario for the word *apprentice:*

> The apprentice must rise before the master, before the first rays of the sun come out. At that time, the apprentice needs to put on the fire, heat up a pitcher for hot water to make the master's tea. Once breakfast is finished, the apprentice needs to prepare the tools for the morning's work. As the master sits down on his bench, the apprentice sits on the side, ready to provide the tools that the master needs, but otherwise watches closely. The master is ready to teach. The apprentice is ready to learn.

Preparing such a scenario requires that the children connect "apprentice" to "master," "learn," and "teach," all crucial concepts. It also requires that the children connect the concept of "apprentice" to a more historical, rural context. Such a scenario cannot be produced without some preteaching by the teacher, but such preteaching would lead to rich learning and might also be a good prereading writing activity for a book that involves an apprenticeship.

Discussion is a powerful way to have children generate connections between new and known information (Stahl & Clark, 1987; Stahl & Vancil, 1986). Discussion makes children active thinkers, because they are trying to make contributions to the discussion. These connections, of course, only occur if an individual child believes that her or his contribution will be accepted and valued by others. Teachers need to make special efforts to create a classroom community in which the contributions of *all* children are equally accepted. Some guidelines for creating an environment in which this can happen can be found in Saunders and Goldenberg (1999). True discussion, in which all children can participate without intervention by the teacher, is a powerful tool for vocabulary learning, but considerable vocabulary learning also can occur in recitation, in which the teacher monitors the turn taking.

As part of their *Text Talk* approach to discussing new books with young children, McKeown and Beck (Beck & McKeown, 2001; McKeown & Beck, 2003) provide a wonderful example of rich vocabulary instruction. Here is the activity they used to teach the word *absurd* as part of their introduction to the story *Burnt Toast on Davenport Street* (Egan, cited in McKeown & Beck, 2003):

> *absurd:* In the story, when the fly told Arthur he could have three wishes if he didn't kill him, Arthur said he thought that was absurd. That means Arthur thought it was silly to believe a fly could grant wishes. When something is absurd—it is ridiculous and hard to believe.

> If I told you that your teacher was going to stand on his/her head to teach you—that would be absurd. If someone told you that dogs could fly—that would be absurd.

I'll say some things, and if you think they are absurd, say: "That's absurd!" If you think they are not absurd, say: "That makes sense."

I have a singing cow for a pet. (absurd)

I saw a tall building that was made of green cheese. (absurd)

Last night I watched a movie on TV. (makes sense)

This morning I saw some birds flying around the sky. (makes sense)

If I said let's fly to the moon this afternoon, that would be absurd. Who can think of an absurd idea? (When a child answers, ask another if they think that was absurd, and if so, to tell the first child: "That's absurd!")

Notice how the researchers provide a bridge from the example of the word's use in the book to examples in different contexts. Also notice that this lesson should be quick-paced, probably no more than 2 minutes, with high participation. Children could respond chorally except to the last item. From this instruction, it is likely that the group would understand *absurd* fairly well in the short period of time.

Providing Multiple Exposures to a Word's Meaning. The third principle of effective vocabulary learning is to provide multiple exposures to a word's meaning. This does *not* mean mere repetition of drill of the word and a synonym or a definition (e.g., *companion* means "friend"), but seeing the word in different contexts—in sentences, with a definition, and with elaborated information. Repetition can be overdone, but a child probably has to see a word more than once to place it firmly in his or her long-term memory.

The picture I have been painting is of vocabulary instruction in a context of rich instruction about texts, rather than the sterile, isolated instruction that we remember from our youth. This rich instruction occurs in oral discussion and collaborative work that fully enables all children in the class to participate. It involves group work and the teacher providing an environment in which equal participation can occur.

Teaching Complex Concepts

Even the more extensive instruction I just discussed is not enough to teach some words. Words such as *flock*, *herd*, *confine*, or *slaughter*, all taken from a Thanksgiving-related magazine article about turkeys, are relatively easy to define and put into various contexts. However, understanding the larger concept of *factory farming* (the point of the article) requires more than learning a definition and coming up with a few selected contexts. This example seems abstract, but children encounter many complex concepts, such as *ecosystem, liberty, circulatory system, representation,* and so on in their content area reading. These concepts cannot be neatly defined, but instead must be developed through what Spiro, Coulson, Feltovich, and Anderson (1994) call "criss-crossing" the landscape.

Take, for example, the concept of *liberty*. This is a fairly common concept for children in the upper elementary grades to encounter in their textbooks. A dictionary definition of *liberty* might be: "The freedom to think or act without being constrained by necessity or force." In this definition, the category to which *liberty* belongs is "freedom" and what differentiates it is that the freedom refers to being able to think or act without constraint. But is this *liberty*? Obviously, our society puts constraints on our liberty, beginning with the constraint not to commit criminal acts ranging from murder to speeding, so that we can function as a society. When a constraint is needed to maintain a civil society and when that constraint violates liberty can be a useful topic for discussion, even in a fifth-grade class. *Liberty* can also be personal. Parents differ in terms of the rules and constraints they set for their children; these are variations in liberty as well. In both realms, there are nonexamples. Totalitarian states restrict personal and political liberties; curfews and chaperones restrict personal liberties.

To understand *liberty*, then, one must understand what *liberty* is. A list generated as a result of a rich class discussion might look like the following:

Category:	Freedom
What is different:	To think or act without constraint
Examples:	Personal
	Going to the mall by oneself
	Hanging with friends
	Ability to choose
	Political
	Ability to vote
	Freedom of speech
	Freedom of religion
Nonexamples	
	Personal
	Parents' rules
	Curfews
	Not being able to talk in class
	Political
	Not being able to kill or steal
	Dictatorships
	Not being able to chose one's leader
	Not being allowed to criticize the laws

A class discussion that generated a list such as this would have looked at the concept of *liberty* from a variety of perspectives, not just going through the concept as a dictionary definition, but "criss-crossing" it from the personal and political perspectives, looking at what *liberty* is and what it is not, understanding the boundaries of the concept. In other words, developing a full and rich understanding of the concept.

The discussion needed to develop this rich understanding is more time consuming than the extended instruction discussed earlier and should be reserved only for concepts that need such instruction. This discussion should take place prior to reading, because it is needed to set the stage for unit or theme understanding. The examples just listed are generally content area examples, but the technique can also be used for literary themes, or even discussions of genre (*narrative, exposition, textbook, recipe*, etc.).

One example of an activity that can used to build full and thorough understandings of a concept is the "four-square" vocabulary approach (Eeds & Cockrum, 1985). This approach uses either a printed diagram or, more simply, a piece of paper folded so that it has four squares. Figure 5.1 illustrates the use of such a diagram around a word to be learned, such as *prejudice*. Examples of the word are written in the second box, upper right. For prejudice, these examples might include such things as disliking someone because of skin color or because they do not speak English or because of how they dress. Nonexamples are written in the next box, lower right. For *prejudice*, nonexamples might be such things as acceptance or reaching out to people who are different from oneself. Finally, in the last box, the definition of the word is written. The completed box has been illustrated with the word *prejudice*.

Four-square boxes can be done as whole-class activities or by groups of children working together. What I like about this activity is its ease and the possibility of its spontaneous use to discuss a particularly gnarly concept that might arise during reading. The activity is flexible enough to use on less complex concepts, but adaptable to even fairly abstract ideas.

Learning About Words

English is made up of words that come from everywhere. Many words come from Anglo-Saxon, yes; but they also come from other languages as familiar as French (*chauffeur*) and as exotic as Icelandic (*mukluk*) or Chinese (*abacus*). Some come from the military (*snafu*), from the names of people (*sandwich*), or from songs (*Yankee Doodle*). A great many of the academic words that are important to school success come from Latin and Greek. Scholars in the Renaissance and beyond, being trained in these "learned" languages, created neologisms (the word itself from the Greek, *neo-* [new], *logos* [word]) to de-

Prejudice	Disliking someone because of their beliefs or appearance
Hatred or dislike because a person is different	Acceptance Tolerance of differences

FIG. 5.1.   Four-square diagram for the teaching the word *prejudice*.

scribe the many new concepts they were discovering. Thus, our language is full of words that contain *quad-*, *bio-*, *loq-*, *fed-*, and so on.

For students, word-part instruction can be truly boring, full of the memorization of lists and definitions. However, such instruction also can be an opportunity for students to engage in a thoughtful exploration of the roots of English.

Teaching word parts in Grades 3–5 can help children learn a great deal of words. Simple prefixes and suffixes can provide a significant amount of vocabulary growth in those grades (Anglin, 1993). According to analyses conducted by White, Sowell, and Yanigihara (1989), 11 prefixes account for 81% of all prefixed words and six suffixes account for 80% of all suffixed words. Teaching children this group of high-leverage prefixes and suffixes ensures that students generalize their knowledge of both root words (to affixed words) and the changes in meaning indicated by affixes. This group of affixes from White et al. (1989) that accounts for approximately 80% of all affixed words is listed in Table 5.1.

A discussion of word parts should become an integral part of word-learning instruction. Discussions that include stories about word origins and derivations can stir interest in learning more about language—that is, build word consciousness. Stories that help children to see and understand how similarities in word spellings may show similarities in meaning, may solidify and expand their word knowledge. For example, the seemingly dissimilar words *loquacious*, *colloquium*, and *elocution* all come from the root word *loq*, meaning "to talk." Knowing this connection may make it easier for children to remember the words. Words stories can stay with a student for a long time. In high school, I learned that *sanguine*, meaning "cheerfully optimistic," comes from the same root as *sanguinary*, meaning "involving blood-

TABLE 5.1

Prefixes and Suffixes That Account for Approximately 80% of Affixed Words

Prefixes	% of All Prefixed Words (Cumulative)	Suffixes	% of All Suffixed Words (Cumulative)
1. Un- (not)	26	-S, -es	31
2. Re- (again)	40	-ed	51
3. In-, im-, il-, ir- (not)	51	-ing	65
4. Dis (	58	-ly	72
5. En-, em-	62	-Er, -or (agent)	76
6. non	66	-Ion, -tion, -ation, ition	80
7. In-, im- (in)	69		
8. over-	72		
9. mis-	75		
10. sub-	78		
11. pre-	81		

Note. Adapted from Tables 1 and 2 of White, T. G., Sowell, J., & Yanagihara, A. (1989). Teaching elementary students to use word-part clues. *The Reading Teacher, 42*(4), 302–308 with permission of the International Reading Association (© 1989).

shed or death." Both words come from the medieval theory of "humors," which held that a person's health was controlled by a series of humors—black bile (*melan-*), white bile, blood, and phlegm. Thus, we have *melancholy, bilious, sanguine* and *phlegmatic,* words that originally described an overabundance of one humor over the others.

CONCLUSION: WORD MEANINGS AND WORLD MEANINGS

To have an impact on children's comprehension, vocabulary teaching should be rich, intensive, and full of interesting information. It needs to cover a great many words and cover them well. Active vocabulary instruction should permeate a classroom, not just be a brief activity to do before reading a basal story. Discussion of words is discussion of knowledge of the world, and knowledge of the world is knowledge of who we are and where we stand in the world. Vocabulary instruction is not just one of several important aspects of reading, it is a gift of words, a gift that one gives generously to others.

REFERENCES

Adams, M. J. (1990). *Beginning to read: Thinking and learning about print*. Cambridge, MA: MIT Press.

Anglin, J. M. (1993). Vocabulary development: A morphological analysis. *Monographs of the Society for Research in Child Development, Serial No. 238, 58*(10), 1–187.

Baker, L., & Brown, A. L. (1984). Metacognitive skills and reading. In P. D. Pearson, R. Barr, M. L. Kamil, & P. Mosenthal (Eds.), *Handbook of reading research* (pp. 353–394). White Plains, NY: Longman.

Beck, I. L., & McKeown, M. G. (2001). Text talk: Capturing the benefits of read-aloud experiences for young children. *The Reading Teacher, 55*, 10–20.

Beck, I. L., McKeown, M. G., & Caslin, E. S. (1983). Vocabulary development: All contexts are not created equal. *The Elementary School Journal, 83*, 177–181.

Beck, I. L., McKeown, M. G., & Kucan, L. (2002). *Bringing words to life: Robust vocabulary instruction*. New York: The Guilford Press.

Biemiller, A., & Slonim, N. (2001). Estimating root word vocabulary growth in normative and advantaged populations: Evidence for a common sequence of vocabulary acquisition. *Journal of Educational Psychology, 93*, 498–520.

Chomsky, C. (1978). When you still can't read in third grade? After decoding, what? In S. J. Samuels (Ed.), *What research has to say about reading instruction* (pp. 13–30). Newark, DE: International Reading Association.

Cobuild Staff (2002). *Collins Cobuild new student's dictionary*. London, UK: HarperCollins.

D'Anna, C. A., Zechmeister, E. B., & Hall, J. W. (1991). Toward a meaningful definition of vocabulary size. *Journal of Reading Behavior, 23*, 109–122.

Dickinson, D. K., & Tabors, P. O. (2001). *Beginning literacy with language: Young children learning at home and school*. Baltimore, MD: Paul H. Brooks.

Eeds, M., & Cockrum, W. A. (1985). Teaching word meanings by expanding schemata vs. dictionary work vs. reading in context. *Journal of Reading, 28*, 492–497.

Fry, E. B., Fountoukidis, D. L., & Polk, J. K. (1985). *The new reading teacher's book of lists*. Englewood Cliffs, NJ: Prentice-Hall.

Graves, M. F. (2000). A vocabulary program to complement and bolster a middle-grade comprehension program. In B. M. Taylor, M. F. Graves, & P. van den Broek (Eds.), *Reading for meaning: Fostering comprehension in the middle grades* (pp. 116–135). New York: Teachers College Press.

Hart, B., & Risley, T. (1995). *Meaningful differences in the everyday lives of young American children*. Baltimore, MD: Paul H. Brookes.

Hayes, D. P., & Ahrens, M. (1988). Vocabulary simplification for children: A special case of 'motherese.' *Journal of Child Language, 15*, 395–410.

Haynes, M. C., & Jenkins, J. R. (1986). Reading instruction in special education resource rooms. *American Educational Research Journal, 23*, 161–190.

Leinhardt, G., Zigmond, N., & Cooley, W. (1981). Reading instruction and its effects. *American Educational Research Journal, 18*, 343–361.

McKeown, M. G., & Beck, I. L. (2003). Taking advantage of read alouds to help children make sense of decontextualized language. In A. v. Kleeck, S. A. Stahl, & E. B. Bauer (Eds.), *On reading storybooks to children: Parents and teachers*. Mahwah, NJ: Lawrence Erlbaum Associates.

McKeown, M. G., Beck, I. L., Omanson, R. C., & Pople, M. T. (1985). Some effects of the nature and frequency of vocabulary instruction on the knowledge and use of words. *Reading Research Quarterly, 20*, 522–535.

Nagy, W. E., & Anderson, R. C. (1984). How many words are there in printed school English? *Reading Research Quarterly, 19,* 304–330.

National Reading Panel. (2000). *Report of the subgroups: National Reading Panel.* Washington, DC: National Institute of Child Health and Human Development.

Saunders, W. M., & Goldenberg, C. (1999). Effects of instructional conversations and literature logs on limited- and fluent-English-proficient students' story comprehension and thematic understanding. *Elementary School Journal, 99,* 277–301.

Scott, J., & Nagy, W. E. (2004). Developing word consciousness. In J. Baumann & E. Kame'enui (Eds.), *Vocabulary instruction: Research to practice* (pp. 201–217). New York: Guilford.

Spiro, R. J., Coulson, R. L., Feltovich, P. J., & Anderson, D. K. (1994). Cognitive flexibility theory: Advanced knowledge acquisition in ill-structured domains. In R. B. Ruddell, M. R. Ruddell, & H. Singer (Eds.), *Theoretical models and processes of reading* (4th ed., pp. 602–615). Newark, DE: International Reading Association.

Stahl, S. A. (1991). Beyond the instrumentalist hypothesis: Some relationships between word meanings and comprehension. In P. Schwanenfluegel (Ed.), *The psychology of word meanings* (pp. 157–178). Hillsdale, NJ: Lawrence Erlbaum Associates.

Stahl, S. A. (1998). *Vocabulary development.* Cambridge, MA: Brookline Press.

Stahl, S. A., & Clark, C. H. (1987). The effects of participatory expectations in classroom discussion on the learning of science vocabulary. *American Educational Research Journal, 24*(4), 541–555.

Stahl, S. A., & Fairbanks, M. M. (1986). The effects of vocabulary instruction: A model-based meta-analysis. *Review of Educational Research, 56*(1), 72–110.

Stahl, S. A., & Nagy, W. E. (in press). *The words we use: Teaching vocabulary.* Mahwah, NJ: Lawrence Erlbaum Associates.

Stahl, S. A., Richek, M. G., & Vandevier, R. (1991). Learning word meanings through listening: A sixth grade replication. In J. Zutell & S. McCormick (Eds.), *Learning factors/teacher factors: Issues in literacy research. Fortieth yearbook of the National Reading Conference* (pp. 185–192). Chicago: National Reading Conference.

Stahl, S. A., & Vancil, S. J. (1986). Discussion is what makes semantic maps work. *The Reading Teacher, 40,* 62–67.

Stanovich, K. E. (1986). Matthew effects in reading: Some consequences of individual differences in the acquisition of literacy. *Reading Research Quarterly, 21,* 360–407.

White, T. G., Graves, M. F., & Slater, W. H. (1990). Growth of reading vocabulary in diverse elementary schools: Decoding and word meaning. *Journal of Educational Psychology, 82,* 281–290.

White, T. G., Sowell, J., & Yanagihara, A. (1989). Teaching elementary students to use word-part clues. *The Reading Teacher, 42,* 302–309.

Wiles, D. (2001). *Freedom summer.* New York: Atheneum.

Chapter 6

Bringing Words to Life in Classrooms With English-Language Learners

Margarita Calderón
Johns Hopkins University

Diane August
August and Associates

Robert Slavin and Daniel Duran
Johns Hopkins University

Nancy Madden and Alan Cheung
Success for All Foundation

Large and growing numbers of students in the United States come from homes where English is not the primary language. According to the National Center for Educational Statistics (2002), the number of English-language learners continued to increase in both absolute terms and as a percentage of total student enrollment in 2000–2001. An estimated 4,584,946 English-language learners were enrolled in public schools, representing approximately 9.6% of the total school enrollment in prekindergarten through Grade 12. Since the 1990–1991 school year, the English-language learner population has grown approximately 105%, whereas the general school population has grown by only 12%. However, the schools and, more generally, the educational system have not been adequately prepared to respond to the rapidly changing student demographics. Such conditions combine and probably interact to produce educational outcomes that demand attention. For example, for the 41 State Educational

Agencies (SEAs) reporting on both the participation and the success of English-language learners in English reading comprehension—the ultimate purpose of reading—only 18.7% of the students assessed scored above the state-established norm.[1]

THEORETICAL BACKGROUND

A major determinant of reading comprehension for all children is vocabulary. Cunningham and Stanovich (1997) reported that vocabulary assessed in first grade predicted over 30% of reading comprehension variance in eleventh grade. Students reading in their first language have already learned on the order of 5,000 to 7,000 words before they begin formal reading instruction in schools (Biemiller & Slonim, 2001). However, second-language learners typically have not already learned a large store of oral language vocabulary in the second language (Singer, cited in Grabe, 1991). Even middle to high socioeconomic status and use of English in addition to a first language (in this case Spanish) does not appear to mitigate lack of second-language vocabulary knowledge for English-language learners (Umbel, Pearson, Fernandez, & Oller, 1992). The researchers tested the receptive vocabulary of Hispanic children in Miami in both English and Spanish with the Peabody Picture Vocabulary Test (PPVT) and its Spanish equivalent, the Test de Vocabulario en Imagenes Peabody (TVIP). The 105 bilingual first graders, of middle to high socioeconomic status relative to national norms, were divided according to the language spoken in their homes (English and Spanish or Spanish only). Both groups performed near the mean of 100 in Spanish, but the English and Spanish group scored more than one standard deviation higher in English than the Spanish-only group. However, both groups were significantly below the mean of the norming sample in English, even when the socioeconomic status of the English-language learners was higher than that of the norming sample. Poor vocabulary is a serious issue for English-language learners. Although skilled readers can tolerate a small proportion of unknown words in a text without disruption of comprehension, comprehension is disrupted if the proportion of unknown words is too high. A series of studies underscores that vocabulary learning results in comprehension gains and improvement on semantic tasks. For example, McKeown, Beck, Omanson, and Perfetti (1983) found that vocabulary instruction had a strong relation to text comprehension in fourth graders.

---

[1]Currently available state data do not offer a clear picture of English-language learners' reading achievement. First, assessment tools and testing policies differ from state to state and even within districts within a state. Furthermore, data are gathered for different grade levels.

Findings from the National Reading Panel (2000) indicate that various methods improve students' vocabulary, depending on the age of the children. First, computer use bolsters vocabulary learning when compared with traditional methods (Davidson, Elcock, & Noyes, 1996). The National Reading Panel also cited the keyword method as having a substantial research base. Although it may significantly augment recall, the method works best with particular kinds of words and requires substantial teacher effort (Kamil & Hiebert, chapter 1, this volume). Other methods have also proven successful. Vocabulary can be acquired through incidental exposure (Schwanenflugel, Stahl, & McFalls, 1997) or reinforced through student-initiated talk and active participation during storybook reading (Dickinson & Smith, 1994; Drevno, Kimball, Possi, Heward, Gardner, & Barbetta, 1994; Senechal, 1997). A focus on high-frequency words and multiple, repeated exposures to vocabulary is important, as is the application of words to multiple contexts (Daniels, 1994; Leung, 1992; Senechal, 1997). Some studies (Brett, Rothlein, & Hurley, 1996; Carney, Anderson, Blackburn, & Blessing, 1984; Wixson, 1986) suggest that preinstruction of vocabulary facilitates vocabulary acquisition and comprehension. Others advocate restructuring materials or procedures (e.g., substituting easy for hard words in a passage, teaching what components make a good definition, selecting relevant words for vocabulary learning, conducting group-assisted reading in dyads rather than unassisted groups) in order to bolster comprehension (Scott & Nagy, 1997). Stahl (1983) reported that a mix of contextual and definitional approaches work better than either approach alone, whereas Margosein, Pascarella, & Pflaum, 1982) found specific gains from a single approach (semantic mapping over context-rich or target-word treatment). Several other researchers have reported that direct instruction in learning word meanings is helpful (Tomesen & Aarnoutse, 1998; White, Graves, & Slater, 1990).

Despite the importance of vocabulary to comprehension for English-language learners, there have been only four experimental studies conducted since 1980 examining the effectiveness of interventions designed to build vocabulary among language minority students learning English as a societal language. The findings indicate that research-based strategies used with first-language learners (National Reading Panel, 2000) are effective with second-language learners, although the strategies must be adapted to the strengths and needs of second language learners. In one study, Carlo et al. (2004) developed, implemented, and assessed an intervention designed to enrich the vocabulary knowledge and bolster the reading comprehension of Spanish-speaking, fifth-grade English-language learners and their English-only peers. The participants were 254 bilingual (Spanish–English) and monolingual English-speaking children from nine fifth-grade classrooms in four schools in California, Virginia, and Massachusetts. The study employed a quasiexperimental design in which classrooms at each site were randomly assigned to the treatment and comparison conditions. This procedure resulted in the assignment of three classes to the treatment while six classrooms served as comparisons.

Students in the treatment groups participated in 15 weeks of instruction, with an emphasis on 10 to 12 words per week. Vocabulary instruction lasted for 30 to 45 minutes per day for 4 days per week, with one additional day per week devoted to review. The vocabulary was presented thematically and included homework assignments and a weekly test. Activities were designed to build depth of word meaning and provide students with strategies to acquire new words. In addition, activities built on students' first-language knowledge by teaching students to take advantage of cognate knowledge and providing Spanish previews of the text students were to read in English. Students in the comparison classrooms did not receive special instruction other than that normally included in the school curriculum, although their teachers did participate as members of school teams in professional development activities focused on vocabulary teaching 2 years prior to the introduction of the intervention.

Students in the intervention and comparison classrooms were tested in the fall and the spring of the academic year on a series of tests designed to reflect the skills the curriculum taught. The assessments measured breadth of vocabulary (Peabody Picture Vocabulary Test Revised, or PPVT-R) as well as the students' ability to form deeper representations of word knowledge (word association test), to master the vocabulary words that had been taught (mastery test), to understand the multiple meanings of words (polysemy production test), to analyze the morphology of words (morphology test), and to comprehend text (cloze). The PPVT-R was used as a covariate to reduce effects associated with differences in initial English proficiency and with site differences in populations being served. The mastery, word association, polysemy, and cloze tests all showed the same general pattern of results, demonstrating the impact of the intervention: The intervention group showed greater gain in the course of the school year than the comparison group.

A second experimental vocabulary study focused on presenting words to first-grade Spanish-dominant students (Vaughn-Shavuo, 1990). In this doctoral dissertation, students were randomly assigned to two groups. Both groups received vocabulary instruction during a 30-minute daily ESL class. One group worked on learning words that were presented in random sentence contexts, while the other worked on words that were embedded in meaningful narratives about which the students dictated sentences. These students were also shown picture cards that illustrated the word meanings. During 3 weeks of instruction, 31 words were presented to each group, and by the end of the training, the experimental group showed better ability to use the English vocabulary than did the control group (21 words learned versus 9).

Perez (1981) reported on a third vocabulary study targeting 75 Mexican-American language minority third graders. The children received 3 months of oral instruction for 20 minutes each day, focusing on compound words, synonyms, antonyms, and multiple meanings. The experimental group children showed significant improvement over a control group on the Prescriptive Reading Inventory.

In a fourth study, a method called *suggestopedia* was used with Spanish-language background third graders (Ramirez, 1986). Suggestopedia is an alternative language learning method developed by Dr. Georgi Lozarov in the 1970s. Lozarov believed the use of music, comfortable chairs, and soft lighting in the classroom created levels of relaxed concentration that enabled students to better learn and retain new material. In the Raimirez study, the suggestopedia procedure was applied with 10 new words per day. These 10 new words were presented through scripted lessons that made use of recordings, filmstrips, and short tests of each lesson. Students in both the control group and the experimental group were presented with 40 words over a 4-day period in class sessions that were 40 minutes in duration. This teaching was delivered to three groups of 10 students each (one control group, and two experimental groups—one that received suggestopedia, and one that received this method without imagery training). The groups were compared on the vocabulary section of the Metropolitan Achievement Tests (MAT) and the Primary Acquisition of Languages Oral Dominance measure and found to be equivalent. The two experimental groups performed significantly better than the control group; moreover, the suggestopedia approach was found to be most successful with the students with the highest levels of English proficiency.

The intervention described in this chapter builds on previous work on vocabulary conducted with English-only students as well as English-language learners. The intervention was designed for use with English language learners who have just transitioned from native language (Spanish) literacy instruction to English literacy instruction. It is estimated that 57% of English-language learners are in some form of transitional bilingual program in which they typically receive literacy and content area instruction in their first language (L1) while learning to speak and comprehend English as a second language (L2; August & Hakuta, 1997). Once students have acquired a certain level of L1 literacy and adequate listening and speaking skills in English, they make the "transition" to English. That is, they are immersed in English-only mainstream classrooms where literacy and other academic subjects are taught in English. The transition into the mainstream usually takes place during the second, third, fourth, or even fifth grade, depending on school, district, or state policy. However, because of the No

Child Left Behind legislation, more schools are leaning toward a second- or third-grade transition.

To date, only two empirical studies (Calderón, Hertz-Lazarowitz, & Slavin, 1998; Saunders & Goldenberg, 2001) have provided experimental evidence on the best way to instruct children during the critical period of transition. Both interventions reported in these studies focused on developing vocabulary to help students with the sudden immersion into English-content reading. The program developed and investigated by Saunders and Goldenberg (2001) is a 3-year transition program implemented in Grades 3–5. The 3-year design presumes that students receive a coherent program of language arts instruction from Grades 3–5, from primary language through transitional language arts. Research results indicate that this transition program does a better job of cultivating literacy than the 3- to 6-month transition program students typically receive. Project students scored significantly higher than nonproject students in reading across Grades 3–5 on both standardized and performance-based assessments, regardless of language. At Grade 5, when most students took English standardized tests and all students took English performance assessments, project students scored significantly higher than nonproject students on every measure taken.

In the other study, Calderón, Hertz-Lazarowitz, and Slavin (1998) investigated the Bilingual Cooperative Integrated Reading and Composition (BCIRC) program. The study was conducted in three experimental ($n =$ 250) and four control ($n = 250$) schools in El Paso, Texas. Students were pretested with the district's language proficiency test and posttested after second and third grades in English reading and writing with the Texas Assessment of Academic Skills and the Norm-Referenced Assessment Program for Texas standardized tests. By the end of third grade, BCIRC students scored almost one standard deviation higher than comparison students in reading (ES = +0.87). In this study, vocabulary was taught in the context of reading, first with simple sequenced readers, then building up to grade-level readers. Redundancy of vocabulary was achieved through prereading, during reading, and postreading activities as students applied the new words orally and in written form.

The purpose of the present study was to evaluate an intervention for children transitioning from Spanish to English reading that was based on current understandings of how to build vocabulary, decoding skills, and comprehension in a second language. The intervention included cooperative learning, extensive teaching of vocabulary strategies, direct teaching of comprehension skills, many opportunities for independent reading, and so on. The Success for All reading program (SFA; Slavin & Madden, 2001) provided the base for the transition model but incorporated vocabulary enhancement strategies derived from the work of several researchers. This study is important in that it provides a first evaluation of a promising strategy to enhance Spanish-to-English transition.

METHOD

Design

The year-long study employed a matched control design. A total of eight experimental and eight control classrooms in Texas schools participated in the study. All experimental classrooms were in four SFA schools in two districts. The experimental students participated in the program described here, designed to facilitate transition from Spanish into English reading. The control students participated in the two districts' regular programs for Spanish-to-English transition, which consist of a basal series and instructional approaches called readers' workshop and writers' workshop. Both programs transition students at the same grade levels and devote one year to introducing reading and writing in English. The principal goal of both SFA and the districts' transition programs is to have all English-language learners ready to meet the districts' criteria for moving into mainstream English classes at the end of the school year.

The experimental and control schools were matched on the percentage of English-language learners and the percentage of free and reduced lunch eligibility (see Table 6.1). Participants in the study were predominately socioeconomically disadvantaged, as an average of 90% received full or reduced lunch subsidies. All schools enrolled a high percentage of English-language learners, ranging from a low of 47% to a high of 76%, with an

TABLE 6.1

Characteristics of Participating Schools

	% English Language Learners	% Free and Reduced Lunch
Experimental School A	60%	85%
Control School B	67%	79%
Experimental School C	55%	93%
Control School D	47%	88%
Experimental School E	55%	90%
Control School F	76%	96%
Experimental School G	71%	96%
Control School H	54%	91%

average of 60%. Pretests were also given to ensure the comparability of the treatment and control groups and were used as covariates in the main analyses to adjust for any initial difference between the two groups.

Participants

Subjects were 293 Spanish-dominant third-grade students enrolled in eight elementary schools in two school districts in El Paso, Texas. The children had been identified by their schools as "ready to begin their transition into English." All participants were pretested and found to be limited English proficient and reading at a second-grade level in Spanish. Both the experimental and control students had been instructed in Spanish for reading, language arts, and content areas since kindergarten.

Overview of the Intervention

The transition intervention was implemented for a period of 22 to 25 weeks. The implementation began at the end of October 2002 (in one case at the beginning of December) and terminated at the end of March 2003, when Texas Assessment of Knowledge and Skills (TAKS) testing preparation began.

The experimental intervention was an adaptation of the Success for All reading program. In this approach, students worked in four-member learning teams, using a series of minibooks containing phonetically decodable texts, children's literature, and ancillary student and teacher materials (Slavin & Madden, 2001). In fast-paced 90-minute lessons, students learned letter sounds, sound blending, sight words, vocabulary, and comprehension skills in English. Because students could already read in Spanish, the instructional pace for teaching English reading was rapid, spending little time on skills common to Spanish and English but stopping to focus on areas in which the languages differ. A major focus was on vocabulary.

Vocabulary activities were designed to build multiple literacy skills in English, including phonological awareness, pronunciation, Spanish–English contrasting sounds, cognate meaning awareness, word reading, decoding, fluency, grammar, reading comprehension, and writing. Vocabulary was taught in two contexts: through the decodable books and through children's literature. To build word knowledge through decodable texts, DVDs were used to preview the vocabulary. The DVDs contained skits that illustrated key vocabulary appearing in the decodable books. However, 30 minutes per day of oral language activities revolving around grade-level children's literature provided the primary method for building children's vocabulary knowledge. Teachers pretaught vocabulary, developed vocabulary through "text talk," and reinforced vocabulary through oral language activities occurring after the story had been read. Students listened to and discussed children's literature (50 books during the year) and worked on daily oral language activities to build word knowledge for key words appearing in the children's literature. Cynthia Rylant's (1993) *The Relatives Came* and John Burningham's (2001) *John Patrick Norman McHennessy: The Boy Who Was Always Late* illustrate the kind of literature that was used in the program. To illustrate the nature of instruction in this chapter, we have chosen Burningham's text to elaborate on the activities of the program. Except for a final set of grammar activities, the complete lesson with which teachers were provided to teach this text is provided in the appendix.

Selecting Words to Teach and the Methods to Teach Them. The selection of words to preteach was based on research by Beck and colleagues (Beck, McKeown, & Kucan, 2002), as well as on the work of the Vocabulary Improvement Project (Carlo et al., 2004) and the BCIRC study (Calderón et al., 1998). Beck and colleagues have developed a systematic method of selecting vocabulary to teach to students. Words are grouped into three tiers, and words in Tier Two are those targeted for instruction. Tier One words are words English-speaking students already know; Tier Three words are words students are unlikely to know, but that are not frequently used across a variety of domains.

We borrowed the tiers concept from Beck and colleagues as a means of categorizing words. However, with English-language learners, we have found it necessary to modify the approach. We take it for granted that native English speakers know most Tier One words, but this is not the case for English-language learners. Many Tier One words that are unknown to English-language learners may be key to the comprehension of a passage. Furthermore, English-language learners may not have sufficient background to use context to figure out the words that Beck et al. have designated as Tier Three Consequently, we developed a set of selection criteria for choosing words. The four criteria include: (a) the nature of the word (i.e., is it concrete? Can it be demonstrated?); (b) cognate status; (c) depth of meaning (i.e., the number and richness of the way a word is used); and (d) utility.

In identifying critical Tier One words, we recognize that English-language learners typically know the concept in their primary language. They simply may not know the label in English. For example, a Tier One word might be *butterfly*. English-language learners may not know this word, but it can be easily taught by pointing to a picture of a butterfly during text discussion. Another Tier One word might be *bug*. Words like *bug* (insect) or *march* (move like a soldier) may be easily instructed during text discussion by pointing to a picture of a bug or marching in place, but because the words are polysemous, they merit further instruction. This can be accomplished in oral language activities that follow the text discussion.

There are some Tier One words that cannot be demonstrated and are not polysemous but that students will need to know (e.g., *uncle*). A simple explanation of the word's meaning during the story reading will suffice, or if the teacher and students are bilingual, a translation is sufficient. Idioms and everyday expressions (e.g., "make up your mind"; "let's hit the books"; "once upon a time") are also composed of Tier One words, and teachers will need to explain their meanings to students. Other Tier One words are cognates (e.g., *family/familia; preparation/preparación*). The cognates in this category consist of words that are high-frequency words in Spanish and English; they do not require substantial instruction because students know the word meanings in Spanish. In this case, the teacher merely states the English cognate and students provide the Spanish cognate or the teacher provides the English cognate and students provide both the English word and Spanish cognate. False cognates also need to be pointed out by the teacher and the correct translation given. For example, *assist* is usually translated as *asistir*, but the correct translation is *atender*, and *attend* means *asistir;* other examples of words that are false cognates are: *rope/ropa; embarrassed/embarasada.*

Tier Two words include: (a) words that have importance and utility (i.e., they are characteristic of mature language users and appear frequently across a variety of domains); (b) words that have instructional potential (i.e., they can be worked with in a variety of ways so that students can build rich representations of them and their connections to other words and concepts); and (c) words that provide precision and specificity in describing ideas for which students already have a basic conceptual understanding. These words often appear in grade-level texts. Tier Two words that are demonstrable may not need elaborate discussion. In addition, many Tier Two words are cognates (in this tier they are often high-frequency words in Spanish and low-frequency words in English). Children whose first language shares cognates with English will have a head start with these words (e.g., *coincidence/coincidencia, industrious/industrioso, fortunate/afortunado*) because they will know both the concept and an approximation of the label in English. (For children whose first language is not Latin-based and does not share cognates with English, such a procedure needs to be adapted.) The Tier Two words that should be targeted for preteaching include words that cannot be demonstrated and are not cognates.

Furthermore, although Beck et al. (2003) focus on Tier Two words and not Tier Three words, many English-language learners may not have the background to use context to figure out the rare, context-bound words of Tier Three. Tier Three words that are not demonstrable or cognates should be translated or briefly explained in the first language but not elaborated in English. They are low-frequency words and are not encountered across a multitude of domains.

Preteaching Vocabulary.   For this intervention, the project staff se-lected the vocabulary for each of the 50 children's literature books that were used in the teacher read-alouds throughout the program. The criteria that were developed in the previous section were used to select words.

Activities were then developed for each of the chosen words by the pro-ject staff. The basis for these activities was the vocabulary process developed by Beck and colleagues (Beck, McKeown, & Kucan, 2002). Second-lan-guage strategies were integrated with the basic preteaching process to achieve five steps.

First, the teacher says a target word in both English and Spanish; second, teachers provide a definition of the word based on its use in the story; third, they provide another example of the word by using it in a sentence whose context clarifies the word's meaning; fourth, they ask students to repeat the word several times to build a phonological representation of the word; and fifth, they have students become "engaged with the word" through oral lan-guage activities. The fifth activity can be carried out with a partner. For in-stance, the teacher might say, "Tell your partner about a time you were *mesmerized*." After a minute of sharing with partners, the teacher may ask two or three students to share what their partner said.

The cycle of preteaching vocabulary is demonstrated in the appendix for the six key vocabulary words for the book *John Patrick Norman McHennessy: The Boy Who Was Always Late* (Burningman, 2001)—*satchel, snapped, tore, swept, cling,* and *lie*.

Developing Vocabulary Through Discourse Around Text.   Vocabulary is also developed through ongoing text-related dialogue between the teacher and students during the read-alouds. Teachers stop at specific in-tervals in the text to elicit discussion. Different methods are used depend-ing on the nature of the word, its cognate status, its depth of meaning, and its utility. Concrete words are demonstrated; for cognates, teachers tell students the cognate in Spanish or ask students for the English cognate. Tier Two words that have been pretaught are reinforced through ques-tions that require students to use and understand the words. Teachers provide Spanish definitions of Tier Three words (if they cannot be dem-onstrated) or simple English explanations. Teachers also use different kinds of questions to encourage vocabulary development. They ask initial questions that prompt students to talk about ideas rather than constrained questions that elicit one-word responses, and they use follow-up questions to help students develop their likely sparse first responses. They also use questions to help students move beyond using pictures and background knowledge in these responses and to encourage more elaborated re-sponses tied to the text. An example of such a question with *John Patrick Norman McHennessy: The Boy Who Was Always Late* can be seen in the appendix: What are the consequences for John Patrick? Have you ever invented excuses/escusas because you were late?

Oral Language Activities to Build Vocabulary. The language development activities that follow the story are based in large part on the story's words. Different stories lend themselves to different kinds of activities. But the key focus is on developing conceptual knowledge about the words and reinforcing labels for the word. This is also an opportunity for students to use the word in extended discourse through story retelling or in a different context such as in story mapping or dramatization. The section usually closes with written exercises for reinforcing word meaning and using multiple meanings of words in sentences.

There are also ongoing activities designed to review words from previous stories and help students listen for and use words outside of the language arts class. Word Wizard is used to promote word use outside of class. The children take home their Partner Activities Book with a Word Wizard page where they can record the target vocabulary they hear outside of class. The Partner Books also contain activities to conduct with parents, older siblings, or for self-review, such as additional passages with the vocabulary learned that day through the DVDs and their decodable books. The classroom has word walls that contain pictures of the words and labels or words organized by category. Student writing is posted, as are posters containing reminders about grammar, syntax, and cognates. Examples of all these activities can be found in the appendix.

Assessment

Children in both conditions were pretested in fall 2002 and posttested in spring 2003. Children were pretested at their schools during the period from November 4 to November 24, 2002. At pretest, children were administered four subtests of the Woodcock Language Proficiency Battery-Revised (WLPB-R) in both Spanish and English forms: Picture Vocabulary, Letter–Word Identification, Word Attack, and Passage Comprehension. The WLPB-R is a comprehensive set of individually administered standardized tests for measuring abilities and achievement in oral language, reading, and written language. Testing sessions required, on average, 40 minutes per child for each language.

The Picture Vocabulary subtest measures the ability to name familiar and unfamiliar pictured objects. The WLPB-R Letter–Word Identification and Word Attack subtests were used to measure orthographic skills. In the Letter–Word Identification task, the first five letter–word identification items measure symbolic learning, or the ability to match a rebus (pictographic representation of a word) with an actual picture of an object. The remaining objects measure the student's reading identification skills with isolated letters and words. The student does not need to know the meaning of any of the words presented but must be able to respond to letters or words he or she may not have seen before. Word Attack measures the student's skill in applying phonic and structural analysis skills to the pronunciation of unfamiliar printed words. The subject reads aloud letter combinations that are linguistically logical in English, but either do not form actual words or form low-frequency words. The first four Passage Comprehension items are presented in a multiple-choice format that requires the participant to point to the picture represented by a phrase. The remaining items measure the participant's skill in reading a short passage and identifying a missing key word. The WLPB-R was normed on a national sample of children, and the internal reliability for the four subtests used is 0.863, 0.918, 0.902, and 0.914, respectively.

Children were posttested at the end of third grade during the period from May 1 to May 20, 2003. Although children were posttested using the same measures used during the pretests, for the purposes of this chapter we report on the picture vocabulary subtest of the WLPB-R in English and Spanish forms.

Examiners for all assessments were full-time, experienced bilingual testers hired and trained by the Johns Hopkins University in El Paso, Texas. Testers were unaware of the assignment of children to condition.

Attrition

Attrition resulted in the loss of 54 students (20 in the experimental group and 27 in the control group) between fall 2002 and spring 2003. This generated a sample size of 239 for the present analyses of effects on achievement outcomes. Attrition for each school is summarized in Table 6.2. As Table 6.2 shows, the attrition rate for both groups was similar—17% in the experimental group and 15% in the control group.

Analyses

The study employed a series of analyses of covariance (ANCOVA) with condition as the independent variable, the WLPB-R vocabulary subtest as the dependent measure, and both Spanish and English pretests as covariates to adjust for initial difference between the treatment group and the control group. Thus analyses for Spanish and English Picture Vocabulary used both Spanish and English Picture Vocabulary at pretests as covariates.

TABLE 6.2
Attrition for Participating Schools

	Number of Participants		
Experimental Group	**Fall 2002**	**Spring 2003**	**Left school**
School A	38	30	8
School C	44	35	9
School E	38	32	6
School G	32	28	4
Total	152	125	27 (17%)
Control Group			
School B	34	31	3
School D	37	30	7
School F	32	27	5
School H	31	26	5
Total	134	114	20 (15%)

RESULTS

Pretests

The results of the WLPB-R testing are summarized in Table 6.3. As the table shows, experimental and control schools were very well matched at pretest on the English Woodcock scales, but the Success for All students scored somewhat higher on all four Spanish pretests.

English Posttests

After adjusting for the initial pretest difference, the experimental group outperformed the control group on three of the four measures. The experimental group scored significantly higher than the control group on Word Attack ($F_{1,235} = 6.209$, $p = 0.013$) with an effect size of +0.21 and Passage Comprehension ($F_{1,235} = 3.753$, $p = 0.05$) with an effect size of +0.16. The difference between the experimental and the control group scores was marginally significant on Picture Vocabulary ($F_{1,235} = 3.042$, $p = 0.08$) with an effect size of +0.11. No significant difference was found between the two groups on the Letter–Word Identification subtest.

Spanish Posttests

For the Spanish subtests, the experimental group scored significantly higher than the control group in Letter–Word Identification ($F_{1,235} = 4.864$,

TABLE 6.3

Effects of the Bilingual Transition Program
on English and Spanish Reading

English Woodcock	Success for All			Control			Effect Size[a]
	Pre	Post	Adj. Post[b]	Pre	Post	Adj. Post[b]	
Picture Vocabulary							
M	450.09	459.91	459.78	451.06	457.43	457.57	+0.11*
SD	(19.89)	(16.57)		(20.21)	(19.51)		
Passage Comprehension							
M	465.41	476.01	475.45	467.56	472.06	472.67	'+0.16**
SD	(23.54)	(16.79)		(23.81)	(17.87)		
Letter Word ID							
M		486.96	485.18		483.13	485.09	
SD		(20.51)		472.68	(21.74)		+0.00
	476.07			(23.19)			
	(22.57)						
Word Attack							
M	478.41	490.32	490.05	478.22	485.54	485.84	'+0.21**
SD	(14.63)	(14.29)		(16.29)	(19.84)		
N	125	125		114	114		
Spanish Woodcock							
Picture Vocabulary							
M	500.69	499.91	497.50	491.86	492.25	494.89	+0.14*
SD	(17.43)	(12.12)		(19.30)	(18.60)		
Passage Comprehension							
M	486.24	488.93	486.85	479.42	484.06	486.34	+0.05
SD	(8.13)	(8.64)		(9.33)	(10.18)		
Letter Word ID							
M	534.64	541.42	539.89	527.51	534.25	535.94	'+0.26**
SD	(15.35)	(15.76)		(19.32)	(15.21)		
Word Attack							
M	512.54	514.70	514.01	508.91	513.18	513.95	+0.00
SD	(12.67)	(11.87)		(13.44)	(12.44)		
N	125	125		114	114		

Notes. [a]Effect size = Adj. Post (Exp) -Adj. Post (control) / Unadjusted SD (control). [b]Adjusted for Spanish and English Pretests. *$p < .10$. **$p < .05$.

$p = 0.028$) with an effect size of $+0.26$, and scored higher with marginal significance in Picture Vocabulary ($F_{1,235} = 2.874, p = 0.091$) with an effect size of $+0.14$. No statistically significant difference was found on the Passage Comprehension and Word Attack subtests.

The effects on Spanish measures were unexpected, as the emphasis of the program was on English reading, but the focus of the program on building vocabulary, on Spanish cognates (and false cognates), and other program features may have contributed to the experimental group's superior performance in Spanish. However, the more interesting impacts were those seen on the English measures, where Success for All students showed modest but positive effects, compared to controls, on the English vocabulary measures.

DISCUSSION

Even with an intervention that was implemented for less than a full year, modest positive benefits were seen on measures of English vocabulary. In addition, gains on scales assessing Spanish vocabulary indicate that the bilingual transition model may also be beneficial in promoting children's reading skills in their home language, even though this was not a primary goal of the intervention. Thus, carefully designed direct vocabulary instruction improves vocabulary knowledge. The evaluation reported here is a first step in a program of research that we expect will produce an effective, replicable program to build word knowledge in English and facilitate Spanish-to-English transition following a Spanish reading program. For the 2003–2004 year, we are carrying out a second evaluation involving at least 30 weeks of implementation of the transition intervention, this time including approximately 600 second-, third-, and fourth-grade students.

As we extend on this line of research, we are particularly cognizant of information learned from follow-up interviews with the teachers who participated in this project. Teachers reported that having the lessons fully developed was critical to the implementation. They mentioned that it would have been an insurmountable task to preselect vocabulary from the different tiers, sort words into the appropriate categories, and create a variety of strategies for teaching each word. Teachers also reported that without lessons, they probably would have selected an inappropriate meaning or would have been unsure of how to state the meaning.

Even though this study was an initial effort, the research findings, observations, and follow-up interviews with teachers suggest directions for policymakers and practitioners. First, this study underscores the critical role of vocabulary, if patterns of English-language learners' comprehension are to be altered. The students in the SFA transition program outperformed students in the control group on reading comprehension, verifying a pattern with English-language learners that has been reported with native English speakers (McKeown et al., 1983; National Reading Panel, 2000; Stahl, 1983).

Second, vocabulary must be explicitly taught to English-language learners if they are to catch up to grade-level standards. At the same time, this vocabulary instruction must be part of a comprehensive language/literacy program. Explicit instruction on word knowledge consisting of phonemic, phonological, and morphemic awareness, decoding, and understanding of the multiple meanings of the words should occur in the context of teaching reading and using texts.

ACKNOWLEDGMENT

Adapted from Calderón, M., August, D., Slavin, R.E., Cheung, A., Madden, N., & Duran, D. (2004). *The evaluation of a bilingual transition program for Success for All: A technical report*. Baltimore, MD: Johns Hopkins University, Center for Research on the Education of Students Placed at Risk.

APPENDIX

STaR Story: *John Patrick Norman McHennessy—the Boy Who Was Always Late* by John Burningham

Materials *John Patrick Norman McHennessy—the Boy Who Was Always Late*

Preparation:
- Highlight or underline with yellow all the key vocabulary; with pink all the cognates; with green all the receptive vocabulary and/or advanced vocabulary.
- Insert the labels with questions on the appropriate pages.

Story Summary: This story is about a boy named John Patrick Norman McHennessy. Strange things happen to him on the way to school which make him late. His teacher does not believe him and he is punished. Finally, a strange thing happens to the teacher and John Patrick Norman McHennessy tells him that he does not believe him!

Vocabulary Summary for Teachers

   Key Vocabulary: satchel (2), snapped (5), tore (10), swept (19), cling (21), lie (7)

Cognates or approximations: crocodile/cocodrilo (2), lion/léon (10), manage/manejar, ingeniarse (13), gorilla/gorila (28)

Receptive/advanced vocabulary: bushes (10), tidal wave/oleada (19)

Multiple-meaning words: drain (2), lie (7)

Idioms: set off (1), hurried off (9), on time (26)

Preteaching Vocabulary
Satchel / mochila(2)
A bag carried over the shoulder
Say satchel three times: satchel, satchel, satchel
  Let's open our invisible satchels. What can we put in there?
    Say: I'm putting _____ in my satchel.

Snapped / estalló (5)
1. To speak sharply or angrily. Please don't snap at me!
2. A sudden cracking sound. The alligator's mouth closed with a snap.
Say snap three times: snap, snap, snap
Let's do 'my turn, your turn'—do what I do and say what I say:
  Snap your fingers 3 times.
  Snap your arms like an alligator
  Step on the branch and make a big snap!
  Don't snap at me or I'll cry.

Tore / rompió, desgarró (10)
  To make a hole by pulling. The nail on the door tore my jacket.
Say tore three times: tore, tore, tore
  Have you ever torn your clothing on something?

Swept / arrastró, barrió (19)
1. To move or carry rapidly and forcefully. The fire swept through the building.
2. To clean or clear away with a broom or a brush.
Say swept three times: swept, swept, swept
Let's do 'my turn, your turn'—do what I do and say what I say:
  Let's sweep this floor clean.
  The river swept my plastic boat.
  The surprise swept me off my chair.
  Sweep the dust off your desk.

Cling / pegarse (21)
To stick to or to hold on to something or someone very tightly. He was very scared so he wanted to cling to my arm throughout the movie.
Say cling three times: cling, cling, cling
Answer the following questions in complete sentences.
    Does a spider cling to its web?
    Does a baby cling to its mother?
    What clings to your clothes?

Lie / mentira, mentir, recostado, estar en una parte (7)
1. To get into or be in a flat, horizontal position. Let's all lie down on the floor.
2. A statement that is not true. I told a lie yesterday.
3. To say something that is not true. I lied about my age. I'm really 25 years old.
Say lie three times: lie, lie, lie
I'm going to say some things. If it's a lie, say "that's a lie;" if it's the truth, say "that's the truth."
    Our school principal is 15 years old.
    I am lying on the grass right now.
    My students love to learn.
    I have never told a lie.
    My students love to read.

Before Reading: Story Preview

Student Background Knowledge:
Show the two pages before the story starts, where John Patrick has written "I must not tell lies …" Ask the students: What do you think this is? Have you ever had to write something many times like this? What do you think happened?

During Reading: Interactive Story Reading
Begin reading the story, stopping after the page number indicated to ask predictive, summative, and inferential questions that will motivate students to interact with the story. In addition, you will be making the key vocabulary, idioms, cognates, and receptive vocabulary comprehensible. We have scripted the key words and receptive vocabulary, but you should let the students know which words are cognates and also explain the idioms to them. Remember to ask the questions after you have read the page.

Page 1:   What do you think is the "road to learn?"

Page 2:   What do you think John Patrick has in his satchel?

Pgs. 4–5:   How did John Patrick get his satchel back?

Page 6:   Did John Patrick tell his teacher the truth? Will his teacher believe him?

Page 7:   What was the consequence for John Patrick? Have you ever invented excuses/escusas because you were late?

Page 10:   What happened the next day on his way to school?

Page 13:   What do you think the consequences will be for being late again?

Page 15:   Is he in trouble again? What is his punishment this time?

Page 16:   Repeat what he has to say.

Page 17:   John Patrick is on his way to school again. Turn to your partner and predict what might happen on his way to school.

Pgs. 18–19: What happened this time?

Page 21:   What do you think the consequences will be this time?

Page 23:   What does John Patrick have to do this time? Repeat what he must write.

Page 25:   Turn to your partner and make another prediction about what's going to happen this time.

Pgs. 26-27: Now the teacher is asking John Patrick for help. Why do you think he said that to the teacher?

Page 28:   Did anyone predict something like this was going to happen?

Pgs. 29–30: So, what did John Patrick learn?

After Reading:

- Fact Review and Story Structure Review: Encourage students to recall the story elements by retelling the story in sequence. Create a sequence chain such as the following on the overhead or board, and record the students' contributions.

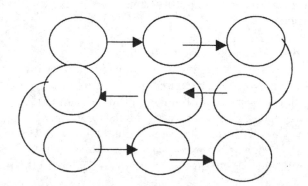

- Story Critique

Did you like the story? [use words like: fantastic, exceptional, exciting, mediocre because ...]

What did you like about this story?

REFERENCES

August, D., & Hakuta, K. (1997). *Improving schooling for language-minority children: A research agenda*. Washington, DC: National Research Council.

Beck, I. L., McKeown, M. G., & Kucan, L. (2002). *Bringing words to life*. New York: Guilford Press.

Biemiller, A., & Slonim, N. (2001). Estimating root word vocabulary growth in normative and advantaged populations: Evidence for a common sequence of vocabulary acquisition. *Journal of Educational Psychology, 93*(3), 498–520.

Brett, A., Rothlein, L., & Hurley, M. (1996). Vocabulary acquisition from listening to stories and explanations of target words. *Elementary School Journal, 96*(4), 415–422.

Burningham, J. (2001). *John Patrick Norman McHennessy—The boy who was always late*. New York: SeaStar Books.

Calderón, M., Hertz-Lazarowitz, R., & Slavin, R. E. (1998). Effects of bilingual cooperative integrated reading and composition on students making the transition from Spanish to English reading. *The Elementary School Journal, 99*(2), 153–165.

Carlo, M., August, D., McLaughlin, B., Snow, C., Dressler, C., Lippman, D., Lively, T., & White, C. (2004). Closing the gap: Addressing the vocabulary needs of English language learners in bilingual and mainstream classrooms. *Reading Research Quarterly, 40.*

Carney, J. J., Anderson, D., Blackburn, C., & Blessing, D. (1984). Preteaching vocabulary and the comprehension of social studies materials by elementary school children. *Social Education, 48*(3), 195–196.

Cunningham, A. E., & Stanovich, K. E. (1997). Early reading acquisition and its relation to reading experience and ability 10 years later. *Developmental Psychology, 33*(6), 934–945.

Daniels, M. (1994). The effects of sign language on hearing children's language development. *Communication Education, 43*(4), 291–298.

Davidson, J., Elcock, J., & Noyes, P. (1996). A preliminary study of the effect of computer-assisted practice on reading attainment. *Journal of Research in Reading, 19*(2), 102–110.

Dickinson, D. K., & Smith, M. W. (1994). Long-term effects of preschool teachers' book readings on low-income children's vocabulary and story comprehension. *Reading Research Quarterly, 29,* 104–122.

Drevno, G. E., Kimball, J. W., Possi, M. K., Heward, W. L., Gardner, R., & Barbetta, P. M. (1994). Effects of active student response during error correction on the acquisition, maintenance, and generalization of science vocabulary by elementary students: A systematic replication. *Journal of Applied Behavior Analysis, 27*(1), 179–180.

Grabe, W. (1991). Current developments in second language reading research. *TESOL Quarterly, 25,* 375–406.

Leung, C. B. (1992). Effects of word-related variables on vocabulary growth through repeated read-aloud events. In C. K. Kinzer & D. J. Leu (Eds.), *Literacy research, theory, and practice: Views from many perspectives. Forty-first yearbook of the National Reading Conference* (pp. 491–498). Chicago: National Reading Conference.

Margosein, C. M., Pascarella, E. T., & Pflaum, S. W. (1982). The effects of instruction using semantic mapping on vocabulary and comprehension. *Journal of Early Adolescence, 2*(2), 185–194.

McKeown, M. G., Beck, I. L., Omanson, R. C., & Perfetti, C. A. (1983). The effects of long-term vocabulary instruction on reading comprehension: A replication. *Journal of Reading Behavior, 15*(1), 3–18.

National Center for Education Statistics. (2002). *Public school student, staff, and graduate counts by state, school year 2000–2001*. Washington, DC: Author.

National Reading Panel. (2000). *Teaching children to read: An evidence-based assessment of the scientific research literature on reading and its implications for reading instruction.* Rockville, MD: National Institute of Child Health and Human Development.

Perez, E. (1981). Oral language competence improves reading skills of Mexican American third graders. *Reading Teacher, 35*(1), 24–27.

Ramirez, S. Z. (1986). The effects of Suggestopedia in teaching English vocabulary to Spanish-dominant Chicano third graders. *Elementary School Journal, 86*(3), 325–333.

Rylant, C. (1993). *The relatives came.* Parsippany, NJ: Pearson Learning Group.

Saunders, W., & Goldenberg, C. (2001). Strengthening the transition in transitional bilingual education. In D. Christian & F. Genesee (Eds.), *Bilingual education* (pp. 41–56). Alexandria, VA: Teachers of English to Speakers of Other Languages, Inc.

Schwanenflugel, P. J., Stahl, S. A., & McFalls, E. L. (1997). Partial word knowledge and vocabulary growth during reading comprehension. *Journal of Literacy Research, 20*, 531–553.

Scott, J., & Nagy, W. (1997). Understanding the definitions of unfamiliar verbs. *Reading Research Quarterly, 32*, 184–200.

Senechal, M. (1997). The differential effect of storybook reading on preschoolers' acquisition of expressive and receptive vocabulary. *Journal of Child Language, 24*(1), 123–138.

Slavin, R. E., & Madden, N. A. (2001). *One million children: Success for All.* Thousand Oaks, CA: Corwin.

Stahl, S. A. (1983). Differential word knowledge and reading comprehension. *Journal of Reading Behavior, 15*(4), 33–50.

Tomesen, M., & Aarnoutse, C. (1998). Effects of an instructional programme for deriving word meanings. *Educational Studies, 24*(1), 107–128.

Umbel, V. M., Pearson, B., Fernandez, M. C., & Oller, D. K. (1992). Measuring bilingual children's receptive vocabularies. *Child Development, 63*, 1012–1020.

Vaughn-Shavuo, F. (1990). *Using story grammar and language experience for improving recall and comprehension in the teaching of ESL to Spanish-dominant first-graders.* Unpublished doctoral dissertation, Hofstra University, New York.

White, T. G., Graves, M. F., & Slater, W. H. (1990). Growth of reading vocabulary in diverse elementary schools: Decoding and word meaning. *Journal of Educational Psychology, 82*(2), 281–290.

Wixson, K. K. (1986). Vocabulary instruction and children's comprehension of basal stories. *Reading Research Quarterly, 21*(3), 317–329.

Sustained Vocabulary-Learning Strategy Instruction for English-Language Learners

María S. Carlo
University of Miami

Diane August
Center for Applied Linguistics

Catherine E. Snow
Harvard Graduate School of Education

Data collected for the National Assessment of Educational Progress during the years 1994–2000 show a difference of approximately 25 points in reading between fourth-, eighth-, and tenth-grade students who routinely speak a language other than English at home and students who speak only English at home (Campbell, Hombo, & Mazzeo, 2000). Research addressing differential outcomes in school performance of linguistic minority and majority children has taught us that explanations for these differences must address a complex set of factors including, but not limited to, differences in socioeconomic, linguistic, cultural, and sociopolitical circumstances. We know of the overrepresentation of language minority children in high poverty schools, in chronically low-achieving schools, and in communities with low levels of formal education and low levels of economic resources of the type that translate into access to artifacts and experiences that are valued by schools. We know also that amid this picture of seeming deficit there exists a wealth of individual, family, and community resources that enrich the lives of language minority children, but in ways that are not often captured by indicators of educational attainment. This is so because, by design, the intellectual and social resources of a particular minority group do not form part of the set of core values and knowledge targeted by most mainstream assessments of learning, which attempt to reflect the values and knowledge of a majority.

In this chapter we describe an instructional intervention that addresses the English instructional needs of English-language learners (ELLs). This intervention, which we refer to as the Vocabulary Improvement Project (VIP), uses what ELLs do know—their first language—as a starting point of instruction. Specifically, this vocabulary intervention teaches children about academic English words while using their conceptual knowledge of these words in Spanish as a springboard to new learning. Before describing this intervention in depth and then the results of a reanalysis of data in which we considered long-term effects of the study, we provide an overview of why this aspect was chosen.

ISSUES OF VOCABULARY AND NATIVE SPANISH SPEAKERS READING IN ENGLISH

Previous work (García, 1991; Nagy, 1997; Verhoeven, 1990) suggests that one major determinant of poor reading comprehension for English-language learners is low vocabulary. Lack of knowledge of the lower frequency academic words encountered in textbooks impedes reading comprehension. This situation is elegantly illustrated in García's (1991) account of Spanish-speaking children's think-alouds while completing a standardized reading assessment. In one telling example, a student in the study named Evita was asked about her understanding of the word *handicap* in the stem of the standardized reading item, "A serious handicap for growth in trade is...." Evita explained that "the handicapped can't go through there" (García, 1991, p. 383), indicating that to her this word functioned as an adjective and referred only to people. With such an understanding of the word, it is little wonder that Evita missed this item.

This example illustrates the reading difficulties created by lack of breadth and depth of English vocabulary for ELLs. Lack of familiarity with a high proportion of the vocabulary in text reduces opportunities for productive contextual analysis. Likewise, unfamiliarity with less frequent meanings of words with multiple meanings, coupled with lack of awareness that many English words are polysemous, leads to faulty interpretations of text.

Given that the vocabulary difficulties of ELLs can stem from lack of *breadth* of English vocabulary (not knowing as many English words as their English speaking peers) as well as *depth* (not knowing as much as they need to know about the words that they do know), a short-term intervention, from all indications in previous research, does not appear to be the solution (García, 2000; Hart & Risley, 1995; Verhallen & Schoonen, 1993). Likewise, given what we know about the inefficiency of direct vocabulary instruction relative to the magnitude of vocabulary growth of school children, which Nagy and Anderson (1984) estimate to be around 3,000 words annually, it is unlikely that interventions that only teach word meanings will close the vocabulary gap between ELLs and their English-speaking peers. Rather, ELLs require interventions that strengthen their ability to apply strategies for independent vocabulary learning as well as provide direct instruction in word meanings.

THE VOCABULARY IMPROVEMENT PROJECT

The development effort that underlies VIP has addressed two components in particular: (a) a curriculum and (b) an instructional routine. We begin here with the curriculum because it involves the selection of words and also the kinds of knowledge about words that students require. For example, because developing morphological connections across words was a critical part of the goals for students, the instructional routine needed to be designed to include activities that support this goal.

The project has a third component—professional development—that is essential to student success. However, as the uniqueness of the project lies in the vocabulary curriculum and instructional routine, the professional development component is not described as fully as the other two components in this chapter.

Research and development of the curriculum and the instructional routine have been conducted in a two-stage process. Both stages occurred in the same schools in three school districts across the country and, in some cases, with the same students over a 2-year period. In Study One, the curriculum and instructional routine were implemented with fourth-graders and, in Study Two, fifth-graders (some of whom had been participants in Study One as fourth-graders). The number of students who participated in the two studies is presented in Table 7.1. We describe the curriculum and instructional routine for Study One as well as the influence of these components on student achievement first, followed by a short description of Study Two where adjustments were made to the curriculum and instructional routine to make them more challenging for fifth graders.

Study One

As shown in Table 7.1, 259 students participated in the first study, which consisted of 10 lessons. A "lesson" consisted of eight components that occurred for 30–45 minutes in daily sessions on 4 days of each of 2 weeks. For

TABLE 7.1

Number of Participants in Two Studies

Language Proficiency	Monolingual (English-Only speakers)		English Language Learners (Native Spanish Speakers)	
	Experimental	Comparison	Experimental	Comparison
Study One: Grade 4	108	48	71	32
Study Two: Grade 5 only	42	29	52	36
Study Two: Grade 5 & previous Grade 4)	29	16	34	16

seven of the sessions, students participated in learning and instructional activities. The eighth session involved an assessment of content that had been covered over the lesson. Four lessons developed new content, whereas every fifth week was devoted to review of the previous 4 weeks' target words.

Curriculum.   The VIP curriculum aims to develop a deeper and richer understanding of a target word's meanings and words and concepts related to a target word. In addition, however, the curriculum is based on the recognition that students require strategies that extend to unfamiliar words in their reading. Prior research led us to emphasize two types of strategies. The first consisted of strategies that support inference making of the meanings of words in the context of text. Reviews by Fukkink and de Glopper (1998) and Kuhn and Stahl (1998) served as the foundation for this emphasis in the VIP curriculum.

Prior research also shows that students benefit from specific strategies that support them in using roots, affixes (Baumann, Font, Edwards, & Boland, chapter 9, this volume), morphological relationships (Carlisle, 2003), and cognates (García & Nagy, 1993). In particular, cognates are a potentially powerful tool for native Spanish speakers because of both the close tie of Spanish to French, which was a source for modern English, and the direct link between Spanish and Latin, from which many scientific words originate (Calfee & Drum, 1986). Many native Spanish speakers learning to read in English, however, need to be made aware of these connections through instruction (Nagy, García, Durgunoglu, & Hancin-Bhatt, 1993).

If students are to apply strategies independently while reading texts, the texts that are used for instruction need to contain exemplars that teachers can use for modeling and scaffolding. We were also interested in using texts that were appropriate for and of interest to learners. In addition, we wanted texts that were available in Spanish as well as English, to ensure that ELLs could access conceptual knowledge available to them in the first language by using their knowledge of words that were translation equivalents to the English words and by highlighting the presence of cognates in the texts.

The texts for the first study came from Arnold Lobel's (1983) *Fables*. Fables, with their classic narrative text structure (Stein & Nezworkski, 1978), seemed like a good starting point for a curriculum. Furthermore, Lobel's *Fables* had been translated from English to Spanish, and Spanish versions of the text were available. A different fable with 10 to 12 target words was the focus of each of the eight lessons where new content was presented. Two of the 10 lessons were devoted to reviewing previously taught vocabulary and vocabulary strategies.

For the most part, the English-language learners in our samples had sufficient oral English vocabulary for everyday communication but lacked in-depth knowledge of many words they encountered in their classroom textbooks. Consequently, our curriculum focused on words that had high frequencies of occurrence across content areas texts but were less frequently encountered in oral language (Beck, McKeown & Kucan, 2002). To illustrate the words that were chosen, we use Lesson 7 of the VIP fourth-grade program where the focus was around Lobel's "The pig at the candy store." The 12 words chosen by the research team for that fable are listed in Table 7.2. The words and activities of other lessons can be found in Lively, August, Carlo, and Snow (2003a).

In addition to the definitions of these target words, teachers were also provided with additional information about the vocabulary in a fable. The idiomatic use of language can be particularly challenging to English-language learners, so the curricular materials also highlighted those for teachers (e.g., *on second thought*), as well as a group of words that may require attention but not at the level of the target words (e.g., *peppermints, wrappers, gumdrops*).

TABLE 7.2

Words in Lesson 7 of the Fourth- and Fifth-Grade VIP Curriculum

	Grade 4	Grade 5
Spanish cognates	Contained, journey	Common, congregate, elevated, humanity, monotonous, rival, torment, ultimatum, unfamiliar
Noncognates	Discourage, glow, halfway, heartburn, likely, sprout, spin, tempt, twinkle, willpower	Arouse, dank, pitched, battle, relief, stifling

Several features of the target words are clear from studying the words in Table 7.2. First, words such as *likely, contain, halfway, journey* and *discourage* are ones that students can be expected to encounter in content area and literary texts in the future. Second, as Nagy and Anderson's (1984) work suggests, some of the targeted words were part of fairly large semantic families. An example of such a word is *discourage* (e.g., *discouragement, encourage, courage, courageous*). Third, many of the words had multiple meanings. The word *spin*, for example, can refer to the action of a weaver or spider as well as a particular perspective on telling or relating information or a story. Fourth, several of the English words share a cognate with Spanish: contained/contener and journey/jornada. For another group of words, the commonly used Spanish word is a cognate for a sophisticated synonym for the word: sprouted/*germinar; likely/probable,* and *glowing/candente*.

Instructional Routine. The principles of vocabulary learning and teaching that underlie the instructional routine of the intervention were drawn from previous work on native English-speaking monolinguals and English-language learners (e.g., Beck, McKeown, & Omanson, 1987; Blachowicz & Fisher, 1996; Nagy, 1988; Nagy & Scott, 2000; National Reading Panel, 2000; Stahl & Fairbanks, 1986). The instructional routine that was used appears in the second column of Table 7.3.

The lesson format seen in Table 7.3 emphasized text comprehension as well as vocabulary instruction. The emphasis on the vocabulary instruction, as can be seen particularly in the content for sessions 3, 4, and 6, was to develop a strategic stance to acquiring word meaning rather than only teaching specific word meanings. This devotion of time to strategic knowledge for understanding unfamiliar words, rather than simply to building vocabulary size, was a deliberate choice. As Graves (2000) noted, students need to know *about* words, not simply acquire new words, if they are to be successful in understanding unfamiliar vocabulary in their reading.

Professional Development. The professional development had begun a year before the implementation of the first study. In that year, both fourth- and fifth-grade teachers and their administrators at the three sites were involved in professional development activities. The curriculum materials provided to the teachers included detailed lesson plans and quasiscripted lesson guides, as well as overhead transparencies, worksheets, homework assignments, and all necessary reading materials. These materials and the words to be taught were previewed in meetings with the teachers.

Assessments and Results. The assessments that were gathered at the end of each lesson were useful to the research team to understand what aspects of students' vocabulary were aided by the VIP curriculum and instruc-

TABLE 7.3

Lesson Format: Fourth- and Fifth-Grade VIP Instructional Routine

Session	Grade 4	Grade 5
1	• Text introduction: Prediction, listen to teacher read aloud, discussion of fable	• Preview for ELLs., including listening to Spanish summary of text, reading text, and previewing target words
2	• Vocabulary introduction: Go over target words and their definitions, assign vocabulary review homework, address cognates	• Story introduction, including making predictions of text content, reading text, participating in "circle vocabulary" and "extract definition" activities, assign homework
3	• Expand meaning instruction (e.g., word association); distribute Word Wizard list	• Activities with words: (a) words in context and (b) cloze sentences (in peer groups)
4	• Instruction on Tools to Develop Vocabulary (e.g., multiple meanings)	• Instruction on expanding meaning (with content such as word roots)
5	• Using Words in Context (small group activity)	• Instruction on tools to develop vocabulary (with content such as using cognates)
6	• Instruction: Tools to develop vocabulary (e.g., affixes)	
7	• Word Wizard Review	
8	• Vocabulary Assessment	

tion. To establish the efficacy of the strategy overall, however, we administered an extensive battery of tests to the VIP students and students in classes in the same schools who had been randomly assigned to the comparison group.

At the beginning and the end of the VIP intervention, students were assessed on: (a) the Peabody Picture Vocabulary Test Revised (PPVT-R); (b) polysemy production: generating many sentences to convey different meanings of polysemous words such as *ring* or *check*; (c) three multiple-choice cloze passages with six content words deleted at random per passage (including some words that were targeted in the intervention); (d) word mastery: 36 target words, each with four short, multiple-choice definitions; (e) a word association task (Schoonen & Verhallen, 1998) in which 20 target words (approximately half from the target curriculum) were presented individually, each surrounded by six other words of which students were to chose three to best define the word (e.g., *debate* has immutable associations to the words "rival," "discussion," and "opinion" but only circumstantial associations to the words "president," "television," and "fight"; (f) morphology: a paper-and-pencil adaptation of Carlisle's (1988) extract, the base task of 27 items (less than a third of which were intervention words) where students needed to provide the base form of a derived word (e.g., *discussion* was stated, followed by a lean sentence context: What did he want to _____).

Large differences were found for language status (English-language learners versus English-only children) on all the measures, as well as site differences (i.e., Boston, Miami, and Santa Cruz, California). Impact of the intervention (condition by time interactions) was found, though, only for the Mastery test, which was designed to determine whether the children had learned and retained the vocabulary words taught in the curriculum.

Overall, the evaluation of the first vocabulary intervention was disappointing. Clear treatment effects were not found for depth of word knowledge measures or for reading comprehension. However, there were significant interactions between school and gain and between school, condition, and gain, suggesting that the intervention may have been successful in particular schools. Thus, we built on these lessons in extending the intervention to the fifth grade, introducing a number of changes.

Study Two

The fifth-grade intervention was designed to be considerably more challenging in words taught and level and variety of reading materials provided. To support this increased challenge, the level of professional support to teachers and monitoring of the implementation were increased to minimize site differences. The full report of this fifth-grade intervention is reported in Carlo et al. (2004). In this context, we give only an overview of the changes in the curriculum and instruction from Study One.

Curriculum. For the fifth graders, the content of the intervention shifted from the more familiar content of fables to a social studies topic. The chosen topic was immigration—a topic about which we believed our students (many of them immigrants or children of immigrants) had a vast store of background knowledge.

This shift to a content area topic also meant that the types of texts that students read changed in genre. Over the 15 lessons of Study Two, students read four texts. All were informational in nature but took different forms: (a) a diary, *Dear America: A Journey to the New World* (Lasky, 1996); (b) a descriptive text, *Immigrant Dids* (Freedman, 1995); (c) oral histories of immigrant teens, *New Kids in Town* (Bode, 1995); and (d) A *New York Times* article entitled *The New Immigrant Tide: A Shuttle Between Worlds* (1998).

By virtue of the topic, the words were more complex. The increased complexity of the words is evident in examining the words from Lesson 7 of the fifth-grade intervention that are given in Table 7.2. (For the content of other lessons, readers can refer to Lively, August, Carlo, and Snow (2003b).)

As with the fourth-grade curriculum, the same principles can be seen at work in the choice of words. Once more, a substantial number of the words are part of semantic families with several or more members such as *humanity* (e.g., *human, humanitarian)* and *unfamiliar (unfamiliarity, familiarity, familiar)*. Furthermore, many words have multiple meanings such as *pitched* and *battle*.

Within a content topic such as immigration, however, some of the words would be expected to occur with somewhat less frequency than the words in fables. For example, *ultimatum* is part of a semantic family with more frequent members (*ultimate, ultimately*), but this word will appear with less frequency than many of the fourth-grade words. As many of the content area words have Spanish cognates, in learning a word such as *ultimatum* (and connecting this word to other members of the semantic family), the existing vocabularies of Spanish speakers provide a foundation for this instruction. The foundation that Spanish speakers bring to the content areas has also been reported for content words in science. Bravo , Hiebert, and Pearson (in review) examined sets of words that science educators targeted as critical to four topics: (a) 13 general process words (e.g., *investigate, observe)*; (b) 25 words pertaining to soil (e.g., *nutrients, decomposition)*; (c) 24 words pertaining to shoreline habitats (*survive, adaptation)*; and (d) 19 words pertaining to chemical mixtures (e.g., *acid, invent)*. In examining the cognates of these words, Bravo et al. (2004) distinguished between high-frequency and low-frequency cognates. The latter are Spanish/English cognates but are more than likely unfamiliar words to Spanish students. Among the 81 words that were analyzed, 50% were classified as high-frequency cognates, 24% were low-frequency cognates, and 26% were noncognates.

Instruction Routine. Several adjustments were made to the intervention for Study Two. First, the intervention was 15 lessons rather than the 10 lessons of Study One. Furthermore, as can be seen with the content of sessions within a lesson in Table 7.3, a lesson did not have as many sessions. The cycle of four lessons with new vocabulary followed by a review lesson was sustained in Study Two. However, because the number of components per lesson was condensed and because the number of lessons was increased, the number of words targeted in Study Two increased substantially, from approximately 100 to 180 words.

Another adaptation provided Spanish speakers with the text (in both written and audiotaped versions) to preview in Spanish on Monday before its introduction in English on Tuesday. The Tuesday whole-group lessons involved presentation of the English text and target words, followed by an activity that involved identifying target words in the text whose meanings could be inferred by context. Wednesday lessons involved work in heterogeneous language groups of four to six where English was used. In these peer groups, students completed two types of cloze tasks with the target words. The first cloze task always involved sentence contexts that were consistent with the theme of the instructional text. A second cloze activity involved sentences that employed the target words in contexts that were distant in theme from the instructional text, designed to help students understand and use related meanings for the target words and, in the process, develop a sense that most words are polysemous.

The word-learning strategies aimed at supporting students' generalization of vocabulary strategies and knowledge occurred on Days 4 and 5. The content of these sessions over the 15-week intervention is provided in Table 7.4. The "Expanding Meaning" lessons were intended to promote depth of word knowledge (word association tasks, synonym/antonym tasks, semantic feature analysis, etc.). The "Tool" lessons were designed to promote word analysis capacities in general, not specifically to reinforce learning of the target words.

TABLE 7.4

Expanding Meaning (Day 4 of Cycle) and "Tools"
to Develop Vocabulary (Day 5 of Cycle)

Week	Expanding Word Meaning	Tools to Develop Vocabulary
1.	Word Roots	Cognates
2.	Deep Processing	Affixes
3.	Deep Processing	Idioms
4.	Multiple Meanings	Root words
5.	Word Guess	Posttest
6.	Antonyms/Synonyms	Inferencing
7.	Deep Processing	Cognates
8.	Word Substitution	Affixes
9.	Related Words	Root Words
10.	Word Sort	Posttest
11.	Synonyms/Antonyms	Dictionaries
12.	Synonyms/Antonyms	Root Words
13.	Word Substitution	Cognates
14.	Deep Processing	Multiple Meanings
15.	Word Bee	Posttest

Additionally, Teacher Learning Communities that met on a biweekly basis were formed during the implementation of the fifth-grade intervention to preview the materials and the instructional techniques. At these meetings, practices that had worked well in previous lessons and aspects of the curriculum that had been problematic were discussed. These meetings were meant to provide support to the teachers throughout the implementation of the curriculum, and information to the researchers about aspects of the curriculum that were working well or not. The curriculum itself was not modified as a result of the meetings with the treatment teachers.

Results. To summarize the results reported in Carlo et al. (2004), a multivariate analysis of variance—with the five dependent measures (Mastery, Word Association, Polysemy, Cloze, Morphology) and time (fall, spring) and predicator variables of site, language status, and condition—revealed overall between-subjects effects for site and language status. Tests of within-subjects effects showed significant gains over time as well as a significant interaction between gain over time and condition. These results justified analyses of each of the outcome variables individually (Myers & Well, 1991).

These individual analyses were conducted on five dependent measures. Scores on the PPVT were used as a covariate as the patterns on the PPVT were higher for language status (EO students scored higher than ELL students) and for time (spring scores were higher than fall scores) but not for treatment. On the Mastery, Word Association, Polysemy, and Cloze measures, the intervention group had greater gains from fall to spring than the comparison group. These results were interpreted to mean that the students in intervention classrooms gained knowledge of the words that were explicitly taught as well as generative knowledge of words as evidenced by performances on morphological structure, about cognates, and about polysemy.

REVISITING THE DATA: THE EFFECTS OF SUSTAINED VOCABULARY LEARNING STRATEGY INSTRUCTION

Having developed and implemented two vocabulary interventions with ELLs, we became curious about the cumulative effects of strategy instruction on English-language learners' learning of English words. Inasmuch as a portion of the children in the fifth-grade *Immigration* intervention had also been part of the fourth-grade *Fables* intervention, it became possible for us to evaluate differences in the performance of children who had experienced the vocabulary strategy instruction for 2 consecutive years relative to those who received only one year of strategy instruction or no instruction at all. What follows is a report of the results of our inquiry into the effects of sustained vocabulary learning strategy instruction.

An Overview of School Contexts

An overview of the participants has already been provided (Table 7.1), as have the assessments. What is critical to bear in mind is the comprehensiveness of the contexts in capturing the Spanish speakers in the United States. The VIP project was carried out in three sites: (a) two California schools that served largely working-class Mexican American children, either in bilingual or in mainstream programs, (b) a Massachusetts school that served working-class, mostly Puerto Rican and Dominican students, again in either bilingual or mainstream classrooms, and (c) a magnet, English-medium school in Virginia that served mainly working-class Spanish speakers from the Caribbean and from Central America, native speakers of many other languages, and middle-class English-only (EO) speakers attracted by its excellent programs.

Findings of the Reanalyses

As mentioned previously, the fourth-grade intervention did not produce generalizable effects on all measures or all sites. The fifth-grade intervention, on the other hand, showed clear effects on our measures of target word mastery, knowledge of polysemy, depth of word knowledge, and reading comprehension. The only outcomes not impacted by the fifth-grade intervention were PPVT performance and morphological awareness.

To consider the effects of participation in both the fourth- and fifth-grade units on students' vocabulary knowledge and strategies, an analyses of covariance was conducted. This analysis controlled for English PPVT assessed in spring of fifth grade. Means for the various groups of students on the five measures appear in Table 7.5. The results suggested that learning word analysis skills in fourth grade enhanced the value of the fifth-grade curriculum. For most outcome measures, children who had received the fourth-grade *Fables* curriculum in addition to the immigration stories curriculum scored higher than children who had received only one or the other. In addition, the fifth-grade curriculum by itself generated greater gains than the fourth-grade curriculum by itself—an unsurprising outcome because the fourth-grade curriculum was our pilot study and, as evaluated at its conclusion, did not appear to affect test scores. The fifth-grade curriculum was both better designed and more challenging.

Table 7.6 contains the results of t-tests comparing difference scores for performance on each of the vocabulary and reading outcomes over the duration of the fifth-grade intervention by intervention group (fifth-grade participation only vs. fourth- and fifth-grade participation). Participation in the fourth-grade curriculum enhanced the vocabulary learning of ELL children while they were in the fifth-grade curriculum with regard to their

TABLE 7.5

Means for Five Measures: Across Time of Test, Language Group,
and Amount of Intervention

Treatment Group	Fall					Spring				
	Word Assoc.	Mastery	Cloze	Polysemy	Mor-phology	Word Assoc.	Mastery	Cloze	Polysemy	Mor-phology
ELL never	34.1	13.9	8.7	7.2	42.5	35.1	16.1	8.8	8.2	54.8
EO never	43.6	21.9	13.4	12.4	87.1	45.8	23.5	13.7	12.8	100.7
ELL: Gr. 4	32.2	15.1	8.2	8.2	56.7	35.4	17.5	8.7	8.3	65.1
EO: Gr. 4	40.3	19.3	10.9	12.0	71.1	42.4	20.2	12.9	12.7	79.7
ELL: Gr. 5	35.7	16.1	8.9	7.8	55.4	40.3	23.9	11.5	10.0	69.6
EO: Gr. 5	41.2	20.6	12.0	10.6	80.4	44.4	29.5	13.9	11.9	95.7
ELL: Grs. 4, 5	35.7	15.3	9.4	8.6	55.4	40.5	25.8	11.1	11.3	78.4
EO: Grs. 4, 5	38.4	22.3	12.8	12	87.4	48.9	30.4	15.6	13.7	102.6

TABLE 7.6

Results of Independent Samples *t* Tests of Differences in Performance
Between ELL Students Receiving the 5th-Grade Intervention Only
and Those Receiving Both the 4th- and 5th-Grade Interventions

Assessment	t	df	Sig. (2-tailed)	Mean Difference
Morphology	−2.075	85	< .05	−6.97
Polysemy	−.702	84	> .05	−.39
Cloze	1.104	82	> .05	.74
Word Association	−.205	84	> .05	−.37
Mastery	−2.420	85	< .05	−2.76

performance on morphology and mastery assessments. The additional year of vocabulary instruction appears to have strengthened the ELL children's ability to engage in structural analysis of words. It should be noted that this effect is not a curriculum-specific effect, given that the words on this assessment were not targeted in the curriculum. Also, this assessment was not administered during the pilot year, thus satisfying any concerns that the differences could be attributed to test practice effects. More importantly, however, is the fact that significant growth on the morphology measure was not found for the fifth graders, suggesting that growth in structural analysis of words requires sustained and longer term instruction.

Understanding that many words in English have multiple meanings—polysemy—and even serve multiple functions is a critical understanding for nonnative English speakers. As is depicted in Fig. 7.1, participation for 2 years in the intervention led to a higher level of understanding of this aspect of English, especially for English-language learners.

It is also worth noting that the children who received 2 years of the intervention learned more of the target words in the fifth-grade curriculum than children who only got the fifth-grade intervention. This again may be interpreted as a general effect on vocabulary learning because none of the target words had been instructed in the fourth grade. This suggests that the children's ability to learn from instruction of the target was bolstered by having participated in the intervention the prior year.

IMPLICATIONS FOR EDUCATIONAL PRACTICE AND POLICY

The evaluation of the fifth-grade curriculum (Carlo et al., 2004) suggests that a well-designed, challenging curriculum focusing on teaching academic words, awareness of polysemy, strategies for inferring word meaning from context, and tools for analyzing morphological and cross-linguistic aspects of word meaning can improve ELLs children's knowledge of words

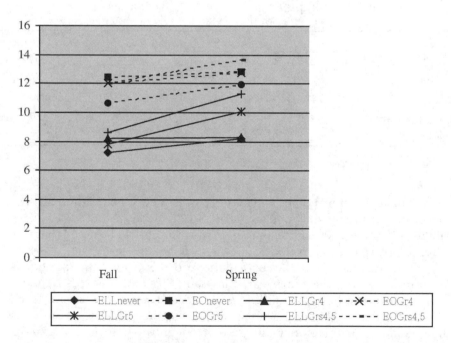

FIG. 7.1.   Average performance as a function of time of test, language group, and amount of intervention: Polysemy.

and about words. Furthermore, children's ability to comprehend texts that have challenging words can be facilitated as well.

These gains meant making particular kinds of choices. The curriculum introduced only 12 to 14 words a week. An additional 10 to 15 words (available in the books that were part of the intervention) were not taught in order to focus instruction on strategies for using the contexts of sentences and texts, checking the likelihood that a word had a Spanish cognate, and analyzing morphological structure for cues to meaning. This attention to strategies paid off. These strategies appear to have ongoing value to all students, including ELL students.

Furthermore, the reanalysis presented here suggests that sustained direct vocabulary instruction can enhance ELLs' ability for word learning. The reanalysis also suggests that some aspects of ELLs' knowledge about words (e.g., morphological analysis) require a long-term commitment to instruction that develops this knowledge.

REFERENCES

Beck, I., McKeown, M. G., & Kucan, L. (2002). *Bringing words to life: Robust vocabulary instruction.* New York: Guilford.

Beck, I., McKeown, M. G., & Omanson, R. C. (1987). The effects and uses of diverse vocabulary instructional techniques. In M. G. McKeown & M. E. Curtis (Eds.), *The nature of vocabulary acquisition* (pp. 147–163). Hillsdale, NJ: Lawrence Erlbaum Associates.

Blachowicz , C. & Fisher, P. (1996). *Teaching vocabulary in all classrooms.* Columbus, OH: Prentice Hall.

Bode, J. (1995). *New kids in town.* New York: Scholastic.

Bravo, M., Hiebert, E. H., & Pearson, P. D. (in review). *Native Spanish speakers & science texts: Building on the existing vocabulary knowledge.* Paper submitted for presentation at the annual meeting of the American Educational Research Association, Montreal, Quebec.

Calfee, R. C., & Drum, P. A. (1986). Research on teaching reading. In M. D. Wittrock (Ed.), *Handbook of research on teaching* (3rd ed., pp. 804–849). New York: Macmillan.

Campbell, J.R., Hombo, C.., & Mazzeo, J. (2000). *Trends in academic progress: Three decades of student performance.* Washington, DC: National Center for Education Statistics.

Carlisle, J. F. (1988). Knowledge of derivational morphology and spelling ability in fourth, sixth and eighth graders. *Applied Psycholinguistics, 9,* 247–266.

Carlisle, J. F. (2003). Morphology matters in learning to read: A commentary. *Reading Psychology, 24,* 291–322.

Carlo, M., August, D., McLaughlin, B., Snow, C. E., Dressler, C., Lippman, D. N., Lively, T. J., & White, C. E. (2004). Closing the gap: Addressing the vocabulary needs of English-language learners in bilingual and mainstream classrooms. *Reading Research Quarterly, 39,* 188–215.

Freedman, R. (1995). *Immigrant kids.* New York: Puffin.

Fukkink, R. G., & de Glopper, K. (1998). Effects of instruction in deriving word meaning from context: A meta-analysis. *Review of Educational Research, 68*(4), 450–468.

García, G. E. (1991). Factors influencing the English reading test performance of Spanish-speaking Hispanic students. *Reading Research Quarterly, 26,* 371–392.

García, G. E. (2000). Bilingual children's reading. In M. L. Kamil., P. Mosenthal, P. D. Pearson, & R. Barr (Eds.), *Handbook of reading research* (Vol. III, pp. 813–834). Mahwah, NJ: Lawrence Erlbaum Associates.

García, G. E., & Nagy, W. E. (1993). Latino students' concept of cognates. In D. J. Leu & C. K. Kinzer (Eds.), *Examining central issues in literacy research, theory, and practice* (pp. 361–373). Chicago: National Reading Conference.

Graves, M.F. (2000). A vocabulary program to complement and bolster a middle-grade comprehension program. In B.M. Taylor, M. F. Graves, & P. van den Broek (Eds), *Reading for meaning: Fostering comprehension in the middle grades* (pp. 116–135). New York: Teachers College Press; Newark, DE: International Reading Association.

Hart, B., & Risley, T. R. (1995). *Meaningful differences in the everyday experience of young American children.* Baltimore, MD: Paul H. Brookes.

Kuhn, M. R., & Stahl, S. A. (1998). Teaching children to learn word meanings from context: A synthesis and some questions. *Journal of Literacy Research, 30*(1), 19–38.

Lasky, K. (1996). *A journey to the new world: The diary of Remember Patience Whipple, Mayflower, 1620 (Dear America Series).* New York: Scholastic.

Lively, T., August, D., Carlo, M., & Snow, C. E. (2003a). *Vocabulary improvement program for English language learners and their classmates: 4th grade.* Baltimore, MD: Paul H Brookes.

Lively, T., August, D., Carlo, M., & Snow, C. E. (2003b). *Vocabulary improvement program for English language learners and their classmates: 5th grade.* Baltimore, MD: Paul H Brookes.

Lobel, A. (1983). *Fables.* New York: HarperTrophy.

Myers, J., & Well, A. (1991). *Research design and statistical analysis.* New York: HarperCollins.

Nagy, W. (1997). On the role of context in first- and second-language vocabulary learning. In N. Schmitt & M. McCarthy (Eds.), *Vocabulary: Description, acquisition and pedagogy* (pp. 64–83). Cambridge: Cambridge University Press.

Nagy, W. E. (1988). *Teaching vocabulary to improve reading comprehension.* Newark, DE: International Reading Association.

Nagy, W. E., & Anderson, R. C. (1984). How many words are there in printed school English? *Reading Research Quarterly, 19,* 304–330.

Nagy, W. E., Garcia, G. E., Durgunoglu, A., & Hancin-Bhatt, B. (1993). Spanish–English bilingual students' use of cognates in English reading. *Journal of Reading Behavior, 25,* 241–259.

Nagy, W. E., & Scott, J. A. (2000). Vocabulary processes. In M. L. Kamil, P. Mosenthal, P. D. Pearson, & R. Barr (Eds.), *Handbook of reading research* (Vol. III, pp. 269–284). Mahwah, NJ: Lawrence Earlbaum Associates.

National Reading Panel. (2000). *Teaching children to read: An evidence-based assessment of the scientific research literature on reading and its implications for reading instruction.* Washington, DC: NICHD.

Schoonen, R., & Verhallen, M. (1998). Kennis van woorden: de toetsing van diepe woordkennis [Knowledge of words: Testing deep word knowledge]. *Pedagogische Studiën, 75,* 153–168.

Stahl, S., & Fairbanks, M. (1986). The effects of vocabulary instruction: A model-based meta-analysis. *Review of Educational Research, 56,* 72–110.

Stein, N. L., & Nezworkski, T. (1978). The effects of organization and instructional set on story memory. *Discourse Processes*, *1*, 177–193.

Verhallen, M., & Schoonen, R. (1993). Vocabulary knowledge of monolingual and bilingual children. *Applied Linguistics*, *14*, 344–363.

Verhoeven, L. T. (1990) Acquisition of reading in a second language. *Reading Research Quarterly*, *25*(2), 90–114.

Chapter 8

Classroom Practices for Vocabulary Enhancement in Prekindergarten: Lessons From PAVEd for Success

Paula J. Schwanenflugel,
Claire E. Hamilton
University of Georgia

Barbara A. Bradley
University of Kansas

Hilary P. Ruston
Stacey Neuharth-Pritchett
University of Georgia

M. Adelaida Restrepo
Arizona State University

As is the case with many children across the United States, one out of five children in the state in which we live and work lives below the poverty line (U.S. Census Bureau, 2004). This poverty puts children at risk of reading problems (Conger, Conger, & Elder, 1997; Duncan, Young, Brooks-Gunn, & Smith, 1998; McLoyd, 1998). Preschoolers living in poverty are more likely to have poorly developed vocabulary and language skills (Graves, Brunetti, & Slater, 1982; Hart & Risley, 1992, 1995; Smith, Brooks-Gunn, & Klebanov, 1997; Washington & Craig, 1999). These depressed language skills for poor preschoolers may not be directly related to poverty per se, but to parent–child interaction styles, home environmental factors, and reading practices associated with poverty (Adams, 1990). The national focus on the provision of prekindergarten services is designed to ameliorate some of the negative effects of poverty on children's preacademic skills.

Given the early intervention emphasis, targeting vocabulary may be particularly important. Young children's vocabulary has a large impact on early reading achievement. Children who begin school with small vocabularies are more prone to have difficulty in learning to read and are at risk for long-term reading problems (Copeland & Edwards, 1990; Snow, Burns, & Griffin, 1999; Storch & Whitehurst, 2002), particularly with comprehension issues (Cunningham & Stanovich, 1997). A meta-analysis conducted by Scarborough (2001) found a significant correlation between young children's receptive vocabulary and reading achievement (Median $r = .40$). Thus, finding ways to enhance the vocabularies of children who enter school with limited vocabulary seems key to improving later reading comprehension and even early word decoding skills (Schwanenflugel & Noyes, 1996).

The gap in children's vocabularies upon school entry is enormous. The vocabulary gap between high and low SES children entering kindergarten is estimated at around 3,000 words (Hart & Risley 1995), and is even larger later in elementary school (Baker, Simmons, & Kame'enui, 1998). For teachers seeking to remediate these vocabulary deficits, the task is enormous. Providing a multitude of opportunities for vocabulary growth within the classroom seems necessary. Yet, existing preschool curricula provide teachers with little guidance in how to do this.

We know that attending preschools with better general preschool classroom quality promotes children's preacademic skills (Bryant, Burchinal, Lau, & Sparling, 1994), verbal cognition (Bryant et al., 1994), and language abilities (Dunn, Beach, & Kontos, 1994), regardless of their home status. Language experiences tend to be particularly poor in low quality preschool classrooms (Bryant et al., 1994; Helburn, 1995). Thus, one goal for improving preschool quality is the development of teacher practices designed to promote children's linguistic and vocabulary growth.

This chapter focuses on assessing the implementation, sustainability, and effectiveness of one effort to promote the use of classroom practices designed to enhance the vocabularies of prekindergarten children through a program we developed called *PAVEd for Success* (which stands for *P*honological *A*wareness and *V*ocabulary *E*nhancement, two of the experimental features of the program). Through this work, we have learned much regarding which classroom practices are likely to be implemented by prekindergarten teachers. This is critical given that, although some programs have been effective in the short term, these efforts to enhance vocabulary have met with teacher resistance (Lonigan & Whitehurst, 1998). Currently, there is little to no research to guide policymakers regarding which classroom practices for 4-year-olds show the best *implementation* and *sustainability* in the classroom, and *benefits* in terms of improved vocabulary skills in children.

For our purposes here, we distinguish between *implicit* and *explicit practices* for enhancing children's vocabularies. By *implicit,* we mean that the practice encourages the growth of children's vocabulary without being the direct focus of the activity, such that vocabulary growth is a positive by-product in the service of other goals; in our case, these practices were: encouraging teacher–child talk *(Building Bridges)*, and interactive storybook reading *(CAR Talk)*. In contrast, by *explicit,* we mean that word learning is the direct focus of the activity, and both children and teachers are aware of this focus; in our case, these practices were didactic–interactional book reading, having vocabulary-explicit targets, and using a novel-name nameless category (N3C) presentation strategy.

IMPLICIT APPROACHES TO ENHANCING CHILDREN'S VOCABULARIES

Building Bridges

Both the quality and quantity of teacher talk is critical in affecting the size and quality of children's vocabulary. To increase the quality and quantity of teacher talk, we developed a set of practices we called *Building Bridges* that drew on both the teacher talk and the student-teacher relationships literature (Howes & Hamilton, 1992; Howes, Hamilton, & Phillipsen, 1998; Pianta & Steinberg, 1992).

A first priority in designing the Building Bridges component of the intervention was to increase the number of conversational interactions between individual students and their teachers. Individual conversations between students and teachers are infrequent in most preschool settings (Dickinson & Tabors, 2002; Dunn, Beach, & Kontos, 1994). However, the amount of talk between children and adults predicts their oral language development (Wiezman & Snow, 2001). For example, Wells (1985) found "a clear relationship between children's rate of language learning and the amount of conversations they experienced" (p. 44), and of particular importance was that "the child's experience of conversation should be in a one-to-one situation in which the adult is talking about matters that are of interest and concern to the child" (p. 44).

To address this issue, we asked teachers to systematically engage each child in a 5-minute conversation at least three times per week and we provided guidelines for structuring consistent times that would be "teacher talk" or Building Bridges times. Building Bridges was loosely based on Pianta's (1999) intervention for remediating problematic student–teacher relationships. Building Bridges provided students with a consistent time in which teachers were available and open to individual interactions with students. From a language perspective, the goal of Building Bridges was to ensure that *all* children in the classroom had opportunities to engage in extended conversations with their teachers, but student–teacher relationships were also expected to benefit.

A second goal of the Building Bridges program was to increase the richness of the conversations preschool teachers had with their students. Although most verbal interactions between preschool teachers and their students tend to be positive (e.g., praise, redirection; Wilcox-Herzog & Kontos, 1998), those verbal interactions are frequently related to routine matters (Dunn, Beach, & Kontos, 1994). Routine talk is concrete or "here and now," (e.g., *How many do you see? What is this?*). In contrast, cognitively challenging talk asks children to interpret information and speculate or hypothesize about alternative reasons (Hughes & Westgate, 1998; Kontos & Wilcox-Herzog, 1997), as well as to discuss vocabulary, summarize, and clarify one's thinking (Dickinson & Smith, 1994). Cognitively challenging talk in the classroom has been linked to the understanding of literate acts (Rosemary & Roskos, 2002), emergent literacy development (Smith & Dickinson, 1994), and growth in reading achievement (Taylor, Peterson, Rodriguez, & Pearson, 2003). To make classroom conversations between teachers and children more meaningful and cognitively challenging, we stipulated that conversational topics should be the child's choice rather than instructionally related (Soundy & Stout, 2002).

CAR Talk

A second, implicit component of our vocabulary program involved increased opportunities for and interaction around storybook reading. To make it memorable for teachers, we called this set of practices *CAR Talk*. Specifically, *CAR* is an acronym that stands for the kinds of questions we wanted teachers to ask children while they were reading: *Competence* questions, *Abstract* thinking, and *Relate* talk. The aims of CAR Talk were derived from research on storybook reading.

One aim of CAR Talk was to increase the amount of storybook reading and the quality of interaction around the reading. Whereas the amount of storybook reading has increased in elementary schools over the past 40 years (Austin & Morrison, 1963; Lickteig & Russell, 1993; Jacobs, Morrison, & Swinyard, 2000), a similar change has not occurred in preschools. In 42 Head Start classrooms, Dickinson and Sprague (2001) found that in 2 days of observation, only 65% of classrooms had any storybook reading time at all and those that did spent an average of 2 minutes on it, with little interaction around the books. (The situation was even worse for non-Head Start classrooms serving low-income children.)

Another aim of CAR Talk was enhancing the quality of interactions around the reading, including the size of groups to whom the stories were read. Probably the single most important aspect of storybook reading in the development of vocabulary is the interaction that takes place between the adult reader of storybooks and the child listeners (Biemiller, 2001). Although reading books aloud straight through is correlated with low reading achievement scores (Allison & Watson, 1994; Morrow, Rand, & Smith, 1995; Share, Jorm, MacLean, & Matthews, 1984), positive benefits have been reported when teachers read interactively (Whitehurst, Arnold, Epstein, Angell, Smith, & Fischel, 1994). In interactive reading (also called dialogical or coconstructive; Dickinson & Smith, 1994), open-ended questions are asked throughout the storybook reading to promote high-level participation. The book, then, merely serves as a stimulus around which a high degree of interaction should take place.

We further specified that CAR talk be carried out in small groups no larger than five to encourage the participation of individual children. Reading interactively in small groups has been shown to be effective for enhancing vocabulary in children living in poverty (Whitehurst et al., 1994). Children who hear stories in small interactive groups understand and recall story elements better than children listening in large groups (Cornell, Senechal, & Broda, 1988; Morrow & Smith, 1990). They are more likely to ask their teachers the meanings of words outside of reading time. The teachers, themselves, are more likely to use challenging vocabulary than other teachers (Wasik & Bond, 2001). One potential difficulty in implementation is that teachers seem to have difficulty arranging small-group reading (Wasik & Bond, 2001; Whitehurst et al., 1994).

To implement CAR Talk, we suggested the following: (a) Prior to reading a book, create a set of competence questions to allow children to practice skills they have already mastered (e.g., Can you find the [object] in the picture? Who said, "[phrase]"?), a set of abstract thinking questions (e.g., What is [character] thinking? What will happen next? How do you think [character] feels? How are [two objects] different?), and a set of related questions that link the text to the students' experiences (How is [character] the same as you? What would you do if you could [action]?); (b) put each question on a *Post-it* note in the book at the proper page, so it would be readily available when needed; (c) read to children in small-group settings.

We also focused on the value of rereading storybooks. Prevailing practices in preschools do not emphasize repeated readings. Two or more readings of a book may be necessary for a significant improvement in vocabulary (Jenkins, Stein, & Wysocki, 1984; Senechal, 1997; Stahl & Fairbanks, 1986). However, repeated readings may not be necessary for vocabulary improvement in preschoolers if the words are explained during the story (Brett, Rothlein, & Hurley, 1996; Ewers & Brownson, 1999). However, as an implicit vocabulary practice, rereadings might provide some benefit in vocabulary development.

EXPLICIT VOCABULARY LEARNING STRATEGIES

Despite the ubiquity of the problem of low vocabulary levels in preschoolers, there is remarkably little research describing explicit practices for highlighting the importance of vocabulary to preschoolers. Next, we describe three explicit strategies that we believe may have some value in promoting vocabulary development.

Didactic–Interactional Book Reading

Didactic–interactional book reading represents an effort to balance building vocabulary and comprehension. In the didactic–interactional style, teachers often pull out the vocabulary word and provide a synonym or recast to broaden the definition of the target word. This strategy may require minimal interaction from children (children passively listen to the target words defined or simply repeat) to more extensive expressive interaction (children expressively use the word in response to a question or in choral repetition; Justice, 2002). Significant gains in vocabulary have been found for the didactic-interactional style of reading, even with minimal interaction, compared to straight-through reading (Brabham & Lynch-Brown, 2002). Elley (1989) found that vocabulary learning nearly doubled for 7- and 8-year-olds even when the reader merely stopped and provided a definition of vocabulary words immediately following their occurrence, compared to straight-through reading. Reese and Cox (1999) observed that 4-year-olds with smaller vocabularies may actually do better with the didactic–interactional style compared to a standard interactive style.

In our version, we merely asked teachers to stop and make note of specific new words in the context, describing relations between the words and the context. On subsequent rereadings, they might ask children to make some sort of response when they hear these new words they are learning.

Explicit Targeted Vocabulary

Another strategy for encouraging vocabulary growth is to create set of targeted vocabulary words that are to be directly dealt with in multiple ways. One successful intervention using this approach was by Wasik and Bond (2001). In that study, 4-year-olds were taught 10 target vocabulary words weekly using an integrated package of books, objects, and activities. Children were presented with concrete representations of the words and were provided with definitions prior to book reading. Teachers then inter-actively read two books that contained these words several times over the week. Then, use of these target words was encouraged by classroom activi-ties that allowed children to play with the objects. Children made expres-sive and receptive vocabulary gains for the targeted vocabulary words, and general gains on a standardized test of receptive vocabulary.

In our version, we asked teachers to develop a set of 10 target words weekly, five from each of two books they were planning to reread during the week. Teachers were asked to create activities that would allow children to use the target words elsewhere in the classroom, and they themselves were to use the words expressively in their speech. They created informal assess-ments such as *Vocabulary Bingo* or *Get Caught with the Word* vocabulary logs, which they were asked to use systematically.

Novel-Name Nameless Category (N3C) Presentation Strategy

Usually, between the ages of 1 and 2 years, normally developing children experience what has been called a *vocabulary spurt* (Dromi, 1987), where children move from learning a few words per week to around nine words per day (or 3,000 words per year; Nagy & Anderson, 1984). The responsi-bility for this spurt can be attributed to a number of universal strategies that children develop relating to word learning. Among these is a strategy that has been termed the *novel-name nameless category strategy* (or N3C; Golinkoff, Mervis, & Hirsh-Pasek, 1994; Mervis & Bertrand, 1994) that allows for a quick map between a novel word and an unnamed object. Golinkoff et al. (1994) state that "N3C is a heuristic that moves a single hypothesis for what the novel word might mean to the top of the stack: the novel term maps to an unnamed object" (p. 143). The N3C principle allows 2-year-old children to fast map nouns, verbs, and adjectives (Golinkoff, Hirsch-Pasek, Mervis, Frawley, & Parillo, 1995).

As children develop more complex vocabulary, they are able to move be-yond the N3C principle to more sophisticated context learning strategies. But for prekindergartners still building basic vocabulary, the N3C is a key vocabulary learning strategy. By nesting an unknown picture or object for a new word among pictures or objects of commonly known things, the teacher can evoke the N3C strategy. "Which one is an artichoke?" is likely to elicit a correct response, when an artichoke is displayed between an apple and a banana. Preliminary evidence indicates that the N3C strategy is an ac-tive tool for children's word learning even at 7 years old (Liu, Golinkoff, & Sak, 2001; Sugimura & Maeda, 1997).

Despite the ubiquity of this strategy in research on child word learning, there is virtually no research on its use as a teaching strategy. In our study, the N3C presentation format was promoted as a vocabulary introduction strategy. Specifically, teachers were asked to introduce the five targeted vocabulary words they had selected from their chosen text one at a time, using props (either concrete objects or pictures) in an N3C format (e.g., presenting a representation of an unknown word such as *radish*, next to two representations of known words such as *carrot* and *tomato*). Following their presentation, teachers read the books from which the words were derived using CAR Talk, adding a didactic focus on the words as they appeared in the text. In days following the initial introduction of vocabulary, the props for vocabulary were simply queried for their labels prior to rereading the books.

DESCRIPTION OF THE INTERVENTION

The vocabulary intervention was part of a larger preliteracy intervention whose primary goal was to focus on the use of research-based practices to improve the preliteracy skills of young children. Beyond the vocabulary practices described here, we provided all intervention teachers with professional development on enhanced environmental print standards, understanding the needs of limited English-proficiency preschoolers, and teaching the alphabet. All intervention teachers received training on the implicit vocabulary enhancement practices described earlier (CAR Talk and Building Bridges). Another subset also received training on the explicit vocabulary enhancement practices. A subset of teachers received training on explicit practices for teaching phonological awareness. A secondary goal of the intervention was to rate the value added by these stepped-up explicit variants in an otherwise literacy-rich classroom environment. For the current purposes, we focus on evaluating the implementation and effectiveness of the vocabulary practices we have described and compare it to controls who did not receive any of this professional development.

Our evaluation of the vocabulary program included 425 children attending a free, lottery-funded, prekindergarten program connected with the public school systems in three counties. Two thirds of the children received free or reduced school lunch. Half were female, and 7% had been diagnosed for special education services. According to parental report, 43% of the children were identified as African American, 5% as Asian/Asian American, 2% biracial, 34% European American, and 16% as Latino. Parents reported 78% of children as speaking English as their first language, 17% Spanish, and 4% some other language. Parental report indicated that 23% of mothers had less than a high school education, 49% a high school diploma, 11% some college/technical training, and 18% a BA or better. Children ranged from 4 years, 0 months of age to 5 years, 0 months at the start of the study. Of these 425, 17 children were missing data from one time point, so they were excluded from our evaluation.

This study was conducted in 37 prekindergarten classrooms serving 720 four-year-old children and administered by three local school districts. Classrooms in one district participated as a control site. Each classroom served 20 children and was staffed by one certified teacher and one paraprofessional. Because all teaching staff are viewed as teachers by the children, training was provided to both the teacher and the paraprofessional, but the specific training components varied across classrooms. Teachers in 31 classrooms received training in the implicit vocabulary practices (CAR Talk and Building Bridges). Teachers in 18 classrooms received training in the explicit Vocabulary Enhancement practices as well. Teachers in 6 control classrooms received no training on any of the practices.

Teachers received professional development in a 3-day session prior to the start of the academic year. Training for the explicit Vocabulary Enhancement practices included a discussion of the literature on vocabulary in preschool children and its relationship to later literacy, and we provided a rationale for all implicit and explicit practices based on the research literature. We discussed why chosen practices might be relevant for prekindergartners from different linguistic, cultural, and socioeconomic backgrounds.

The training focused on practice and was rich in examples. Teachers were given time and materials to develop their own lessons. Training sessions were followed by biweekly classroom visits from PAVE preliteracy specialists during the 15-week intervention period. The specialists observed the literacy activities being carried out in the classrooms, conferred with the teachers regarding their implementation of the activities, and supported teachers in the development of materials. The literacy specialist conducted a minimum of five formal observations across the intervention period in each classroom, reviewed lesson plans, and collected surveys from teachers during the intervention period. Fidelity ratings were based on both the quality of the teachers' implementation of practices based on the formal observations and the frequency with which these practices were implemented based on the surveys and lesson plans.

During the sustainability period of the project, teachers were asked to continue completing the weekly surveys. At the conclusion of the project, they were interviewed about the curricular decisions they made and why they did or did not choose to implement or sustain a particular activity.

IMPLEMENTATION BY TEACHERS

Implicit Vocabulary Practices

Car Talk.   Teachers were most successful in implementing CAR Talk than any of our other practices. Eighty-one percent of the teachers effectively implemented CAR Talk. To be considered successful, teachers had to use the CAR Talk questioning strategies as they read each book and provide (story)book reading at least five times per week in a large group and three times per week in small-group settings.

Teachers were generally comfortable with the CAR Talk questioning techniques and easily adopted those into their reading. As one teacher noted:

> It's not something that we didn't do before, I think every good teacher questions in those ways. What I did like was some of the specific ideas about having at least two questions on each of these levels and writing them on a sticky note before you put it in a book to read it. That was good because it made me have to go back and think ... and, because you had to think, you came up with much better questions that generated more discussions.

Large-group reading was already part of teachers' routine so they were familiar and accepting of this structure.

Teachers expressed more concerns about small-group reading. Prior to the intervention, most teachers defined a small group as comprising 10 children and generally divided the class into two groups, each working with either the teacher or the paraprofessional. We defined a small group as having five or fewer children, which required them to adopt a new strategy. Several classrooms accommodated for this requirement by using volunteers—foster grandparents or students from the older grades—to read to small groups of children. Other teachers created a small-group reading center so that they worked with a group of five children while the other children engaged in free choice activities (e.g., puzzles or table toys) in centers around the room.

When we spoke to teachers about the sustainability of these practices, most teachers continued to use CAR Talk although they were less formal in identifying specific questions prior to reading individual books. Like most other small-group intervention programs (Whitehurst & Lonigan, 1998), this practice was largely discontinued after the intervention. Teachers felt that it was simply too time-consuming to continue small groups and that the interactive aspect of book reading could be maintained in a large group. However, teachers did see value in students having had this experience even though they discontinued it: "I think that (small group) has helped build their confidence ... practice that we did with the small groups with them, it might have been practice in coming to the larger group." Thus, they reinterpreted small-group reading as a way of transitioning children

Children have gathered on the rug for large group reading time and they are reading a new book. The teacher holds up the book, points at the title, and asks, "What's this?" A child answers, "Yellow sun." The teacher responds, "Yes there's a yellow sun and the name of the book is the *Very Busy Spider* and the author's name is Eric Carle." She begins to read the book, asking questions and talking about the text and pictures throughout the story. "Let's see what's on this page. What do you think is going on? What is this cow doing with this spider? Have you ever watched a spider make a web? Can you make a sound like a goat?" Children rather noisily begin to "maaa" like goats and she holds up her hand and begins to speak softly, a signal to settle down. The children seem eager to continue the story and the goat noises give way to more attentive listening. This teacher has found that it works best for her to talk through the book the first time she reads it in the large group using a style which includes elements of performance and interactive reading. She rereads the book again in small group using a more constrained but still interactive approach, and then finally she rereads the book for a third time straight through in large group.

Box 1. An example of CAR Talk and interactive storybook reading from PAVEd for Success.

into participating in larger groups. Box 1 illustrates one successful implementation of our storybook reading practices.

Building Bridges. To be considered successful in implementing Building Bridges, teachers had to engage each child individually or in small groups in a conversation lasting about 5 to 10 minutes three times per week. They also had to keep records of the children to whom they had talked. Building Bridges was successfully implemented in 52% of the classrooms. Difficulties in implementing Building Bridges occurred largely because of time and record-keeping factors:

That was the most difficult component of the program. And, it was just because you were having to document when you were talking to the children; I mean, that is something that you naturally do anyway, but three times a week both my paraprofessional and I and then for five minutes. It was just a time issue.

Teachers who were successful found times during their regular routine, typically mealtimes, but even so it was difficult. "Just finding the time to separate yourself from the group because the second you separate yourself, that's when they all want to come and talk to you, you know, one at a time."

Some teachers also struggled with meeting the different language capabilities of individual children in their classrooms. "Trying to have conversations with children who either choose not to interact socially with others or their speech can't be understood or they can't speak English is frustrating—it's just very frustrating." Asking teachers to engage in conversations with a child with whom they did not, at least initially, share a common language was a challenge, and those who were successful began by simply commenting on what the child was doing or using simpler yes/no questions. One teacher described her experience: "You really had to just pull stuff out of them [the nonnative English speakers] and you might get one little short answer and if you just keep talking, they finally got to where they'll open up and talk to you too."

Despite the difficulty some teachers had in systematically implementing this strategy, those that did felt that it paid off, particularly from the perspective of supporting teacher–student relationships. "Before, it would be in one and ear and out the other, so, you get to know your children a lot better. That was a great benefit." Or as one paraprofessional noted, before they began Building Bridges, "There were some kids that probably got left between the cracks because they didn't talk and we just really never noticed that a lot of kids weren't even talking."

Given that many teachers had difficulty implementing *Building Bridges*, it is not surprising that most discontinued it during the sustainability phase of the project. Teachers certainly saw the value of the experience but could not fit it into their schedules as a consistent practice. *"Building Bridges* may have had a big influence … thinking well that's such a good thing to do but when?" Teachers talked about sustaining a focus on engaging children in conversations, but they did not maintain systematic ways of tracking that these conversations took place. Box 2 provides an illustration of how one teacher successfully carried out Building Bridges.

Early on a Monday morning, a group of 8 children and their teacher were sitting at a table in their classroom as 5th grade safety patrol students arrived with a breakfast cart. This teacher had struggled with how to implement *Building Bridges*; there seemed to be no time during the day—mealtimes were too noisy and disruptive in the cafeteria. All of the children seemed to need their naps. She couldn't find a way to schedule it during small group time. Finally, with the support of her principal, she had been able to move breakfast from the cafeteria to the classroom. *Building Bridges* was now part of their regular routine. The teacher and paraprofessional alternated eating with different groups of children. As breakfast began the teacher leaned over to a little boy and asked about his weekend. The child looked up and excitedly said, "I got sick and threwed up." This topic seemed to immediately interest all the children at the table and though they listened, they didn't interrupt, they knew this was "his turn" and that their turn would come.

Box 2. An illustration of classroom use of Building Bridges.

Explicit Vocabulary Practices

The explicit vocabulary intervention posed many challenges for teachers, and just 61% of the teachers implemented the explicit vocabulary enhancement practices in their classrooms with a high degree of fidelity. It appears that the challenges were, in large measure, organizational. Teachers had difficulties deciding on vocabulary-rich units, finding books with interesting vocabulary, and thinking of activities that might support the use of vocabulary. Our intention was to focus on effective practices while providing teachers the freedom they needed to choose themes and materials that worked for them. In reality, this meant that teachers had to expend quite a bit of energy identifying the target vocabulary words, finding appropriate books, finding pictures or objects for the N3C activities, and thinking of extension or assessment activities.

Identifying vocabulary words that clearly related to a theme and specific books had some unexpected pitfalls. For example, many of our teachers began the year exploring the theme of friendship and frequently read the book *The Rainbow Fish* (Pfister, 1992). This book is about a little fish that learns to be a friend and share his pretty scales, and it supports the theme of friendship, but it was difficult to use as a source for target vocabulary. They correctly identified words like *scales, starfish,* or *coral reef* as good vocabulary words, but the words were unrelated to their overall friendship theme. Although we helped teachers identify appropriate themes, books, and target vocabulary words during the intervention phase, it was still hard for teachers to find 10 new target words each week that related to a theme *and* were included in two appropriate books.

Some teachers also had difficulty finding pictures or objects for each target vocabulary word. As one teacher noted, "Nouns seemed to work. There were some other vocabulary areas I wanted them to know, and that was a real challenge ... some ones like *waddle.*" Teachers who were successful used Internet picture resources as a source for pictures to support vocabulary learning. Others used book illustrations as a source of vocabulary pictures. Others incorporated target vocabulary into their classroom through a "show-and-tell" routine by asking children to bring in objects from home for each target vocabulary word.

On the positive side, teachers found that children were very excited about learning new vocabulary words. As one teacher noted:

> It was good to see that they picked up on that kind of stuff. And then to watch them, during the unit, play with the stuff in the room, "That's the *stethoscope!* That's the *tongue depressor!*" ... instead of being the *popsicle stick* (which is what it has been their entire life).

Teachers who effectively implemented the explicit vocabulary practices embedded these practices as part of large-group storybook reading,
free play, center activities, or other ongoing classroom procedures. Many
teachers, even those who were successful, were initially concerned: "It was
just so overwhelming ... it was just like I need 3 more hours added to this
day to get all this stuff done and to feel like it was going to be effective."
Teachers had to reorganize their schedules to incorporate these activities
and they had to work effectively as a team with their paraprofessional. As
one teacher noted, she needed to "keep a lot of what we had been doing
'cause that's what we knew, and just kind of add those in." Another said, "I
incorporated my vocabulary in with my book sharing because that made it
a whole lot better and ... we ended up reading probably two to three times
a day in a large-group setting ... then the next week it's up in the book center and they are reading the books to each other." Teachers also brought
target vocabulary words into free-choice or center activities by including
the target vocabulary words in the writing center, featuring vocabulary as
part of the unit, or having children dictate stories together as a class, which
emphasized the vocabulary words.

Classrooms in which vocabulary assessment was systematic were often
those in which both the teacher and the paraprofessional took an active
role. For example, the teacher might ask questions about the target vocabulary words during large-group time while the paraprofessional assessed individual children's responses using a checklist. One teacher asked children
to raise "thumbs up" when they heard a current target vocabulary word being used and "hands up" for a target word from a previous week. Children
in that classroom loved being the first with "thumbs up" or the only one to
remember a word with "hands up."

To be successful, teachers had to be good organizers. Classrooms in
which explicit vocabulary practices were less effective were those in which
teachers had difficulty "fitting vocabulary into the day" or focusing on specific vocabulary entirely: "It takes looking ahead, I think, and actually planning what you think the children are capable of doing and trying not to be
... overwhelmed."

As we moved into the sustainability phase, teachers seemed to maintain a
focus on vocabulary but dropped the formal implementation guidelines.
Many continued to target specific vocabulary, usually at least five words per
week, and they did continue to incorporate target words into thematic
small-group activities. They did not continue to introduce words using the
N3C strategy, base the target words on specific texts, or systematically assess
vocabulary. Moreover, many teachers throughout the intervention and
sustainability period had incorporated the target vocabulary words into
their parent newsletters: "I got several comments from parents about how

It was two weeks before Halloween and the second day of a unit on spiders. The teacher did not want to emphasize Halloween in her classroom because of the varied religious backgrounds of children and families, but did want to focus on a topic that related to children's current interest in things spooky and scary. The vocabulary words included *arachnid, orb web,* and *hammock web.* She had found pictures representing these words using *google.com* and from the photographs in one of the books she was using. As I walked in the room I noticed the bulletin boards were newly decorated with a multitude of black spiders, each with eight pipe cleaner legs but each also decorated with widely differing configurations of spots. Children were just coming in from outside, stopping momentarily to get a drink of water or wash hands. As they entered the teacher asked them to find their spots on the rug and get ready for *circle time.* As they settled in she took her position at the front of the group while the paraprofessional sat in a small chair towards the back of the group with a pencil and clipboard in hand. She settled the children in and reviewed the vocabulary words she had introduced the day before using N3C. She read through an expository text about spiders paying special attention to the vocabulary words, asking questions, and in some cases summarizing the text because the book was at a third or fourth grade reading level. Throughout the group time, the paraprofessional jotted notes and completed a checklist about children's expressive use of the vocabulary words. When group time ended, the children were sent to various areas throughout the classroom. With the help of the paraprofessional, the children tossed a ball of yarn from one to another to create a giant spider web.

Box 3. An example of classroom activities from the explicit Vocabulary Enhancement program.

impressed they were with some of the vocabulary words." Thus, the focus on target vocabulary may have carried over into children's home environments. Box 3 provides an illustration of the vocabulary program in action.

EFFECTIVENESS OF THE PROGRAM
FOR ENHANCING CHILDREN'S VOCABULARY

Prior to evaluating the effectiveness of the program for improving children's vocabularies, we determined whether each teacher carried out the key aspects of the practice most of the time based on observation notes, interviews, and lesson plans. For each classroom, we decided whether each teacher showed fidelity with CAR Talk, Building Bridges, and the explicit vocabulary enhancement program separately. Recall that not all teachers had received professional development on the explicit features of the program, so they would not have been expected to demonstrate these practices. Moreover, teachers in the control classrooms had not received any of this training, so would have been extremely unlikely to have carried out the practices given the requirements that we set for demonstrating fidelity on given practices. Thus, in some classrooms, children's teachers were observed to have carried out only one of the three practices with fidelity, whereas in others they carried out all of them. In still others, including all the control classrooms, children were not exposed to any of the practices in a systematic way. These differences among classrooms were used as the effective levels of the program (none, one implicit, two implicit, one implicit/one explicit, and all practices) from the point of view of the children, regardless of whether the teacher did not receive professional development on a given practice or simply chose not to carry it out.

Children's receptive and expressive vocabularies were assessed using the Peabody Picture Vocabulary Test-III (Dunn & Dunn, 1997) and the Expressive Vocabulary Test (Williams, 1997). Note that we did not directly assess whether children learned the particular vocabulary teachers had targeted, but rather, whether vocabulary growth would be reflected on standardized tests of vocabulary knowledge, presumably a much tougher standard.

The PPVT-III and EVT were part of a larger battery of preliteracy assessments administered to the children in a quiet area in their school. Each test took approximately 15 to 20 minutes to administer. Children were provided with stickers upon completing each test and they received children's books for their participation in the study. Children were tested once at the start of the intervention, immediately after the 15-week intervention, and then 3 months later at the end of the school year. Standard scores were calculated based the children's chronological age at the time of testing.

Effects of the vocabulary practices were determined using the procedures suggested by Rausch, Maxwell, and Kelley (2003), who reviewed various analytic schemes for pretest–posttest designs, including repeated measures Analysis of Variance, analysis of gain scores, and Hierarchical Linear Modeling. They concluded that an Analysis of Covariance, treating the pretest as the covariate, was the most powerful approach to determining effects of an intervention. ANCOVA, because it allowed the use of regression to control for preexisting ability, had no less power than many of these designs and more parsimony. In this study, we were interested in overall effects of vocabulary practices. However, the use of ANCOVA in this way is conservative because a great deal of variance is accounted for by the covariate, the children's initial vocabulary.

Effects of the program were evaluated for children's receptive vocabulary and expressive vocabulary separately. We also distinguished whether children were designated as native English speakers according to parental report. Overall, children in the intervention started the school year with very low vocabulary levels (PPVT: $M = 83$, $SD = 21$; EVT: $M = 92$, $SD = 17$). A 5-teacher practice level (none, one implicit, two implicit, one implicit/one explicit, or all) X 2 first language (English or Other) X test time (immediate versus delayed posttest) repeated-measures ANCOVA was carried out using the child's pretest scores as a covariate for the PPVT-III and EVT separately.

For the EVT, there were no significant main effects of Time of testing, child's first language, teacher practice, or interactions between any of these factors. However, only 58% of children not speaking English as their native language had enough English proficiency to even attempt EVT testing during pretest, so their data are not included in this analysis. Clearly, the program had little impact on expressive vocabulary.

For the PPVT, the effects of the intervention were much more positive. As seen in Fig. 8.1, there was no main effect of time of test, $F (1, 297) < 1$, suggesting that any effects of the program were fairly stable following the immediate posttest. There was a significant effect of the child's first language, $F (1, 397) = 5.29, p = .022$, partial eta^2 = .013, and first language X time interaction, $F (1, 397) = 4.50, p = .033$, such that English language learners made larger receptive vocabulary gains than native English speakers did across all practices. Clearly, attendance at preschool in general is important for developing the English vocabulary skills of English language

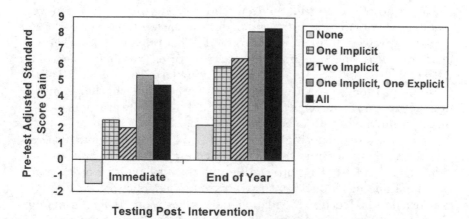

FIG. 8.1.   Changes in children's pretest adjusted PPVT-III standard scores as a function of the number and type of vocabulary practices implemented by their teacher during the 15-week intervention period (None; One Implicit; Two Implicit: One Implicit, One Explicit; All).

learners. However, most importantly for our purposes here, once adjusted for pretest PPVT, there was a main effect of teacher practice, $F(4, 397) = 3.58$, $p = .007$, partial eta^2 = .035, that was similar across native and nonnative English-speaking children, $F(4, 397) = 1.39$, $p = .239$.

Simple contrasts indicated that children whose teachers carried out any combination of program practices with fidelity ended up with higher vocabularies than controls, all $p < .05$. It seems that the more practices teachers engaged in, the better off children appeared to be, particularly if explicit vocabulary practices were used. Adjusting for initial vocabulary level, by the end of the year children whose teachers had carried out all the practices scored 8.2 standard score points and 14 percentile ranks higher than those whose teachers carried out none of them. Clearly, if the practices were carried out through kindergarten, children's vocabularies might well fall within in the normal range.

LESSONS FROM *PAVED FOR SUCCESS*

We have identified a number of promising approaches for enhancing the vocabularies of prekindergarten children. Systematic approaches, both implicit and explicit, were found to have an impact above and beyond enrollment in a quality preschool environment. Clearly, the more ways vocabulary was targeted, the more children's vocabularies improved. Our findings support the view that a comprehensive approach to vocabulary offers the best opportunity for supporting the linguistic needs of young children.

We found that the gains children made during the intervention were maintained following the intervention despite the fact that some of the systematic aspects of program were dropped. What remained, however, was teachers' focus on core practices that supported vocabulary learning. Rather than simply saying, "Focus on vocabulary," or merely, "Talk to kids," we provided very specific guidelines for how and why that should be done. Teachers who had the training were able to modify practices in a way that continued to support vocabulary.

With regard to enhancing teacher–child talk in the classroom, teachers benefited from a structure that made scheduling conversations with individual children part of a routine. Although the systematic record-keeping aspect of Building Bridges was largely discontinued following the intervention, teachers had set up a foundation in their classrooms that made it more likely that children would initiate conversations with them. A classroom climate had been created where such conversation was the norm.

With regard to CAR Talk, we feel that the secret of the teachers' success in the implementation can be attributed to the simplification that we made to other procedures that had been suggested by other researchers. CAR Talk encouraged children to demonstrate both simple and difficult types of knowledge, while motivating them to relate books to their personal experiences. These practices may have fostered children's engagement in the text and averted a difficult period where children were unable to provide answers to the abstract questions that were raised (McKeown & Beck, 2003).

Our interviews and observations convince us that having an explicit focus on vocabulary is something that preschool teachers want. It is also clear that developing an integrated explicit focus on vocabulary (including concrete props, stories, activities, and assessments) is difficult without a program package. If one was provided to them, it is likely that at least relevant parts would be implemented.

For children entering school already at risk for reading failure, this program had a substantive impact on their vocabularies. With some minor modifications, the integrated program we suggest might be feasible. We have described how teachers who were successful in implementing the practices were able to integrate them into their classrooms. Our findings have direct implications for policymakers attempting to improve the preliteracy skills of young children.

ACKNOWLEDGMENTS

The research presented here was carried out as part of the funding from the U.S. Department of Education Early Childhood Educator Professional Development program, 2001. Bradley is affiliated with the Department of Teaching and Learning at the University of Kansas, Lawrence, KS. Restrepo is affiliated with the Department of Speech and Hearing Science, Arizona State University, Tempe, AZ. Hamilton and Neuharth-Pritchell are affiliated with Elementary Education; and Ruston and Schwanenflugel with Educational Psychology, University of Georgia, Athens, GA.

REFERENCES

Adams, M. J. (1990). *Learning to read: Thinking and learning about print*. Cambridge, MA: MIT Press.

Allison, D. T. & Watson, J. A. (1994). The significance of adult storybook reading styles on the development of young children's emergent reading. *Reading Research and Instruction, 34*(1), 57–72.

Austin, M. C., & Morrison, C. (1963). *The first R: The Harvard report on reading in elementary schools*. New York: Macmillan.

Baker, S., Simmons, D., & Kame'enui, E. (1998). Vocabulary acquisition: Research bases. In D. C. Simmons & E. J. Kameenui (Eds.), *What reading research tells us about children with diverse learning needs* (pp. 249–288). Mahwah, NJ: Lawrence Erlbaum Associates.

Biemiller, A. (2001). Teaching vocabulary; early, direct and sequential. *American Educator, 25*, 24–28.

Brabham, E. G., Lynch-Brown, C. (2002). Effects of teachers' reading-aloud styles on vocabulary acquisition and comprehension of students in early elementary grades. *Journal of Educational Psychology, 94*, 465–473.

Brett, A., Rothlein, L., & Hurley, M. (1996). Vocabulary acquisition from listening to stories and explanations of target words. *Elementary School Journal, 96,* 415–422.

Bryant, D. M., Burchinal, M., Lau, L. B., & Sparling, J. J. (1994). Family and classroom correlates of Head Start children's developmental outcomes. *Early Childhood Research Quarterly, 9,* 289–304.

Conger, R. D., Conger, K. J., & Elder, G. (1997). Family economic hardship and adolescent academic performance: Mediating and moderating processes. In G. Duncan & J. Brooks-Gunn (Eds.), *Consequences of growing up poor* (pp. 288–310). New York: Russell Sage Foundation.

Copeland, K. A., & Edwards, P. A., (1990). Towards understanding the roles parents play in supporting young children's development in writing. *Early Child Development and Care, 56,* 11–17.

Cornell, E. H., Senechal, M., & Broda, L. S. (1988). Recall of picture books by 3-year-old children: Testing and repetition effects in joint reading activities. *Journal of Educational Psychology, 80,* 537–542

Cunningham, A. E. & Stanovich, K. E. (1997). Early reading acquisition and its relation to reading experience and ability 10 years later. *Developmental Psychology, 33,* 934–945.

Dickinson, D., & Smith, M. (1994). Long term effects of pre-school teachers' book readings on low-income children's vocabulary and story comprehension. *Reading Research Quarterly, 29,* 104–122.

Dickinson, D. K., & Sprague, K. E. (2001). The nature and impact of early childhood care environments on the language and early literacy development of children from low-income families. In S. B. Neuman & D. K. Dickinson (Eds.), *Handbook of early literacy research* (pp. 263–280). New York: Guilford Publication.

Dickinson, D. K., & Tabors, P. O. (2001). Fostering language and literacy in classrooms and homes: Supporting language learning. *Young Children, 57,* 10–18.

Dromi, E. (1987). *Early lexical development.* Cambridge, England: Cambridge University Press.

Duncan, G. J., Young, W. J., Brooks-Gunn, J., & Smith, J. R. (1998). How much does poverty affect the life chances of children? *American Sociological Review, 63*(3), 406–423.

Dunn, L., Beach, S. A., & Kontos, S. (1994). Quality of the literacy environment in day care and children's development. *Journal of Research in Childhood Education, 9,* 24–34.

Dunn, L. M., & Dunn, L. M. (1997). Peabody Pictrure Vocabulary Test—third edition (PPVT-III). Circle Pines, MN: AGS Publishing.

Elley, W. B. (1989). Vocabulary acquisition from listening to stories. *Reading Research Quarterly, 24,* 174–187

Ewers, C. A., & Brownson, S.M. (1999). Kindergartners' vocabulary acquisition as a function of active vs. passive storybook reading, prior vocabulary, and working memory. *Journal of Reading Psychology, 20,* 11–20.

Golinkoff, R. M., Mervis, C. B., & Hirsh-Pasek, K. (1994). Early object labels: The case for a developmental lexical principles framework. *Journal of Child Language, 21,* 125–155.

Golinkoff, R. M., Hirsch-Pasek, K., Mervis, C. B., Frawley, W. B., & Parillo, M. (1995). Lexical principles can be extended to the acquisition of verbs. In M. Tomasello & W. E. Merriman (Eds.), *Beyond names for things; Young children's acquisition of verbs* (pp. 185–221). Hillsdale, NJ: Lawrence Erlbaum Associates.

Graves, M. F., Brunetti, G. J., & Slater, W. H. (1982). The reading vocabularies of primary grade children of varying geographic and social backgrounds. In J. A. Niles

& L. A. Harris (Eds.), *New inquiries in reading research and instruction* (pp. 99–104). Rochester, NY: National Reading Conference.

Hart, B., & Risley, T. R. (1992). American parenting of language-learning children: Persisting differences in family–child interactions observed in natural home environments. *Developmental Psychology, 28,* 1096–1105.

Hart, B., & Risley, T. R. (1995). *Meaningful differences in the everyday experiences of young American children.* Baltimore, MD: Paul Brookes.

Helburn, S. W. (1995). *Cost, quality, and child outcomes in child care centers.* Technical Report, Public Report, and Executive Summary. Denver, CO: University of Colorado.

Howes, C., & Hamilton, C. E. (1992). Children's relationships with caregivers: Mothers and child-care teachers. *Child Development, 63,* 859–866.

Howes, C., Hamilton, C. E., & Phillipsen, L. C. (1998). Stability and continuity of child–caregiver and child–peer relationships. *Child Development, 69,* 418–426.

Hughes, M., & Westgate, D. (1998). Possible enabling strategies in teacher-led talk with young pupils. *Language and Education, 12,* 174–191.

Jacobs, J. S., Morrison, T. G., & Swinyard, W. R. (2000). Reading aloud to students: A national probability study of classroom reading practices of elementary school teachers. *Reading Psychology, 21,* 171–194.

Jenkins, J. R., Stein, M. L., & Wysocki, K. (1984). Learning vocabulary through reading. *American Educational Research Journal, 21,* 767–787.

Justice, L. (2002). Word exposure conditions and preschoolers' novel word learning during shared storybook reading. *Reading Psychology, 23,* 87–106.

Kontos, S., & Wilcox-Herzog, A. (1997). Influences on children's competence in early childhood classrooms. *Early Childhood Research Quarterly, 12,* 247–262.

Lickteig, M. J., & Russell, J. F., (1993). Elementary teachers' read-aloud practices. *Reading Improvement, 30,* 202–208.

Liu, J., Golinkoff, R. M., & Sak, K. (2001). One cow does not an animal make: Young children can extend novel words at the superordinate level. *Child Development, 72,* 1674–1694.

Lonigan, C. J., & Whitehurst, G. J. (1998). Relative efficacy of parent and teacher involvement in a shared-reading intervention for preschool children from low-income backgrounds. *Early Childhood Research Quarterly, 13,* 263–290.

McKeown, M., & Beck, I. L. (2003). Taking advantage of read alouds to help children make sense of decontextualized language. In A. van Kleeck, S. A. Stahl, & E. B. Bauer (Eds.), *On reading books to children: Parents and teachers.* Mahwah, NJ: Lawrence Erlbaum Associates.

McLoyd, V. C. (1998). Economic disadvantage and child development. *American Psychologist, 52, 185–204.*

Mervis, C. B., & Bertrand, J. (1994). Acquisition of the Novel-Name-Nameless Category (N3C) Principle. *Child Development, 65,* 1646–1662.

Morrow, L. M., Rand, M. K., & Smith, J. K. (1995). Reading aloud to children: Characteristics and relationships between teachers and student behaviors. *Reading Research & Instruction, 35,* 85–101.

Morrow, L. M., & Smith, J. K, (1990). The effects of group size on interactive storybook reading. *Reading Research Quarterly, 23,* 213–31.

Nagy, W. F., & Anderson, R. C. (1984). How many words are there in printed English? *Reading Research Quarterly, 19,* 304–330.

Pfister, M. (1992). *The rainbow fish.* New York: North-South Books.

Pianta, R. C. (1999). *Enhancing relationships between children and teachers.* Washington, DC: American Psychological Association.

Pianta, R. C., & Steinberg, M. (1992). Relationships between children and kindergarten teachers from the teachers' perspective. In R. C. Pianta (Ed.), *Beyond the parent: The role of other adults in children's lives* (pp. 61–80). San Francisco: Jossey-Bass.

Rausch, J. R., Maxwell, S. E., Kelley, K. (2003). Analytic methods for questions pertaining to a randomized pretest, posttest, follow-up design. *Journal of Clinical Child and Adolescent Psychology, 32,* 467–486.

Reese, E., & Cox, A. (1999). Quality of adult book reading affects children's emergent literacy. *Developmental Psychology, 35,* 20–28.

Rosemary, C. A., & Roskos, K. A. (2002). Literacy conversations between adults and children at childcare: Descriptive observations and hypotheses. *Journal of Research in Childhood Education, 16,* 212–231.

Scarborough, H. S. (2001). Connecting early language and literacy to later reading (dis)abilities: Evidence, theory and practice. In S. Neuman and D. Dickinson (Eds.), *Handbook for research in early literacy* (pp. 97–110). New York: Guilford.

Schwanenflugel, P., & Noyes, C. R. (1996). Context availability and the development of word reading skill. *Journal of Literacy Research, 28,* 35–54.

Share, D. L., Jorm, A. F., MacLean, R., & Matthews, R. (1984). Sources of individual differences in reading acquisition. *Journal of Educational Psychology, 76,* 1309–1324.

Smith, J., Brooks-Gunn, J., & Klebanov, P. (1997). Consequences of living in poverty for young children's cognitive and verbal ability and early school achievement. In G. Duncan & J. Brooks-Gunn (Eds.), *Consequences of growing up poor* (pp. 132–189). New York: Russell Sage Foundation.

Smith, M. W., & Dickinson, D. K. (1994). Describing oral language opportunities and environments in Head Start and other preschool classrooms. *Early Childhood Education Quarterly, 9,* 345–366.

Snow, C., Burns, M., & Griffin, P. (1999). Preventing reading difficulties in young children. In Consortium on Reading Instruction (Ed.), *Reading research anthology: The why? of reading instruction* (pp. 148–155). Novato, CA: Arena Press.

Soundy, C. S., & Stount, N. L. (2002, March) Fostering emotional and language needs of young learners. *Young Children, 57,* 20–24.

Stahl, S. A., & Fairbanks, M. M. (1986). The effects of vocabulary instruction: A model based meta-analysis. *Review of Educational Research, 56*(1), 72–110.

Storch, S. A., & Whitehurst, G. J. (2002). Oral language and code-related precursors to reading: Evidence from a longitudinal structural model. *Developmental Psychology, 38,* 934–947.

Sugimura, T., & Maeda, N. (1997). Relative sensitivity of the mutual exclusivity and novel-name-nameless category assumptions. *Japanese Psychological Research, 39,* 51–55.

Taylor, B. M., Peterson, D. S., Pearson, P. D., & Rodriguez, M. C. (2003). Looking inside classrooms: Reflecting on the "how" as well as the "what" in effective reading instruction. *Reading Teacher, 56,* 270–279.

U.S. Census Bureau (2004, September 8). *Poverty.* Retrieved October 14, 2004, from http://www.census.gov/hhes/www/poverty.html

Washington, J., & Craig, H. (1999). Performance of at-risk African American preschoolers on the Peabody Picture Vocabulary Test - III. *Language, Speech, and Hearing Services in the Schools, 30,* 75–82.

Wasik, B. A., & Bond, M. A. (2001). Beyond the pages of a book: Interactive book reading and language development in preschool classrooms, *Journal of Educational Psychology, 93,* 243–250.

Weizman, Z. O., & Snow, C. E. (2001). Lexical input as related to children's vocabulary acquisition: Effects of sophisticated exposure and support for meaning, *Developmental Psychology, 37,* 265–279.

Wells, C. G. (1985). Preschool literacy-related activities and success in school. In D. Olson, N. Torrance, & A. Hillyard (Eds.), *Literacy, language, and learning: The nature and consequence of literacy* (pp. 229–255). Cambridge, England: Cambridge University Press.

Whitehurst, G. J., Arnold, D. S., Epstein, J. N., Angell, A. L., Smith, M., & Fischel, J. E. (1994). A picture book reading intervention in day care and home for children from low-income families, *Developmental Psychology, 30,* 679–689.

Whitehurst, G. J., & Lonigan, C. J. (1998). Child development and emergent literacy. *Child Development, 69,* 848–872.

Wilcox-Herzog, A., & Kontos, "S. (1998). The nature of teacher talk in early childhood classrooms and its relationship to children's play with objects and peers. *Journal of Genetic Psychology, 159,* 30–44.

Williams, K. T. (1997). *Expressive vocabulary test (EVT).* Circle Pines, MN: AGS Publishing.

Chapter 9

Strategies for Teaching Middle-Grade Students to Use Word-Part and Context Clues to Expand Reading Vocabulary

James F. Baumann
University of Georgia

George Font
Purdue University

Elizabeth Carr Edwards
University of Georgia

Eileen Boland
Fresno, California

In two recent studies (Baumann, Edwards, Boland, Olejnik, & Kame'enui, 2003; Baumann, Edwards, Font, Tereshinski, Kame'enui, & Olejnik, 2002), we explored the effectiveness of teaching middle-grade students to use root words, prefixes, and suffixes to derive word meanings, that is, to use word-part clues. We also taught students to scrutinize the text in sentences and paragraphs around an unfamiliar word to infer its meanings, that is, to use context clues. Results supported the effectiveness of our interventions. Quantitative, or numerical, findings revealed that students learned the meanings of prefixes and suffixes and used that knowledge to derive the meanings of novel words with affixes. The data also demonstrated that students who were taught specific types of context clues were able to use contextual analysis to unlock the meanings of unfamiliar words.

In addition to the numerical data, at the end of the instructional program we conducted interviews and invited participants to complete questionnaires to provide us descriptive information about the interventions. We asked students to explain how they determined the meanings of unknown words, and several students noted that they used word-part clues. For example, one student stated, "I figured out [the meaning of *semiretired*], like I knew what *retired* means, so I just had to figure out what *semi* means. *Semi* means like part or half, so you're almost or half-way retired." Other students commented that they had relied on context: "After I read the sentence [containing *fortitude*], I noticed that it had a comma and then it said *or courage*.... I just used *courage* from what you taught us ... and that was one of the context clues."

When asked about the instructional program, teachers noted that their students were more likely to use context clues (e.g., "[My students] seem to be able to look for context clues better and pick out meanings.") and word-structure information (e.g., "The students have been able to identify word parts now and figure out the meanings of words.") to determine the meanings of difficult vocabulary. Students indicated that they used context (e.g., "I used to skip over [words], but now I go back and read for context clues."), and others stated that they looked for word-part clues (e.g., "I see prefixes in other books I read.").

Given the findings of our research and similar research by others, we have prepared this chapter in order to present strategies that middle-grade teachers (Grades 4–8) might use to instruct students to use word-part and context clues to expand their reading vocabularies. We begin with a brief review of research on vocabulary instruction, with emphasis on teaching word-part and context clues as means to promote word knowledge. Next, we describe the interventions we implemented and provide sample lessons for teaching word-part and context clues in language arts and content area classes. We conclude by acknowledging limits to and extensions of the instructional recommendations we offer.

RESEARCH ON VOCABULARY INSTRUCTION

The Importance of a Multifaceted Vocabulary Instructional Program

Vocabulary is strongly associated with reading comprehension (Anderson & Freebody, 1981; Cunningham & Stanovich, 1997) and is an integral component of reading instructional programs (Beck & McKeown, 1991; Blachowicz & Fisher, 2000). Many researchers and writers have argued that a vocabulary instructional program should be multifaceted, or have multiple components (e.g., Johnson, 2001; Nagy, 1988). Graves (2000) identified four components that possess both intuitive appeal and empirical support for expanding students' reading vocabularies: (a) exposure to written language by engaging in wide, independent reading (Swanborn & de Glopper, 1999); (b) instruction in specific words (Stahl & Fairbanks, 1986); (c) teaching students word-learning strategies for independent vocabulary acquisition (Fukkink & de Glopper, 1998; White, Sowell, & Yanagihara, 1989); and (d) fostering word consciousness to promote motivated, reflective word learning (Graves & Watts-Taffe, 2002; Scott & Nagy, 2004).

In our research, we focused on Graves's (2000) third component—teaching word-learning strategies—specifically, instruction in word-part and context clues. Nagy, Anderson, Schommer, Scott, and Stallman (1989) asserted that "more than 60% of the new words that readers encounter have relatively transparent morphological structure—that is, they can be broken down into [meaningful] parts" (p. 279). In addition, Nagy and Anderson (1984) stated that "for every word a child learns, we estimate that there are an average of one to three additional related words that should also be understandable to the child, the exact number depending on how well the child is able to utilize context and morphology to induce meanings" (p. 304). Thus, there is potential power in skillful use of available word-part and context clues.

Research on Teaching Word-Part and Context Clues

Early research on teaching word-part clues, or morphological analysis, produced mixed findings (cf. Otterman, 1955; Thompson, 1958), but more contemporary studies have indicated that students can be taught various word-parts, most often prefixes and suffixes, to derive the meanings of untaught words (e.g., Graves & Hammond, 1980; Wysocki & Jenkins, 1987). There is also equivocal historic research on teaching context clues (cf. Askov & Kamm, 1976; Hafner, 1965), although more current research supports the efficacy of teaching students to employ linguistic clues to infer word meanings through context (e.g., Buikema & Graves, 1993; Jenkins, Matlock, & Slocum, 1989). Building on and extending this research, we recently conducted two studies involving teaching Grade 5 students to use word-part and context clues.

Study 1. In the first study (Baumann et al., 2002), we wanted to find out if we could teach students morphemic (word-part) and contextual analysis as strategies for learning new vocabulary. We also wondered whether the acquisition of these word-learning strategies would affect students' reading comprehension. To explore this, we conducted a study with fifth-grade students, providing them twelve 50-minute vocabulary strategy lessons.

We included four groups of fifth graders in our study: a Prefix, Context, Combined, and Control group. For the Prefix Group, we taught them the meanings of 20 prefixes organized into families (e.g., the "Not Family" = *in-, im-, un-, dis-*) and how to derive the meanings of new words that contained those prefixes. For the Context Group, we taught nine types of context clues (e.g., direct definition, synonym) and how to use them to infer the meanings of unknown words. For the Combined Group, we taught them the information provided to the Prefix and Context groups, but in an abbreviated fashion. For the Control Group, students read and responded to a children's book, so that we could compare students who did not receive special instruction in word-part and context clues to those who did.

We found that students in either the Prefix or Combined Group were more skillful at deriving the meanings of novel words that contained the prefixes we taught compared to students in the Context Group or Control Group. Similarly, we found that students in the Context or Combined Group outperformed students in the Prefix and Control group on measures that had them use context to infer the meanings of unfamiliar words. We also found that the word-part and context instruction was equally effective when provided either separately (i.e., Prefix or Context Group) or in tandem (i.e., Combined Group). Students both high and low in vocabulary ability prior to the study seemed to benefit equally from the instruction. Finally, there were no group differences on a reading comprehension measure. We concluded that students can be taught to use word-part and context clues to learn vocabulary independently, that combined word-part and context instruction is just as effective as separate instruction, and that this instruction does not necessarily enhance text comprehension.

Study 2.   We were encouraged by our first study, but it was limited in that it was a fairly controlled, or "laboratory," kind of study. At the conclusion of their review of vocabulary research, the National Reading Panel (2000) stated that "the Panel knows a great deal about the ways in which vocabulary increases under highly controlled conditions" but "there is a great need for the conduct of research … in authentic school contexts, with real teachers, under real conditions" (p. 4–27). Therefore, our second study (Baumann, Edwards, et al., 2003) addressed the call for more naturalistic vocabulary research. Specifically, we enlisted the help of regular classroom teachers to provide the instruction (we had taught the lessons in Study 1). We embedded combined word-part and context clue instruction within the adopted school curriculum (a unit on the Civil War from the social studies textbook). And we integrated brief (15-minute) vocabulary strategy lessons into daily 45-minute social studies lessons.

We provided instructional materials and staff development to eight Grade 5 teachers, who were randomly assigned to one of two intervention groups: a Word-Part/Context Group or a Textbook Vocabulary Group. Teachers in the Word-Part/Context Group taught their students 20 prefixes and suffixes and 5 context clue types as strategies for learning new vocabulary. We selected the instructional example words right from the social studies textbook lessons (e.g., *citizenship* was used to teach the suffix *-ship*). Teachers in the Textbook Vocabulary Group spent equivalent instructional time teaching students the meanings of content-specific vocabulary (e.g., *tariff, secede*) from the same social studies textbook lessons. The interventions spanned 2 months, with both groups receiving 25 lessons.

We again found that combined word-part and context clue instruction generally was effective. Students in Word Part/Context Group classes outperformed Textbook Vocabulary Group classes on a test of new words that contained prefixes and suffixes that the students had been taught. They also outperformed the Textbook Vocabulary Group on a delayed test, although not an immediate test, that required students to determine the meanings of novel words included in social studies textbook excerpts the students had not yet read (i.e., words that had the same affixes that had been taught and words that were in contexts similar to the clues the students had been taught). As expected, the Textbook Vocabulary Group outperformed the Word Part/Context Group on a test of the key vocabulary they had been taught. There were no group differences on measures of social studies learning (two textbook chapter tests) or a comprehension measure, and again, students both high and low in initial vocabulary knowledge benefited from the instruction.

In summary, we concluded from our two studies that word-part and context clue instruction can be provided to middle-grade students in an integrated manner that enables them to derive the meanings of novel, transfer words that contain prefixes and suffixes that they had been taught. There also was evidence, although somewhat limited by the results of Study 2, that students could apply knowledge of context clue instruction to infer the meanings of novel, transfer words in experimental and natural texts. We also found that this instruction was effective for students who were initially high or low in vocabulary, although there was no evidence that the vocabulary strategies influenced students' subject matter learning differentially or enhanced their text comprehension. We now turn to a description of the elements of the instructional program employed in these studies.

TEACHING WORD-PART AND CONTEXT CLUES
TO EXPAND READING VOCABULARY

Instructional Content

Word-Part Clues.   Word-part clues are meaningful parts of words (morphemes) that a reader can identify and then assemble to derive the meaning of a previously unfamiliar word. Instruction in word-part clues typically involves teaching root or base words, prefixes, and suffixes. In our research, we provided students instruction primarily in prefixes, which Graves (2004) argues are efficient and effective to teach because prefixes are relatively few in number and have generally consistent spellings and meanings. We also taught a few high-frequency suffixes.

We have listed later in this chapter (see Teaching Chart 3 adjacent to Sample Lesson 2) the prefixes and suffixes that we included in our research, along with additional affixes that we believe are worthy of instruction based on their frequency of occurrence in various empirically and descriptively based listings (e.g., Bear, Invernizzi, Templeton, & Johnston, 1996; Blachowicz & Fisher, 1996; Durkin, 1981; Johnson & Pearson, 1978; White et al., 1989). We found that clustering affixes into groups, or "families," when appropriate helped students to learn, recall, and apply them well, so that is the organization we recommend. We concur with Graves (2004), who suggests that affix instruction be restricted, at least initially, to words in which the affix removal results in an intact English word, or free morpheme (e.g., *pre/approve*), as opposed to those in which affix removal results in a root that cannot stand alone as a word (e.g., *pre/dict*).

Context Clues.   Context clues involve the linguistic (e.g., words, phrases, sentences) and nonlinguistic information (e.g., illustrations, typographic features) available surrounding an unfamiliar word, which a reader can use to infer the word's meaning. Instruction in context clues typically involves teaching students to use linguistic information to predict the meaning of a word (e.g., Blachowicz, 1993; Buikema & Graves, 1993; Durkin, 1981), and that was the focus of our research and the emphasis here.

Various researchers and writers have offered listings of context clue types (e.g., Dale & O'Rourke, 1986; Johnson & Pearson, 1978; Sternberg & Powell, 1983). Drawing from these sources, we identified nine context clues for instruction in our first study. In an attempt to make instruction more efficient, we consolidated and reduced these nine types to five in our second experiment, which we present later (see Teaching Chart 4 adjacent to Sample Lesson 3) and recommend for instruction.

Instructional Framework

In our research, we employed an explicit instruction model (Pearson & Gallagher, 1983) that included a gradual release of responsibility dimension (Pearson & Fielding, 1991). This translated into an instructional framework that included verbal explanation, modeling, guided practice, and independent practice (Duke & Pearson, 2002) of the particular word-part or context clue under consideration. In Study 1, we created instructional texts to teach word-part and context clues. In Study 2, we created a few instructional texts, but we relied primarily on excerpts from the social studies textbook to teach word-part and context clues. We see an appropriate place for the judicious use of both specially constructed instructional texts and regular curricular materials. The former are useful to clearly demonstrate to students how word-part and context clues function; the latter are necessary to promote transfer and application of word-learning strategies to real-world texts.

Sample Lesson Scenario

The sample lessons incorporate instructional principles and examples from our two studies, but they are not lessons directly from the research. Instead, we present four, sequenced sample lessons that reflect our empirical explorations and the strategies and guidelines we recommend for teaching students word-part and context clues (Edwards, Font, Baumann, & Boland, 2004). The lesson sequence includes integrated instruction such that students learn to examine words simultaneously for all available intraword (word-part) and interword (context clue) linguistic information that may help them unlock a word's meaning. For instructional efficiency and clarity, however, we believe that there is a place for separate instruction in word-parts and context clues, as long as the two are integrated ultimately.

To demonstrate how teachers might embed word-part and context clue instruction within their existing curriculum, the lessons reference various subject matter texts and trade books, the latter of which could be read in conjunction with language arts structures such as book club (McMahon, Raphael, Goatley, & Pardo, 1997) or literature circles (Daniels, 2002). It is important to recognize that even though the sample lessons focus on strategies for identifying word meanings, the strategy lessons should not dominate content or language arts instruction. Therefore, we intend for lessons like the following to represent a small amount of the total instructional time, with the majority of class time dedicated to reading, discussing, analyzing, responding to, enjoying, and learning from the trade books and subject matter texts.

Each of the following model lessons is taught by a hypothetical Grade 5 teacher, who might work in an elementary school or in a middle school environment. We have chosen to portray each lesson within a somewhat different instructional context, so that we can demonstrate how the word-learning strategies might be integrated into different curricular areas. Lesson 1 describes how Ms. Jackson uses historical fiction to teach an overview lesson on the combined use of word-part and context clues. In Lesson 2, Mr. Lopez provides instruction in word-part analysis by connecting it to social studies textbook content, and Lesson 3 describes how Ms. Lee uses science class to teach context clues. In Lesson 4, Mr. Olson provides integrated instruction in word-part and context clues through his use of literature circles.

We use the following conventions in the sample lessons. Descriptions of lesson events are presented in regular type, with annotations referring to lesson procedures or teacher or student actions [in brackets]. We do not advocate scripted lessons, but we present possible teacher wordings in **bold type**. Excerpts from published texts and instructional examples we have created are presented in *italic type*. Teaching charts and student work papers are presented as boxed text figures.

Sample Lesson 1: Introducing Word-Parts and Context Clues

Background.   Ms. Jackson is a member of a team of fifth-grade elementary teachers who have decided to focus on vocabulary. Team members have brought articles to team meetings that describe how students can use word-parts and context clues to learn new word meanings. Ms. Jackson has volunteered to begin a month-long effort in the language arts block in which she works explicitly with students on both word-parts and context clues. Because her program has long revolved around the reading and discussion of literature, she knows that the combination of word-part and context clue instruction could go a long way in supporting students' understanding of the rich vocabulary in literature. Ms. Jackson knows that students have received general instruction in prior grades on context clues and structural elements, so she assumes that students know what *context clue, root word, prefix,* and *suffix* mean. Should she find this assumption to be untrue, she would reteach those concepts.

The class has been begun reading Patricia C. McKissack's (1997) *Run Away Home* as a complement to their study of postbellum U.S. history in social studies. *Run Away Home* is historical fiction that builds on McKissack's African American and Native American ancestors and tells the story of how Sarah Jane befriends a runaway Apache boy in southeast Alabama in 1888. Chapters 1 and 2 of the book have been read and discussed in large- and small-group formats.

Verbal Explanation.   Following the instructional framework of Pearson (Duke & Pearson, 2002; Pearson & Gallagher, 1983), Ms. Jackson begins the word-part and context clue instruction with a verbal explanation of why and where the strategies will be useful:

> **Sometimes when you read, you will come across a word for which you are not sure of its meaning. This can make it difficult for you to understand and enjoy the story. There are different things you can do to help you figure out the meanings of unknown words. In several lessons beginning today, we will learn about two strategies: using context clues and looking for word parts like root words, prefixes, and suffixes.** [If necessary, Ms. Jackson would review the concepts of prefixes, suffixes, and root words at this time.] **We will put these together in what I call The Vocabulary Rule, which will give you a strategy to help figure out the meanings of unknown words.** [Ms. Jackson displays Teaching Chart 1 and reads the three steps to the students.] **The Vocabulary Rule will not always work, but it is one more tool you can add to your Reading Strategy Toolbox to help you become independent readers and learners.**

Modeling.   Following verbal explanation, Ms. Jackson moves to the modeling phase of the instructional framework. To support this modeling, she has put part of the text that students have been discussing on an overhead transparency:

> *Buster grew into a big dog, built like a collie, but with a dark reddish coat of a redbone. But Papa's delight turned sour when no amount of training could turn Buster into a fine hunting dog. "Too wild, uncontrollable. Useless," he announced, dismissing Buster as a failure. (McKissack, 1997, pp. 6–7)*

After students have read the text on the transparency, Ms. Jackson demonstrates how to use the vocabulary strategy:

> **Let's say that you are not sure what the word** *uncontrollable* **means. The Vocabulary Rule can help us figure out what it means. I'm going to model the three steps of The Vocabulary Rule.**
>
> **Step 1 says to read the sentences to see if there are any clues.** [She begins reading and stops at *uncontrollable*.] **Hmmm. Papa says that Buster is "Too**

Teaching Chart 1: VOCABULARY RULE

When you come to a word, and you don't know what it means, use:

1. CONTEXT CLUES: Read the sentences around the word to see if there are clues to its meaning.
2. WORD-PART CLUES: See if you can break the word into a root word, prefix, or suffix to help figure out its meaning.
3. CONTEXT CLUES: Read the sentences around the word again to see if you have figured out its meaning.

wild, uncontrollable." I wonder if *uncontrollable* means something like *wild*, for Papa uses those words right after one another? What do you think? [Students reply to Ms. Jackson's query.]

Step 1 also says to read the sentences around the word, so I better read on. It says that Papa called Buster "useless" and thought of "Buster as a failure." These seem like other context clues, for if *uncontrollable* means something like *wild*, then it makes sense that Papa would consider Buster to be useless and a failure as a hunting dog. It also said before that "no amount of training could turn Buster into a fine hunting dog," which seems to go along with the idea that Buster was wild. Does it seem like we're finding useful clues that *uncontrollable* means *wild*? [Students respond.]

Now let's try Step 2, which says to see if you can break the word into a root word and any prefixes or suffixes. It looks as though *control* might be the root word and that *un-* is a prefix and *-able* is a suffix. [She writes the following on the board, as she explains her reasoning for what each word part means: "*control* = to be restrained or to hold back; *un-* = not; *-able* = capable of."] So, if *control* means to be restrained or to hold back and *-able* means capable of, then *controllable* means capable of being held back or restrained, like this. [She writes "*control* + *-able* = *controllable* = capable of being held back or restrained" on the board.] And if *un-* means not, then *uncontrollable* means not capable of being held back or restrained, or not tame. [She writes "*un-* + *control* + *-able* = *uncontrollable* = not capable of being held back or restrained" on the board.]

Step 3 says to check the context again. [She rereads the text on the transparency.] Does the idea of Buster being not capable of being restrained or held back make sense? Do you get the idea that Buster is not tame or wild as Papa said? [Students respond.]

Guided Practice. The third part of the instructional framework involves guided practice, during which students practice applying the skills with support from the teacher as well as other students. Ms. Jackson has a transparency with the following sentences ready:

- *Rashad was a disbeliever. He never accepted what anyone had to say or what he read. We expected him to question everything he heard and to view what he read with suspicion.*
- *My Mom said that she thought that the winner of the reality TV show was predetermined. She said that the people who put on the show had already decided which performer would win the grand prize.*

She reminds students of the three steps to figure out the meaning of the word *disbeliever* in the first example, referring them to the three steps on The Vocabulary Rule poster. After giving students time to apply the strategy, she asks for a volunteer to explain the use of the Vocabulary Rule to figure out the meaning of *disbeliever*. She reinforces and reteaches The Vocabulary Rule as needed to help students apply it independently. She then repeats the process for the *predetermined* example.

Independent Practice. The final step of the instructional framework is for students to apply the strategy independently. Several features of this independent practice are important to note. First, Ms. Jackson has identified several instances from *Run Away Home* in preparation for this practice, to which she refers students in the book. Second, she does not ask students to go through all instances all at once.

In conjunction with the assigned independent reading of chapters 3 and 4 of *Run Away Home*, Ms. Jackson has students use The Vocabulary Rule to try to determine the meanings of *southbound* (p. 11), *sureness* (p. 13), *overlooked* (p. 18), and *unnatural* (p. 19), recording their answers on paper. Time is given in class to start the assignment, so that Ms. Jackson can monitor students' understanding of the strategies and help those who need assistance. Students are to come back the following day with descriptions of the usefulness of The Vocabulary Rule with these words.

The next day, Ms. Jackson begins her lesson with students' descriptions, including their explanations of why and where the strategy was useful. When students' explanations show misunderstandings, she leads them in applying the strategy appropriately. The Vocabulary Rule on the poster will be revisited frequently over the next month through discussions of strategy use and, when necessary, modeling of the use of the strategy. The poster will remain visible in the classroom even after the month-long period, and Ms. Jackson will ask students to review the strategy periodically as unknown words are encountered in texts and discussions.

Sample Lesson 2: Teaching Word-Part Analysis

Background. Mr. Lopez teaches social studies in a middle school. He has determined that comprehension of the social studies textbook is a problem for a number of his students, which he sees as impeding the students' learning. Having recently taken a university course in content area reading, he is aware of the importance of word knowledge to text understanding and subject matter learning. Thus, he has decided to implement a multifaceted vocabulary initiative this school year (Graves, 2000). As one component of his program, he has decided to teach his students strategies for independent word learning by relying on word-part and contextual information.

Mr. Lopez has planned a series of lessons on teaching word-part and context clues that he will implement as he teaches a unit on the Civil War using the adopted social studies textbook. Several days ago, he taught an introductory lesson on The Vocabulary Rule that was similar to Ms. Jackson's preceding lesson. He now moves into teaching specific word-part clues. This lesson, just like the other sample lessons, follows the instructional framework of verbal explanation, modeling, guided practice, and independent practice (Duke & Pearson, 2002; Pearson & Gallagher, 1983). Mr. Lopez assumes that his students possess general knowledge of structural elements, although he is prepared to review or reteach those concepts as needed.

Verbal Explanation.   He begins the lesson by connecting it to his preceding introductory lesson and then explaining how to analyze words for meaningful parts as a strategy for deriving their meanings:

> **We have learned about The Vocabulary Rule** [pointing to Teaching Chart 1] **as a way to use context and word-part clues to help us figure out the meanings of difficult or new words. It says to first use context, second to look for word-part clues, and third to use context again.**
>
> **Today we will take a closer look at Step 2, using word-part clues. Please look at this second chart, which tells us more about how to use word-part clues.** [He displays and reads Teaching Chart 2, explaining briefly each of the four steps to the students.] **Knowing how to look for and use word parts to figure out word meanings is important because many root words have prefixes and suffixes, and we can use that information to help figure out the meanings of new words that contain those word parts.**

Modeling.   Mr. Lopez now demonstrates how to analyze the meaningful parts of words as a strategy for deriving word meanings. He displays the following section of the students' social studies textbook on a transparency, invites a volunteer to read it aloud, and then proceeds to model strategy use:

> *Differences among Americans help make the United States strong. Sometimes, however, differences come between people. In the mid-1800s differences became disagree-*

Teaching Chart 2: WORD-PART CLUES

1. Look for the ROOT WORD, which is a single word that cannot be broken into smaller words or word parts. See if you know what the root word means.
2. Look for a PREFIX, which is a word part added to the beginning of a word that changes its meaning. See if you know what the prefix means.
3. Look for a SUFFIX, which is a word part added to the end of a word that changes its meaning. See if you know what the suffix means.
4. Put the meanings of the ROOT WORD and any PREFIX or SUFFIX together and see if you can build the meaning of the word.

ments between Americans living in two regions—the North and the South. (Boehm et al., 2000, p. 129)

Let's say that you are reading and come to the word *disagreements*, and you are not sure what it means. You can try to figure out its meaning using the strategy in Chart 2. Step 1 says to look for the root word, which, I think, is *agree*, and which means to share the same view or opinion of something with another person. Step 2 says to look for a prefix. I see the prefix *dis-*, which means not or opposite. Step 3 says to look for a suffix, and I see *-ments*, which means the state or quality of something. Step 4 says to put the word parts together. If *dis-* means not and *agree* means to have the same view, then to *disagree* means to have a different or opposite opinion. If we add *-ments*, then *disagreements* means the state of having a different or opposite opinion.

Mr. Lopez explains that there are many prefixes and suffixes and that one way to think about and learn them is to group them together into families, noting that just as families of people have things in common, families of prefixes and suffixes have meanings in common.

We'll begin by looking at the Not Prefix Family, of which *dis-* is one member. The top part of Chart 3 [displaying the chart] **presents the Not Prefix Family, which has seven members: *dis-*, *un-*, *in-*, *im-*, *il-*, *ir-*, and *non-*. Next is the meaning of each prefix. As you can see, all of these prefixes are grouped into the Not Prefix Family because they share the common meaning of "not." Let's look at some example words. For instance, *dislike* means to not like, *impolite* means the opposite of *polite*, and so forth.**

You may also see that some of the later example words get a little harder. Does anyone know what *inedible* means? [Student responds, "not edible."] **Good; it means not edible, but you have to know what *edible* means. Does anyone know?** [Student responds.] **Yes, *edible* means something that is fit to eat or eatable.** [If no student knows the meaning, Mr. Lopez could provide it, or a student could consult a dictionary or thesaurus.] **Therefore, *inedible* means something that is not fit to eat. For example, you could say that *Because the potato salad was left out of the refrigerator all night, it spoiled and was inedible*.**

Guided Practice. Mr. Lopez now has the students begin to use the word-part strategy themselves but still under his supervision, so he can support, correct, or extend their application of it. Students also support one another through dialogue. He has them turn to and read the following section of their social studies book and continues with the lesson:

Teaching Chart 3: PREFIX AND SUFFIX FAMILIES

Family	Prefix or Suffix	Meaning	Example Words
"Not" Prefix Family	dis-	not, opposite	dislike, disloyal, disentangle, disparity, disrepute
	un-	not, opposite	unafraid, unhappy, undefeated, unsympathetic
	in-	not, opposite	invisible, incurable, inappropriate, inedible, infallible
	im-	not, opposite	imperfect, impolite, imprecise, immobile, immortal
	il-	not, opposite	illogical, illegal, illiterate, illegible, illimitable
	ir-	not, opposite	irresponsible, irreplaceable, irrestible, irreleveant
	non-	not, opposite	nonfiction, nonstop, nonliving, nonviolent, nonverbal
"Position" Prefix Family	pre-	before	preview, predawn, prehistoric, prepublication
	fore-	before	forewarn, foreleg, forenoon, forethought, foreshadow
	mid-	middle	midnight, midair, midland, midlife, midterm
	inter-	between, among	intercity, intermix, interaction, international, intergalactic
	post-	after	postwar, posttest, postdate, postoperative
"Over/ Under" Prefix Family	super-	over, high, big, extreme	superheat, superhuman, superdeluxe, supercompetitive
	over-	more than, too much	oversleep, overload, overheat, overqualified, overexert
	sub-	more than, too much	subset, substation, subcontinent, subtropical
"Together Prefix Family"	com-	together with	compress, composition, compatriot, compassion
	con-	together	conform, concentric, conjoin, configure
	co-	together with	coauthor, cosign, coequal, cooperative
"Bad" Prefix Family	mis-	bad, wrong, not	misuse, misread, misunderstand, mismanage, misquote
	mal-	bad, ill	malpractice, malodor, malnourished, maladjusted

(continued on next page)

Teaching Chart 3: PREFIX AND SUFFIX FAMILIES

Family	Prefix or Suffix	Meaning	Example Words
"Against Prefix Family"	anti-	against	antifreeze, antibiotic, antisocial, antipollutiona
	contra-	against, opposite	contraband, contradict, contraindicate, contravene
"Number" Prefix Family	uni-	one	unicycle, unicorn, unidirectional, unicellular
	mono-	one	monorail, monosyllable, monogram, monotone, monocle
	bi-	two	bicycle, biweekly, bicolor, biplane, bnomial
	tri-	three	triangle, tricycle, tricolor, triathlon, tripod
	quad-	four	quadrilateral, quadruplets, quadrennial, quadrangle
	penta-	five	pentagon, pentameter, pentagram, pentathlon
	dec-	ten	decagon, decade, decapod, decibel
	cent-	hundred	centimeter, centipede, centennial, centigram
	semi-	half, part	semicircle, semiyearly, semiprivate, semiretired
Other Useful Prefixes	re-	again, back	redo, reorder, rearrange, reposition, reconnect
	trans-	across, through	transport, transatlantic, transmit, transfusion
	de-	take away	defrost, deforest, deodorize, deflate, deactivate
	ex-	out of, away from	export, exhale, extinguish, exclude, excise
	under-	low, to little	underweight, underachieve, underestimate, underappreciated
"Person" Suffix Family	-ee	person who	employee, referee, trainee, interviewee
	-er	person/thing that does something	writer, teacher, composer, reporter, consumer
	-or	person/thing that does something	actor, governor, dictator, juror, donor
Other Useful Suffixes	-ful	full of, characterized by	joyful, beautiful, successful, delightful, pitiful
	-Able -ible	can be, worthy of, inclined to	valuable, comfortable, dependable, impressionable, terrible, responsible, reversible, compatible
	-less	without, free of	helpless, hopeless, bottomless, expressionless

For most Africans, however, life was very hard no matter where they lived. They were unwelcome in many places and often were treated unfairly. State laws in both the North and South gave them little freedom. (Boehm et al., 2000, p. 141)

Do you see any words that have prefixes from the Not Family? [Students respond.] **Yes, *unwelcome* and *unfairly* contain the prefix *un-*. So what do these words mean?** [Students respond "not welcome" and "not fairly."] **Could someone reread the sentences and substitute "not welcome" for *unwelcome* and "not fairly" for *unfairly*? Do the sentences still make sense?** [Students respond.]

Practice using word-part clues by completing this paper. [He distributes the Work Paper.] **Let's do the first one together. In the first row, you must break the word into the Not Prefix and the root word. Where would you break *unafraid*?** [Student responds.] **Yes, *unafraid* can be broken into *un-* and *afraid*. Next write what the root means. What does afraid mean?** [Student responds *scared*, and students writes that.] **Finally, what does the whole word *unafraid* mean?** [Student responds and students write *not scared* or *brave*.] **Good. Now complete the rest of the paper by working with a partner. You may use a dictionary or thesaurus to help you figure out the meanings of root words you may not know.**

When students have finished, Mr. Lopez does a group-check of their work, and he provides reinforcement and reteaching as necessary to guide students in their use of the word-part strategy.

Independent Practice.   As a final portion of the lesson, Mr. Lopez has students apply the strategy on their own. He accomplishes this by having the students read the next section in the textbook, identify words that contain Not Prefixes, and write down the words and their meanings. The next day, students share their lists, Mr. Lopez reviews the Word-Part Clues strategy, and students explain the meanings of words they included on their lists.

As part of this discussion, Mr. Lopez notes that there are exceptions to the word-part strategy. For example, he draws attention to *understand* and *imaginary*, which are from page 142 of the social studies textbook. He has

Work Paper: "Not" Prefix Family Practice

Break the Word	Root Means	Full Word Means
un/afraid	scared	Not scared, brave
imperfect		
illiterate		
disunite		
irreparable		

students evaluate whether these words actually include the prefixes *un-* and *im-* and can be figured out according to the word-part strategy. He uses these "nonexamples" as an opportunity to point out that not all words that begin with *dis-, un-, in-, im-, il-, ir-,* and *non-* are necessarily prefixes, displaying and discussing *uncle, imagination,* and *iron* to demonstrate that readers must be careful when using the word-part strategy. He also asks students to volunteer other nonexamples that they know. Finally, Mr. Lopez introduces and teaches the additional prefix and suffix families on Teaching Chart 3 in subsequent lessons, providing students cumulative practice on the application of the word-part strategy as each new family is introduced.

Sample Lesson 3: Teaching Contextual Analysis

Background. Ms. Lee teaches science on an elementary school fifth-grade team. Following a recent staff development series on the importance of vocabulary teaching and learning, Ms. Lee and her colleagues have decided to emphasize vocabulary strategies in their reading/language arts and subject-matter classes. Ms. Lee incorporates young adult trade books into her science lessons, which are grounded on the adopted science textbook. She has created a series of vocabulary lessons to integrate into an upcoming science unit on life cycles and ecosystems. To extend the science unit topics such as food chains, biomes, and animal behavior, her class will read Jean Craighead George's *Julie's Wolf Pack* (1997), the 6-year story of an Alaskan wolf named Kapu and his pack. This lesson on contextual analysis follows an introductory lesson like that taught by Ms. Jackson and several word-part lessons like the preceding one by Mr. Lopez. Ms. Lee's lesson adheres to the same instructional framework (Duke & Pearson, 2002; Pearson & Gallagher, 1983) as Sample Lessons 1 and 2. She also assumes that her students possess general knowledge of context clues, but she is prepared to review and reteach these basic concepts if necessary.

Verbal Explanation. Ms. Lee begins her explanation of the use of context clues by embedding it within the overall vocabulary strategy presented in prior lessons:

> **We have been learning about The Vocabulary Rule.** [She calls students' attention to Chart 1, rereads the three steps, and reviews each.] **Let's focus today on Steps 1 and 3, which involve context clues. *Context clues* are words or phrases that give readers clues or ideas to the meanings of other words. For example, look at this sentence.** [Ms. Lee writes the following (from Baumann et al., 2002) on the board.]*When the sun hit its zenith, which means right overhead, I could tell it was noon by the tremendous heat.*
>
> **Can anyone tell me what the word *zenith* in the sentence means?** [Student responds "right overhead."] **Yes, it says right in the sentence that zenith means right overhead. Sometimes context clues are very strong and give readers a**

clear idea of what a word means, as in this example. Sometimes, however, context clues are not so obvious, and readers must think hard to use them. Still other times there may be no context clues for hard words, or there might even be ideas that confuse you regarding a word's meaning. Even though context clues may differ in strength, they are important to learn about, for they are useful tools to add to your Reading Strategy Toolbox to help you figure out word meanings and understand selections you read.

Modeling.   Next, Ms. Lee presents an excerpt from the science textbook on a transparency. She invites a student to read it aloud and then proceeds to model the use of context clues.

A single organization in an environment is called an individual. One grasshopper in a field is an individual. (Frank et al., 2002, p. B28)

I'm looking at the word *individual* and trying to figure out what it means. I see that the author writes, "A single organization in an environment is called an individual," so I guess that *individual* refers to or means just one living thing. This seems to be supported by the second sentence that says that "One grasshopper in a field is an individual." These seem to be pretty good context clues. Could anyone look up *individual* in the dictionary? [Student finds "a single organism as distinguished from a group" (Merriam-Webster, 2002, p. 592).] All right; it seems as though our guess from the use of context was a good one.

Ms. Lee then presents Chart 4, which tells about different kinds of context clues, and continues with her instruction and modeling.

Could someone read number 1 on Chart 4? [Student reads the Definition entry.] See how *brambles* is defined as "prickly vines and shrubs" just like *individual* was defined as "a single organism in an environment." So one type of context clue is Definition, in which an author explains the meaning of a word right in the sentences.

Let's look at the other context clue types. [Ms. Lee has students read the remaining four types in Chart 4 and briefly discusses each.] Does anyone see another context clue type for *individual*? [She refers students back to the transparency, and one student responds that there might be an Example context clue.] Yes, the second sentence, "One grasshopper in a field is an individual," gives an example of an individual, in this case one individual grasshopper. So sometimes there might be more than one kind of context clue to help you out.

Guided Practice.   In the third part of the instructional framework, Ms. Lee invites students to use the context clue types to infer word meanings,

Teaching Chart 4: CONTEXT CLUES

Context Clue Type	Example
1. **Definition**: the author explains the meaning of the word right in the sentence or selection.	When Sara was hiking, she accidentally walked through a patch of **brambles**, *prickly vines and shrubs*, which resulted in many scratches to her legs.
2. **Synonym**: the author uses a word similar in meaning.	Josh walked into the living room and accidentally tripped over the **ottoman**. He then mumbled "I wish people would not leave the *footstool* right in the middle of the room. That's dangerous!"
3. **Antonym**: the author uses a word nearly opposite in meaning.	The supermarket manager complained, "Why do we have such a **plethora** of boxes of cereal on the shelves? In contrast, we have a real *shortage* of pancake and waffle mix. We've got to do a better job ordering."
4. **Example**: the author provides one or more example words or ideas.	There are many members of the **canine** family. For example, *wolves, foxes, coyotes*, and pets such as *collies, beagles*, and *golden retrievers* are all canines.
5. **General**: the author provides several words or statements that give clues to the word's meaning.	It was a **sultry** day. The day was very *hot and humid*. If you moved at all, you would *break out in a sweat*. It was one of those days to *drink water* and *stay in the shade*.

Note: Words in italic provide context clues for bold words.

calling students' attention to another textbook excerpt she has presented on a transparency:

> *Individuals of the same kind living in the same environment make up a population. All the grasshoppers in a field are the grasshopper population. (Frank et al., 2002, p. B28).*

Look at the word *population* and see if you can find a context clue for it? [Student responds that there is a Definition clue.] **Yes, *population* is defined as "individuals of the same kind living in the same environment." Does anyone see another type of context clue?** [Student responds that there is an Example context clue in the second sentence.] **Yes, the author has given you Definition and Example context clues for *population*, just as the author had done for *individual*.**

Now try to find and use context clues for the words *instinct* and *learned behaviors*, which also come from your science textbook. [Ms. Lee displays the following transparency and distributes paper copies to the students.] **On your paper copy, underline Definition and Example context clues that help you understand each word's meaning.**

- *Some behaviors are inherited and some are learned. An instinct is a behavior that an organism inherits. An instinct isn't unique to an individual. Instead, it is a behavior shared by an entire population, or by all the males or all the females of a population. Herding aphids, for example, is an instinct for certain populations of ants. (Frank et al., 2002, p. B46)*
- *Many animals show learned behaviors, which are behaviors they have learned from their parents, not inherited from them. Lions, for example, are born with the instinct to kill and eat other animals. To survive, however, young lions must learn hunting skills from adult lions. Both the instinct to hunt and the learned behavior, skillful hunting, help the lion survive. (Frank et al., 2002, p. B46)*

Ms. Lee guides the students in their application of Definition and Example context clues to infer the meanings of *instinct* and *learned behaviors*. She provides support and reteaching as necessary. She also notes that sometimes authors use commas to set off definitions, as in *learned behaviors*, and she makes a mental note to bring up the idea of Definition context clues and the linguistic device of appositive later during their writing workshop.

Independent Practice.   In her afternoon language arts period, Ms. Lee provides students an opportunity to practice the context clue strategy. She introduces *Julie's Wolf Pack* (George, 1997), the story of a wolf pack in the Alaskan arctic. This book connects nicely with the science unit, for it includes concepts such as food chains and the instinctual and learned behaviors of animals. Ms. Lee has students read the first section of *Julie's Wolf Pack*, which is titled "Kapu, The Alpha." She writes *alpha* and *beta* on the board and asks students to use what they learned about context clues in the morning's science lesson to see if they can figure what each word means (e.g., *beta* is in the context, "... Zing—the beta, or second in command—enjoyed the joke even more than Kapu...."; George, 1997, p. 4). She asks students to be prepared to discuss whether they found context clues in the book to help them figure out the meanings of *alpha* and *beta*. Ms. Lee plans additional lessons for teaching the other context clues types in conjunction with the science content and their reading of *Julie's Wolf Pack*.

Sample Lesson 4: Integrating the Use of Word-Part and Context Clues

Background.   Mr. Olson is a fifth-grade language arts teacher. He employs various instructional structures in his language arts classes, one of which is literature circles (Daniels, 2002). Mr. Olson has identified seven realistic fiction and humorous titles from which the students will select books for the next round of literature circles. He plans to conduct brief book talks and to allow the students to browse and preview the titles before they select books to read and form circles.

Similar to the other teachers described in the preceding sample lessons, Mr. Olson has chosen to focus on vocabulary-learning strategies this academic year. Previously, he completed lessons on word-part and context clues parallel to Sample Lessons 1–3. To extend this instruction, Mr. Olson wishes to emphasize how students can integrate the use of word-part and context clues as strategies for inferring or deriving word meanings. As a complement to the book talks he will do, Mr. Olson has prepared the following lesson.

Verbal Explanation.   Mr. Olson begins by reviewing with students the content of the prior lessons on the use of word-part and context clues, emphasizing how the two sources of information can be used together to try to determine the meanings of words:

> **You have learned about The Vocabulary Rule** [pointing to Chart 1]. **This includes three steps.** [He reads and reviews how each step functions.] **We have also learned how to use word-part clues and context clues** [pointing to Charts 2 and 3, respectively] **to help you figure out the meanings of new or hard words.** [He reads and reviews briefly the information on these charts.]

> **As we prepare today for our next set of literature circles, let's use these strategies for figuring out word meanings. All of you will take on the role of word finder as one of your literature circle activities. You will identify new and interesting vocabulary in the books you choose to read. We will review how The Vocabulary Rule works, looking especially hard at how to combine the use of context clues and any word-part clues to determine word meanings. This should help you figure out the meanings of interesting words you come across as you read the books you select.**

Modeling.   Mr. Olson models how to combine context clue and word-part information to determine word meanings, using one of the titles available to students for the literature circles:

> **One of the books you might choose to read is** *The Music of Dolphins* **by Karen Hesse (1996). It's a story of how a young girl, Mila, raised by dolphins, learns what it is like to live with humans. Here's how the story begins when Mila is swimming with dolphins** [excerpt presented on a transparency].

> *I swim out to them on the murmuring sea. As I reach them, their circle opens to let me in, then re-forms. The dolphins rise and blow, floating, one eye open, the other shut in half sleep. (Hesse, 1996, p.1)*

> **Let's use The Vocabulary Rule to see if we can figure out what the word** *re-forms* **means. Step 1 says to look for context clues. Are there any available?** [Student says that "their circle opens to let me in" provides the idea that the circle opens and then closes back up.] **All right; we get the idea**

that there's this circle of dolphins, which opens up to let Mila in and then closes up.

What about word-part clues, Step 2? [Student responds that *re-forms* has the root word *forms* and the prefix *re-*.] Yes. Does anyone know what the root word *form* or *forms* means, especially when it is showing action and is a verb as it is in this part of the story? [Student responds that it means to make or take shape as when the P.E. teacher says, "Class, form a big circle."] Good. Now what about *re-*? What does it mean? [Student responds that it's on Chart 3 and means again or back.] Now put the word parts together. [Student responds that *re-forms* might mean to form back, to form again, or to make the shape of a circle again.]

Step 3 says to check the context again. Do the meanings for *re-form* you suggested make sense? [Students affirm that they do.] Yes, we get the idea that the dolphins are in a circle, which they open to let Mila in, and then they make the circle again, or *re-form* it, to enclose her in it.

Guided Practice.   Using the same text excerpt, Mr. Olson invites students to participate more in the application of The Vocabulary Rule. He also focuses on the flexible use of the strategy as well as its limits:

Please examine the word *murmuring* in this same section. Can we use The Vocabulary Rule to help us figure out the meaning of it? [Mr. Olson guides students as they work through the rule, recognizing that there are not very strong context clues and no prefixes or suffixes that help identify its meaning.] Here's a situation in which The Vocabulary Rule may not work very well. Does anyone have any guesses as to what *murmuring* means? [Students suggest words such as *calm*, *wavy*, *dark green*, and *bubbling*.] Those are good ideas, for all are adjectives that could describe how the sea might look or act.

Does anyone know what the word *murmur* means? Could someone look in the dictionary? [Student looks up *murmur* and reads, "a low indistinct but often continuous sound" and "a soft or gentle utterance" (Merriam-Webster, 2002, p. 764).] Hmm. So it seems like *murmur* has to do with a sound, maybe a low, soft, and continuous sound. Would this make sense in the sentence *I swim out to them on the murmuring sea*? [Student responds that waves and water make sounds and that a writer might describe the sound of the sea as being low and continuous.]

Here's an example of where there are no prefixes or suffixes and the context clues only tell you that the word describes the sea. This is a good lesson when it comes to using context clues. Sometimes context clues are not strong, and in those cases, the best you can do is to make a general guess as to what a word means and read on to see if there might be more clues to come. If you are really curious about a word's meaning or you think that

the word is important to understanding a selection, then you might check a dictionary or thesaurus, ask a friend, or ask me.

Independent Practice.   Mr. Olson proceeds to conduct book talks on the additional books he has identified for possible literature circles. Following the book talks, he invites students to practice The Vocabulary Rule by using context and word-part clues (when applicable) to identify the meanings of *incapable* in *The Watsons Go to Birmingham—1963* (Curtis, 1995, p. 24), *flailed* in *Bad Girls* (Voigt, 1996, p. 35), *inexhaustible* in *Knots in My Yo-yo String* (Spinelli, 1998, p. 11), *sensitivity* in *Later, Gator* (Yep, 1995, p. 63), *peevish* in *Cousins* (Hamilton, 1990, p. 73), and *improvise* in *Yellow Bird and Me* (Hansen, 1986, p. 31).

In subsequent vocabulary lessons, Mr. Olson reinforces the process of analyzing affixed words into meaningful parts, referring to Charts 2 and 3, and the process of identifying different types of and combinations of context clues. He invites students to examine larger text segments as necessary to identify context clues that appear prior to and after an unfamiliar word. He also reiterates the notion that context clues vary in power, and he reminds the students that some words may have misleading or "pseudo" prefixes. After literature circles have been formed and initiated, Mr. Olson provides review of word-part and context clues as needed, while having students assume more responsibility for identifying and applying The Vocabulary Rule.

CONCLUSION

We conclude this presentation with the acknowledgment of several important qualifications of and extensions to the ideas we present. First, one must keep in mind that there are other components to a comprehensive vocabulary instructional program beyond teaching the word-learning strategies of word-part and contextual analysis. For instance, if it were one's goal to teach specific words in order to enhance comprehension of a given text, then word-part and contextual analysis are not efficient strategies; instead, one should teach those words directly (Beck, McKeown, & Kucan, 2002; Stahl & Fairbanks, 1986). It is important, therefore, to recognize that different instructional goals require different teaching strategies, and a total vocabulary program ought to encompass multiple objectives and pedagogical perspectives (Baumann, Kame'enui, & Ash, 2003). We believe that Graves's (2000) four components—engaging in wide reading, teaching individual words, teaching word-learning strategies, and fostering word consciousness—provide a useful framework for crafting a balanced, multifaceted vocabulary instructional program.

Second, the instructional content we present would need to be expanded across time. For example, subsequent word-part instruction should move beyond simple root words (i.e., free morphemes), prefixes, and suffixes to include Latin and Greek word roots (e.g., *vis*, *vid*, light, to see, as in *video*, *television*, *visible*, *preview*, *evidence*, etc.). Templeton's (2004) suggestions for promoting the "vocabulary–spelling connection" provide important ways to extend vocabulary instruction to more complex morphemic associations. Similarly, we refer readers to other excellent sources that address the limits to and place of instruction in context clues (Beck et al., 2002, chapter 6) and provide additional instructional strategies (e.g., Blachowicz & Fisher, 2002, chapter 2; Durkin, 1981, chapter 2; Johnson & Pearson, 1978, chapter 6).

Third, it is important to emphasize that, in practice, it would take more than four lessons to teach the various context clue types and word-part elements in depth. Graves (2000), for example, suggests spending 2 to 4 hours a week during initial instruction in word-learning strategies, with decreasing time weekly later on. Effective instruction in word-part and context clues should be efficient but long-term (Graves, 2000), so that students can internalize the strategies and receive the support required to apply them across multiple contexts over time. On the other hand, it is important to keep word-part and context clue instruction "in its place," that is, not dedicating inordinate amounts of time to such lessons. We believe that the majority of language arts time should be spent on literature discussion and appreciation, and likewise most content lessons should involve subject matter inquiry and study.

Finally, we emphasize that the sample lessons are just that—exemplars from which teachers might develop their own lessons that match their students' needs and their own instructional goals. Effective vocabulary instruction is highly context-dependent. In other words, it is determined by a teacher's judgment about her or his students' knowledge, skills, and needs; by the nature of the specific reading, language arts, and subject-matter curriculum; and by a teacher's unique teaching style. Thus, there is no one-size-fits-all set of lessons that can be constructed and implemented across countless teaching and learning situations. Quality vocabulary instruction occurs ultimately when teachers who are knowledgeable in literacy processes, curriculum content and goals, and sound reading and language arts pedagogy craft their own vocabulary lessons that accommodate their students' unique learning needs.

ACKNOWLEDGMENT

The research on which this chapter is based was supported by a Field-Initiated Study (PR/AWARD NUMBER R305T990271) administered by the National Institute for Student Achievement, Curriculum and Assessment, of the

Office of Educational Research and Improvement within the U.S. Department of Education. The research and practice suggestions expressed herein do not necessarily reflect the position or policies of the National Institute for Student Achievement, Curriculum and Assessment, the Office of Educational Research and Improvement, or the U.S. Department of Education.

REFERENCES

Anderson, R. C., & Freebody, P. (1981). Vocabulary knowledge. In J. T. Guthrie (Ed.), *Comprehension and teaching: Research reviews* (pp. 77–117). Newark, DE: International Reading Association.

Askov, E. N., & Kamm, K. (1976). Context clues: Should we teach children to use a classification system in reading? *Journal of Educational Research, 69,* 341–344.

Baumann, J. F., Edwards, E. C., Boland, E., Olejnik, S., & Kame'enui, E. W. (2003). Vocabulary tricks: Effects of instruction in morphology and context on fifth-grade students' ability to derive and infer word meanings. *American Educational Research Journal, 40,* 447–494.

Baumann, J. F., Edwards, E. C., Font, G., Tereshinski, C. A., Kame'enui, E. J., & Olejnik, S. (2002). Teaching morphemic and contextual analysis to fifth-grade students. *Reading Research Quarterly, 37,* 150–176.

Baumann, J. F., Kame'enui, E. J., & Ash, G. (2003). Research on vocabulary instruction: Voltaire redux. In J. Flood, D. Lapp, J. R. Squire ,&, J. Jensen (Eds.), *Handbook of research on teaching the English Language Arts* (2nd ed., pp. 752–785). Mahwah, NJ: Lawrence Erlbaum Associates.

Bear, D. R., Invernizzi, M., Templeton, S., & Johnston, F. (1996). *Words their way: Word study for phonics, vocabulary, and spelling instruction.* Upper Saddle River, NJ: Merrill.

Beck, I. L., & McKeown, M. G. (1991). Conditions of vocabulary acquisition. In R. Barr, M. Kamil, P. Mosenthal, & P. D. Pearson (Eds.), *Handbook of reading research* (Vol. III, pp. 789–814). New York: Longman.

Beck, I. L., McKeown, M. G., & Kucan, L. (2002). *Bring words to life: Robust vocabulary instruction.* New York: Guilford.

Blachowicz, C. L. Z. (1993). C2QU: Modeling context use in the classroom. *The Reading Teacher, 47,* 268–269.

Blachowicz, C., & Fisher, P. (1996). *Teaching vocabulary in all classrooms.* Englewood Cliffs, NJ: Merrill.

Blachowicz, C. L. Z., & Fisher, P. (2000). Vocabulary instruction. In M. L. Kamil, P. B. Mosenthal, P. D. Pearson, & R. Barr (Eds.), *Handbook of reading research* (Vol. III, pp. 503–523). Mahwah, NJ: Lawrence Erlbaum Associates.

Blachowicz, C. L. Z., & Fisher, P. (2002). *Teaching vocabulary in all classrooms* (2nd ed.). Englewood Cliffs, NJ: Merrill/Prentice Hall.

Boehm, R. G., Hoone, C., McGowan, T. M., McKinney-Browning, M. C., Miramontes, O. B., & Porter, P. H. (2000). *United States in modern times.* Orlando: Harcourt Brace.

Buikema, J. L., & Graves, M. F. (1993). Teaching students to use context cues to infer word meanings. *Journal of Reading, 36,* 450–457.

Cunningham, A. E., & Stanovich, K. E. (1997). Early reading acquisition and its relation to reading experience and ability 10 years later. *Developmental Psychology, 33,* 934–945.

Curtis, C. P. (1995). *The Watsons go to Birmingham—1963.* New York: Delacorte.

Dale, E., & O'Rourke, J. (1986). *Vocabulary building: A process approach*. Columbus, OH: Zaner-Bloser.

Daniels, H. (2002). *Literature circles: Voice and choice in book clubs and reading programs* (2nd ed.). Portland, ME: Stenhouse.

Duke, N. K., & Pearson, P. D. (2002). Effective practices for developing reading comprehension. In A. E. Farstrup & S. J. Samuels (Eds.), *What research has to say about reading instruction* (2nd ed., pp. 205–242). Newark, DE: International Reading Association.

Durkin, D. D. (1981). *Strategies for identifying words: A workbook for teachers and those preparing to teach* (2nd ed.). Boston: Allyn & Bacon.

Edwards, E. C., Font, G., Baumann, J. F., & Boland, E. (2004). Unlocking word meanings: Strategies and guidelines for teaching morphemic and contextual analysis. In J. F. Baumann & E. J. Kame'enui (Eds.), *Vocabulary instruction: Research to practice* (pp. 159–176). New York: Guilford.

Frank, M. S., Jones, R. M., Krockover, G. H., Lang, M. P., McLeod, J. C., Valenta, C. J., & Van Deman, B. A. (2002). *Harcourt science* (Grade 5). Orlando: Harcourt.

Fukkink, R. G., & de Glopper, K. (1998). Effects of instruction in deriving word meaning from context: A meta-analysis. *Review of Educational Research, 68,* 450–469.

George, J. C. (1997). *Julie's wolf pack*. New York: Scholastic.

Graves, M. F. (2000). A vocabulary program to complement and bolster a middle-grade comprehension program. In B. M. Taylor, M. F. Graves, & P. van den Broek (Eds.), *Reading for meaning: Fostering comprehension in the middle grades* (pp. 116–135). Newark, DE: International Reading Association.

Graves, M. F. (2004). Teaching prefixes: As good as it gets? In J. F. Baumann & E. J. Kame'enui, E. J. (Eds.). *Vocabulary instruction: Research to practice* (pp. 81–99). New York: Guilford.

Graves, M. F., & Hammond, H. K. (1980). A validated procedure for teaching prefixes and its effect on students' ability to assign meaning to novel words. In M. L. Kamil & A. J. Moe (Eds.), *Perspectives on reading research and instruction* (pp. 184–188). Washington, DC: National Reading Conference.

Graves, M. F., & Watts-Taffe, S. M. (2002). The place of word consciousness in a research-based vocabulary program. In S. J. Samuels & A. E. Farstrup (Eds.), *What research has to say about reading instruction* (3rd ed., pp. 140–165). Newark, DE: International Reading Association.

Hafner, L. E. (1965). A one-month experiment in teaching context aids in fifth grade. *Journal of Educational Research, 58,* 471–474.

Hamilton, V. (1990). *Cousins*. New York: Scholastic.

Hansen, J. (1986). *Yellow Bird and me*. New York: Clarion.

Hesse, K. (1996). *The music of the dolphins*. New York: Scholastic.

Jenkins, J. R., Matlock, B., & Slocum, T. A. (1989). Approaches to vocabulary instruction: The teaching of individual word meanings and practice in deriving word meaning from context. *Reading Research Quarterly, 24,* 215–235.

Johnson, D. D. (2001). *Vocabulary in the elementary and middle school*. Needham Heights, MA: Allyn & Bacon.

Johnson, D. D., & Pearson, P. D. (1978). *Teaching reading vocabulary*. New York: Holt, Rinehart & Winston.

McKissack, P. C. (1997). *Run away home*. New York: Scholastic.

McMahon, S. I., Raphael, T. E., Goatley, V. J., & Pardo, L. S. (1997). *The book club connection: Literacy learning and classroom talk*. New York: Teachers College Press.

Merriam-Webster's collegiate dictionary (10th ed.). (2002). Springfield, MA: Merriam-Webster.

Nagy, W. E. (1988). *Teaching vocabulary to improve reading comprehension*. Newark, DE: International Reading Association.

Nagy, W. E., & Anderson, R. C. (1984). How many words are there in printed school English? *Reading Research Quarterly, 19*, 303–330.

Nagy, W., Anderson, R. C., Schommer, M., Scott, J. A., & Stallman, A. C. (1989). Morphological families in the internal lexicon. *Reading Research Quarterly, 24*, 263–282.

National Reading Panel. (2000). *National Reading Panel: Teaching children to read: An evidence-based assessment of the scientific research literature on reading and its implications for reading instruction* (NIH Publication No. 00-4754). Washington, DC: National Institute of Health and National Institute of Child Health and Human Development.

Otterman, L. M. (1955). The value of teaching prefixes and word-roots. *Journal of Educational Research, 48*, 611–616.

Pearson, P. D., & Fielding, L. (1991). Comprehension instruction. In R. Barr, M. L. Kamil, P. Mosenthal, & P. D. Pearson (Eds.), *Handbook of reading research* (Vol. II, pp. 814–860). New York: Longman.

Pearson, P. D., & Gallagher, M. (1983). The instruction of reading comprehension. *Contemporary Educational Psychology, 8*, 317–345.

Scott, J. A., & Nagy, W. E. (2004).Developing word consciousness. In J. F. Baumann & E. J. Kame'enui, E. J. (Eds.), *Vocabulary instruction: Research to practice* (pp. 201–217). New York: Guilford.

Spinelli, J. (1998). *Knots in my yo-yo string*. New York: Knopf.

Stahl, S. A., & Fairbanks, M. M. (1986). The effects of vocabulary instruction: A model-based meta-analysis. *Review of Educational Research, 56*, 72–110.

Sternberg, R., & Powell, J. S. (1983). Comprehending verbal discourse. *American Psychologist, 38*, 878–893.

Swanborn, M. S. L., & de Glopper, K. (1999). Incidental word learning while reading: A meta-analysis. *Review of Educational Research, 69*, 261–285.

Templeton, S. (2004). The vocabulary–spelling connection: Orthographic development and morphological knowledge at the intermediate grades and beyond. In J. F. Baumann & E. J. Kame'enui, E. J. (Eds.), *Vocabulary instruction: Research to practice* (pp. 118–138). New York: Guilford.

Thompson, E. (1958). The "master word" approach to vocabulary training. *Journal of Developmental Reading, 2*, 62–66.

Voigt, C. (1996). *Bad girls*. New York: Scholastic.

White, T. G., Sowell, J., & Yanagihara, A. (1989). Teaching elementary students to use word-part clues. *The Reading Teacher, 42*, 302–308.

Wysocki, K., & Jenkins, J. R. (1987). Deriving word meanings through morphological generalization. *Reading Research Quarterly, 22*, 66–81.

Yep, L. (1995). *Later, gator*. New York: Hyperion.

PART III

PERSPECTIVES ON WHICH WORDS TO CHOOSE FOR INSTRUCTION

Chapter 10

Choosing Words to Teach[1]

Isabel L. Beck
Margaret G. McKeown
University of Pittsburgh

Linda Kucan
Appalachian State University

The teacher's edition for a fourth-grade anthology suggests teaching the following words before inviting students to read an excerpt from *Charlotte's Web* (White, 1952): *comfort, cunning, endure, friendless, frolic, lonely, soaked,* and *stealthily.* Why do you think these words were selected? One obvious reason for selecting words to teach is that students do not know the words. Although *cunning, endure, frolic,* and *stealthily* are probably unfamiliar to most fourth graders, *comfort, friendless, lonely,* and *soaked* are probably not. Familiarity does not seem to be the principle used to make the selection. What about importance or usefulness? Are the selected words useful for writing or talking? Would the words be important to know because they appear in other texts with a high degree of frequency? Some—but not all—of the words might be considered useful or important. Thus, the question remains: why were the words selected? The pur-

---

[1]At the Focus on Vocabulary Forum in Dallas in October 2003, Isabel Beck reported on a vocabulary study that she and her colleague Margaret McKeown had conducted in kindergarten and first-grade classrooms. Results of the study showed these very young children could learn, and relished learning, very sophisticated words, words that are not typically part of young children's language experiences. Drs. Beck and McKeown are presently writing a journal article about the findings of that study. (*continued*)

pose of this chapter is to consider what principles might be used for selecting words to teach.

USEFUL WORDS

As a way to begin thinking about which words to teach, consider that words in the language have different levels of utility. In this regard, we have found our notion of tiers to be one helpful lens through which to consider words for instructional attention. Tier One consists of the most basic words—*clock, baby, happy*—rarely requiring instruction in school. Tier Three includes words whose frequency of use is quite low, often being limited to specific domains—*isotope, lathe, peninsula*—and probably best learned when needed in a content area. Tier Two words are high-frequency words for mature language users—*coincidence, absurd, industrious*—and, thus, instruction in these words can add productively to an individual's language ability.

IDENTIFYING TIER TWO WORDS IN TEXTS

To get an idea of the process of identifying Tier Two words, consider an example. Below is the opening paragraph of a retelling of an old tale (Kohnke, 2001, p. 12) about a donkey who is under a magical spell that forces him to do the chores for a group of lazy servants. The story would likely be of interest to third and fourth graders:

> *Johnny Harrington was a kind master who treated his servants fairly. He was also a successful wool merchant, and his business required that he travel often. In his absence, his servants would tend to the fields and cattle and maintain the upkeep of his mansion. They performed their duties happily, for they felt fortunate to have such a benevolent and trusting master.*

The underlined words are those we identified as consistent with the notion of Tier Two words. That is, most of the words are likely to appear frequently in a wide variety of texts and in the written and oral language of mature language users. (Note: We chose this paragraph because there were

(*continued*)   This chapter, "Choosing Words to Teach," is from Isabel L. Beck, Margaret G. McKeown, and Linda Kucan's *Bringing Words to Life: Robust Vocabulary Instruction* (2002), reprinted with permission of The Guilford Press: New York. The chapter is relevant to discussions at the Focus on Vocabulary Forum about choosing words to teach and the value of teaching sophisticated words.

so many candidate Tier Two words; however, most grade-level material would not have so many words in only one paragraph.)

One "test" of whether a word meets the Tier Two criterion of being a useful addition to students' repertoires is to think about whether the students already have ways to express the concepts represented by the words. Would students be able to explain these words using words that are already well known to them? If that is the case, it suggests that the new words offer students more precise or mature ways of referring to ideas they already know about. One way to answer the question is to think about how average third and fourth graders would talk about the concepts represented by the Tier Two words. We think that students would be likely to offer the explanations shown here.

Tier Two Words	Students' Likely Expressions
merchant	Salesperson or clerk
required	Have to
tend	Take care of
maintain	Keep going
performed	did
fortunate	lucky
benevolent	kind

Adding the 7 target words to young students' vocabulary repertoires would seem to be quite productive, because learning the words would allow students to describe with greater specificity people and situations they already have some familiarity with. However, notice that these words are not simple synonyms of the familiar ones, but represent more precise or more complex forms of the familiar words. For example, *maintain* means more than "keep going," but "to continue something in its present condition or at its present level." *Benevolent* has the dimension of tolerance as well as kindness.

SELECTING FROM A POOL OF WORDS

The decision about which words to teach must also take into account how many words to teach in conjunction with any given text or lesson. Given that students are learning vocabulary in social studies and science as well as reading or language arts, there needs to be some basis for limiting the number of words so that students will have the opportunity to learn some words well.

Consider which of the words will be most useful in helping students understand it. For the seven words noted before, our thinking is that *fortunate* is particularly important because the fact that the servants thought they were lucky is an important condition of the story. Similarly, *benevolent* plays an important role in setting up the story, as the servants appreciate their master's kindness, and they do not want to upset their pleasant living situation. If one other word were to be selected, a good choice would be *merchant*. *Merchant* is a word that comes up in fourth- and fifth-grade social studies textbooks in discussions of colonization of the Americas (e.g., European *merchants* were eager to locate new resources like tobacco and indigo, which could be found in the colonies. Colonial *merchants* were dismayed by the taxes on English goods, which meant higher prices for their customers but no more profit for themselves.).

The other candidate words, *tend, required, performed*, and *maintain*, are also words of strong general utility, and the choice of whether to include any more words is based solely on considering how many words one thinks students could usefully handle.

You Try It

Below is another excerpt from the tale about the donkey under the magical spell described earlier (Kohnke, 2001, p.12). You might find it useful to try your hand at identifying Tier Two words. You will get to see our choices after the excerpt, so that you can compare your selections with ours.

> *The servants would never comment on this strange occurrence [finding the kitchen clean even though none of them were seen doing the cleaning.], each servant hoping the other had tended to the chores. Never would they mention the loud noises they'd hear emerging from the kitchen in the middle of the night. Nor would they admit to pulling the covers under their chins as they listened to the sound of haunting laughter that drifted down the halls to their bedrooms each night. In reality, they knew there was a more sinister reason behind their good fortune.*

Which words did you select? Trying to be all-inclusive, selecting any words that might fit Tier Two, we chose: *comment, occurrence, tended, mention, emerging, admit, haunting, reality, sinister,* and *fortune*. We considered them Tier Two words as we viewed them as fairly "general but sophisticated words." That is, they are not the most basic, common ways of expressing ideas, but they are familiar to mature language users as ordinary as opposed to specialized language. The concepts embodied in each word are ones that students already have some understanding of, as shown here.

Tier Two Words	Students' Likely Expressions
comment	Something someone has to say
occurrence	Something happening
tended	Took care of
mention	tell
emerging	Coming out
admit	To say you did something
haunting	scary
Reality	Being read
sinister	scary
fortune	luck

Now, the notion of tiers of words is not a precise one, and the lines between tiers are not clearcut, so your selection may not match ours. Thinking in terms of tiers is just a starting point—a way of framing the task of choosing candidate words for instruction. Even within Tier Two, some words will be more easily familiar and some will be more useful than others. For example, our hunch is that *admit, reality,* and *fortune* are likely known to most fourth or fifth graders; that *tended* is not usually used in a way that is key to understanding, and that fifth graders may already associate *haunting* with scary things—a Halloween context—which is fitting for this story. Thus we ended up with: *comment, occurrence, mention, emerging,* and *sinister.* We judged the first four of these to be most useful across a range of contexts, and we chose *sinister* because it is a strong word with emotional impact that is used in literature to describe fictional characters as well as in nonfiction, such as when describing a group's *sinister* plans to invade another's territory.

Some Criteria for Identifying Tier Two Words

Importance and Utility: words that are characteristic of mature language users and appear frequently across a variety of domains.

Instructional Potential: words that can be worked with in a variety of ways so that students can build rich representations of them and of their connections to other words and concepts.

Conceptual Understanding: words for which students understand the general concept but provide precision and specificity in describing the concept.

CONSIDERATIONS BEYOND TIER TWO

There is nothing scientific about the way words are identified for attention in school materials. Some words are obvious candidates, such as selecting the word *representation* for a social studies unit on the American Revolution-

WHAT IF THERE ARE NOT ENOUGH WORDS?

Now let us consider a text that does not seem to offer much for vocabulary development because all of the words in the text are familiar to students. An approach in such a case could be selecting words whose concepts fit in with the story even though the words do not appear. For example, if the story features a character who is a loner, introduce the words *hermit, isolated,* or *solitary*; if a problem is dealt with, present it as a *dilemma* or *conflict*; if a character is hard-working, consider if she is *diligent* and *conscientious*. Think in terms of words that coordinate with, expand, or play off of words, situations, or characters in a text.

Bringing in words whose concepts fit with a story is especially salient when young children are just learning to read, and there are only the simplest words in their text. Consider a story in which two children (Pam and Matt) try on a number silly hats, some of which are very big, and two of which are exactly alike. A number of words came to mind, and we chose, *absurd, enormous,* and *identical*. We suggest how those words might be introduced to young children.

- In the story, Pam and Matt had very, very silly hats. Another way to say that something is very, very silly is to say that it is absurd. When something is absurd, it is so silly it's hard to believe.
- Some of the hats that Pam and Matt wore were so big that all you could see were their feet. Another way to say that something is very, very big is to say that it is enormous. *Enormous* means "very big—very, very big."
- Pam and Matt put on red hats that were almost exactly alike. A way to say that two things are exactly alike is to say that they are identical. *Identical* means "exactly alike."

Words do not need to be completely unfamiliar to students in order to be good candidates for instructional attention. Words might be selected for attention that may be familiar to students but that illustrate the power of an author's choice of words to reveal information about a character or situation. For example, notice the underlined words in the following excerpt, which is taken from a sixth-grade unit on Egypt (Banks et al., 1997, p. 87). The topic is Hatshepsut, a female pharaoh.

Hatshepsut

Hatshepsut was a princess and the wife of a pharaoh. She seized the chance to become pharaoh herself when her husband died. Her young stepson was supposed to become the new pharaoh of Egypt. Hatshepsut proclaimed, however, that the ten-year-old boy was too young to rule on his own. In this way she succeeded in being named co-ruler.

Hatshepsut's Trading Journey

In the eighth year of her reign, Hatshepsut organized the biggest trading expedition of her career. An expedition is a group of people who go on a trip for a set reason. The goal of Hatshepsut's expedition was to trade with Egypt's neighbors to the south in Punt. Historians think Punt may have been in what is today Ethiopia or Somalia....

The huge caravan of scribes, soldiers, artists, and attendants set off along a dusty road that led east to the Red Sea. There they loaded their cargo onto five sleek ships for the long journey south.

The only word identified for attention by the publisher in this segment is *expedition*, which is explained within the text. The two underlined words—*seized* and *sleek*—offer possibilities for drawing students' attention to the effect of an author's choice of words and help the topic come alive.

That Hatshepsut "seized" the chance to become pharaoh reveals something about her character that would make for interesting discussion. For example: "It says that Hatshepsut seized the chance to become pharaoh. *Seize* means 'to grab something or take control of it firmly.' So, what does that tell us about Hatshepsut? Was she afraid of being pharaoh? Do you think she was eager to become a ruler?"

Similarly, that the expedition sailed off in "sleek" ships communicates the prosperity and style of the Egyptian civilization. Discussion could prompt thinking in that direction: "*Sleek* is a word used to describe something graceful and stylish, that marks its owner as well-to-do. 'They sailed off in sleek ships.' What picture does that give us of Egypt?" Additionally, words like *ambitious* and *calculating* could be introduced to characterize Hatshepsut.

AN EXAMPLE FOR OLDER STUDENTS

The examples provided thus far were drawn from texts for readers in the intermediate grades. Although the same principles apply to selecting words from texts for students in the upper grades, they may play out a bit differently. Thus, we present a discussion of the words that might be selected for Agatha Christie's "In a Glass Darkly" (1934), a story that is likely to be of interest to students in eighth or ninth grade. It is a rather brooding tale that moves from a murderous premonition to unrequited love, jealousy, and near tragedy before resolving happily. The story begins as the narrator, while staying with a friend, sees a vision of a man strangling a woman. The woman turns out to be his friend's sister, with whom he falls in love. But she is engaged—to the man he saw in his vision. He tells her of the vision, and she breaks her engagement. For years, the narrator is unable to tell her of his feelings for her. Finally, love is revealed and they marry. But he is deeply jealous, a feeling that results in his nearly strangling his wife—until he notices in the mirror that he is playing out the scene of his premonition.

The language of the story is sophisticated but not particularly difficult. Most words will likely be at least passingly familiar to many readers in eighth or ninth grade. However, many of the words are probably not of high frequency in the students' vocabularies, and, thus, an opportunity presents itself for students to work with these words and gain fluency with them. Here are the 30 words from the story that we identified as Tier Two words:

essential	appreciated	altered
intervened	decent	well-off
attractive	rambling	prospect
valet	throttling	complication
gravely	upshot	leisure
disinterested	scornfully	devotedly
absurdly	endangering	inevitable
entrenched	gloomy	sullen
savage	unwarranted	abuse
endurance	revelation	sobering

Of the 30 words, we decided to focus on 10 of them: *essential, altered, well-off, devoted, entrenched, inevitable, sobering, revelation, upshot,* and *disinterested.*

Ten words may be a lot to develop effectively for one story, but we see it as a workable number because many of them will already be familiar. Also, two of the words could be introduced rather briefly with little or no follow-up work. These are: *altered,* which could be defined simply as "permanently changed," and *well-off,* which could simply be given the synonym *wealthy.* The reason for attention to these two words is that they could cause confusion at the local level in the story if not understood.

Two other words were also chosen because they could cause confusion in a part of the story. These are *upshot* and *disinterested.* The narrator talks of the *upshot* of his decision to tell Sylvia that he saw a vision of her fiancé choking her. Because of the context and feel of the story, we thought *upshot* might be interpreted as some sort of physical violence, instead of simply "the result of." The word *disinterested* meaning "not being involved in a particular situation" is often confused with *uninterested,* meaning "not interested," and the story provides a good opportunity to introduce that distinction.

Five words seem to convey the mood and emotional impact of story developments: *devoted, entrenched, inevitable, sobering,* and *revelation.* And the word *essential* was chosen because "one essential detail" turns out to be a key plot device—that is, in his premonition, the narrator notices a scar on the left side of the choker's face. The essential detail he fails to account for is that he is seeing this in a mirror, so the scar is actually on the right. The five words can be used to describe the plot as follows: The narrator is *devoted* to Sylvia, although *entrenched* in a jealousy that causes *inevitable* problems. Only a *sobering revelation* (that *essential* detail) saves him, his marriage, and his wife.

A couple of points should be emphasized here. The words were selected not so much because they are essential to comprehension of the story, but because they seem most closely integral to the mood and plot. In this way, the vocabulary work provides for both learning new words and for enriching understanding of literature. This decision was made possible because there was a large pool of words to choose from. Sometimes choices are more limited, and sometimes the best words are not so tied to the story. In such cases, a decision might be made to select words that seem most productive for vocabulary development despite their role in the story.

For the six words we consider to be most important to teach, some characteristics of the words themselves also drove our selections. *Sobering* was selected because its strongest sense for students might be as the opposite of drunk. So, the context of the story provides a good opportunity to overcome that and introduce its more general sense. The others, *essential, devoted, entrenched, inevitable,* and *revelation,* have wide potential for use, and are not limited to specific situations or stereotypic contexts. Yet, they seem to be strongly expressive words that can bring emotional impact to contexts in which they are used.

AN EXAMPLE FOR YOUNG CHILDREN

We turn now to selecting words to enhance the vocabulary repertoires of young children—those who are just learning to read. We make two immediate distinctions between vocabulary work with intermediate and older students and work with students in the earliest grades, typically kindergarten through early second grade. The first is that we find the best sources for new vocabulary are tradebooks that teachers read aloud to children rather than the books children read on their own. The second distinction is that in contrast to introducing words before a story, in our work with young children we have found it most appropriate to engage in vocabulary activities after a story has been read.

There are two reasons we decided that vocabulary activities for young children should occur after a story. First, if a word is needed for comprehension, inasmuch as the teacher is reading the story, she is available to briefly explain the word at the point in the story where it is needed (e.g., "A ukulele is a kind of guitar." "When ducks molt, they lose their feathers and can't fly until new ones grow."). Second, because the words that will be singled out for vocabulary attention are words that are very likely unfamiliar to young children, the context from the story provides a rich example of the word's use and thus strong support for children's initial learning of the word.

The basis for selecting words from tradebooks for young children is that they are Tier Two words and words that are not too difficult to explain to young children. Here, we present our thinking for selecting three words for instructional attention from *The Popcorn Dragon* (Thayer, 1953), a story targeted to kindergartners.

In our review of *The Popcorn Dragon* for Tier Two candidate words, we first identified the following seven: *accidentally, drowsy, pranced, scorched, envious, delighted,* and *forlorn*. From the pool of seven, we decided to provide instruction for three: *envious, delighted,* and *forlorn*. We considered three issues in making our choices. First, we determined that the concept represented by each word was understandable to kindergartners. That is, five-year-olds understand: wanting something someone else has *(envious)*; being very happy *(delighted)*, and being very sad *(forlorn)*. Second, it is not too difficult to explain the meanings of those words in very simple language, as illustrated in the previous sentence! And third, each word has extensive possibilities for use. In particular, the words are found in numerous fairy tales. That is, there is often some character who is envious of another, and characters who are delighted or forlorn about the turn of events. The words, however, are not restricted to make-believe; they can all be used in describing people in common situations.

We found the other candidate words—*pranced, accidentally, scorched,* and *drowsy*—interesting and potentially useful, but, relative to the words we chose, we saw *scorched* and *pranced* as narrower, and *drowsy* and *accidentally* as not quite so interesting as the ones we chose. We hasten to make the point that this is all a matter of judgment. The final decisions about which words to teach may not be as important as thoughtful consideration about why to teach certain words and not others.

WHAT ABOUT WORDS BEING ON GRADE LEVEL?

A concern that surfaces in deciding which words to teach is whether words are appropriate for students at certain grade levels. Key to this concern is to understand that no formula exists for selecting age-appropriate vocabulary words despite lists that identify "fifth-grade words" or "seventh-grade words." There is simply no basis for determining which words students should be learning at different grade levels. For example, that *coincidence* is an "eighth-grade word" according to a frequency index means only that most students do not know the word until eighth grade. It does not mean that students in seventh or even third grade cannot learn the word or should not be taught it.

There are only two things that make a word inappropriate for a certain level. One is not being able to explain the meaning of a word in known terms. If the words used to explain a target word are likely unknown to the students, then the word is too hard.

The other consideration for word selection is that the words be useful and interesting—ones that students will be able to find uses for in their everyday lives. Of course, this is a matter of judgment, best decided by those who know the individual students. Work we have done with kindergarten and first-grade children shows that sophisticated words can be successfully taught to young children.

For example, kindergartners readily applied *nuisance* to disruptive classmates, and identified when a *commotion* occurred in the hall. First graders could easily discern *argumentative* peers from those who acted *dignified!*

IN SUMMARY

In evaluating words as possible candidates for instruction, here are three things to keep in mind:

1. How generally useful is the word? Is it a word that students are likely to meet often in other texts? Will it be of use to students in describing their own experiences? For example, students are likely to find more situations in which to apply *typical* and *dread* than *portage* and *brackish*.

2. How does the word relate to other words, to ideas that students know or have been learning? Does it directly relate to some topic of study in the classroom? Or might it add a dimension to ideas that have been developed? For example, what might knowing the word *hubris* bring to a middle school student's understanding of the battles at Lexington and Concord, which set the Revolutionary War in motion?

3. What does the word bring to a text or situation? What role does the word play in communicating the meaning of the context in which it is used? A word's meaning might be necessary for understanding a text. Or understanding its meaning might allow an enriched insight about the situation being presented, such as in the case of Hatshepsut's seizing power and riding in sleek ships.

Keep in mind that there is no formula for selecting age-appropriate vocabulary words despite lists that identify "fifth-grade words" or "seventh-grade words." As long as the word can be explained in known words and can apply to what students might talk or write about, it is an appropriate word to teach.

Your Turn

We invite you to use what you have learned in this chapter to make some decisions about which words you will teach.

1. Select a text that your students will be reading. It can be a story, or an excerpt from a chapter book or novel, or a social studies textbook.
2. List all the words that are likely to be unfamiliar to students.
3. Analyze the word list.
   • Which words can be categorized as Tier Two words?
   • Which of the Tier Two words are most necessary for comprehension?
   • Are there other words needed for comprehension? Which ones?
4. On the basis of your analysis, which words will you teach?
   • Which will need only brief attention?
   • Which will you give more elaborate attention to?

REFERENCES

Banks, J. A., Beyer, B. K., Contreras, G., Craven, J., Ladson-Billings, G., McFarland, M. A., & Parker, S. C. (1997). *World: Adventures in time and place*. New York: Macmillan/McGraw-Hill.

Christie, A. (1934). In a glass darkly. In L. Mountain, S. Crawley, & E. Fry (Eds.), *Jamestown Heritage Readers* (Book H, pp. 160–167). Providence, RI: Jamestown Publishers.

Edwards, A. (2001). My father, the entomologist. *Cricket, 28*(10), 5–9.

Kohnke, J. M. (2001). The pooka of allihies. *Cricket, 28*(7), 12–16.

Thayer, J. (1953). *The popcorn dragon*. New York: Morrow.

White, E. B. (1952). *Charlotte's web*. New York: Harper & Row.

Chapter 11

Size and Sequence
in Vocabulary Development:

Implications for Choosing Words for Primary
Grade Vocabulary Instruction

Andrew Biemiller
University of Toronto

The importance of English vocabulary for success in English-speaking schools cannot be overestimated. The authors of the National Reading Panel (2000) wrote: "Benefits in understanding text by applying letter–sound correspondences to printed material come about only if the target word is in the learner's oral vocabulary. (ch. 4, p. 3)" Chall, a well-known reading scholar, argued that written vocabulary test was effectively equivalent to reading comprehension testing because the correlation between the two was so high (at $r = .95$ in my own studies), that it is not necessary to test comprehension. Hazenberg and Hulstijn (1996) reported that children with vocabularies of less than 11,000 root words were unable to succeed in college programs. (They noted that this study was done in the Netherlands, and that somewhat higher vocabularies would probably be needed in English.)

A simple example from my own research illustrates the relationship between basic reading skills and vocabulary. When we (Biemiller & Slonim, 2001) conducted our second normative study, we included a simple test of oral reading of 60 words after orally testing vocabulary meanings of the same words. We found that from Grade 3 on, 95% of children could *read* more words than they could *define*. Figure 11.1 illustrates this relationship. One re-

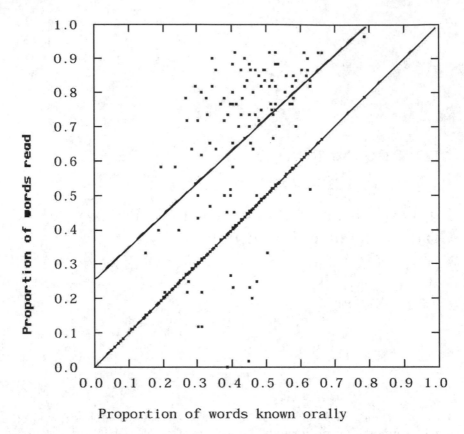

FIG. 11.1.   Defining versus reading words, Grades 3–6.

gression line in the figure simply shows the level of vocabulary known. The other regression line shows accuracy in reading the words tested for vocabulary. Although the number of words read correctly was correlated with the number of words defined ($r = .45$, $N = 92$), after Grade 2, most children could read more words than they could explain. The average difference was 25% to 30% more words read correctly than understood (see Table 11.1).

In another study (Biemiller, 1999), I found a correlation of $r = .81$ (68% of variance) between vocabulary size and reading comprehension (Canadian Test of Basic Skills) across Grades 1–5. Adding grade level to the equation brings the equation to $r = .86$ (74%). Thus grade adds 6% of reading comprehension variance, slightly affecting comprehension performance over and above that predicted by vocabulary, but not very much.

These findings make it not surprising that whereas *identifying words in print* in first grade was *not* predictive of reading comprehension many years

TABLE 11.1

Mean Percentages of Correctly Explaining and Correctly Reading Words
and Difference Between Them, by Grade (Standard Deviations in Parentheses)

Grade	N	Word-Meaning Knowledge	Read Vocabulary	Read-Explain Difference
two	24	37% (11%)	44 (25)	8 (25)
three	28	39 (10)	63 (18)	24 (16)
four	20	44 (9)	70 (16)	26 (18)
five	24	49 (8)	79 (13)	30 (14)
six	20	53 (12)	84 (8)	30 (11)

later in Grade 11, *orally tested vocabulary* in first grade was correlated $r = .55$ with much later reading comprehension (Cunningham & Stanovich, 1997). Numerous other studies show the importance of vocabulary for oral and reading comprehension during the elementary years (Dickinson et al, 2003; Scarborough, 2001). In fact, many more children become "competent readers" in the sense of word recognition than become "competent readers" in the sense of *understanding* grade-level reading content.

In this chapter, I will be discussing the number of root word meanings children need to acquire to become competent readers. I will be emphasizing the fact that words are learned largely in the same order—even when different populations (e.g., advantaged, English Second Language) and varying methods of assessing vocabulary are used. I will then discuss the practical implications for vocabulary instruction, particularly in the primary grades.

VOCABULARY SIZE

How large a vocabulary must a child acquire? If we consider *all* words—meaning all the varied forms of words—plural, singular, past or present tense, not to mention affixes (e.g. preterm, doable)—the number of words children deal with is very large. However, as Anglin (1993) has shown, the number of "derived" words using affixes, compound words, etc. is 3 times the number of "root" words known in Grade 1. By Grade 5, this ratio increases to 5 times as many derived words and idioms as root words. Nagy and Scott (2001) concur with Anglin's estimates of number of root words acquired.

My view is that by and large, "derived words" can be known when encountered or derived from context, as long as the root words and affixes are known. Teaching affixes—e.g., *pre-* or *-able*—typically occurs in the upper

Children's Achievement on Two Different Forms of the Root Word Inventory.

Children who took two different forms of our Root Word Inventory (with different words) scored very similarly on both tests. The correlation between children's scores on these test forms was $r = .88$ across 126 Grade 1–5 children (Biemiller & Slonim, 2001).

Use of Different Context Sentences to Assess the Same Root Word Meaning

In an unpublished study, we examined the use of different context sentences for the same word. This involved 58 words from our "form B" (Biemiller & Slonim, 2001). Procedures were the same as the Biemiller & Slonim study 3. For this comparison, we determined average scores for each word with each sentence in a sample of grade 1 to Grade 4 children. Data was collected in the same laboratory school, with data taken 3 years apart. The correlation for word means from the two forms was $r = .87$ ($N = 58$). Means for grades were reasonably similar (Table 11.3).

Word Order with Normative, Advantaged, and ESL Children

The Biemiller & Slonim (2001) study reported results for both normative and advantaged populations. The average correlation between word means (from Grades 1, 2, 4, and 5) was $r = .94$ for the two test forms. We conducted a subsequent unpublished study with 82 Grade 5 and 6 children in a school where 95% do not speak English at home (drawn from many different ethnicities). The methodology was the same as that used in Biemiller & Slonim (2001), study 1. The correlation between average word means for ESL Grade 5 and 6 children was correlated $r = .91$ with word means for advantaged children

TABLE 11.3

Percentage Correct Means for Alternate Forms B1 and B2
by Grade (Advantaged Population)

Grade	Form B1	Form B2
One	30%	31
Two	40	36
Three	48	44
Four	44	51

Context Sentences: Open-ended Versus Multiple-Choice Methods

In one study, I compared our standard context-sentence method (written version) with multiple choice responses (Biemiller, 1998). Word meanings sampled from *Living Word Vocabulary* levels 4, 6, and 8 were used. Two cohorts were used in each class such that all children had both open-ended and multiple choice tests, and all words in the study were tested both ways. Children from an advantaged population (university laboratory school) and from an ESL population participated in this study in Grades 3, 5, and 6.

Individual children's scores on multiple choice and open-ended tests were correlated $r = .81$ with grade controlled. Test scores using multiple choice were higher than test scores using open-ended (in which children had to write the meaning of a word as presented in a sentence). Table 11.4 shows these results. Not surprisingly, the ESL Grade 6 children had results similar to Grade 3 advantaged children on both multiple choice and open-ended tests. In general, on harder words for younger children there was a larger difference between multiple-choice performance and open-ended performance. I suspect that children who cannot provide plausible meanings for root words will have difficulty understanding texts with those words, at least when the word is central to the text. Thus my best guess is that multiple-choice results may overestimate children's effective vocabulary.

TABLE 11.4

Mean Percentages of 4th, 6th, and 8th Grade Vocabulary Items Passed
on Multiple Choice and Open-Ended Tests by Student Background

	Grade and Word Level										
		Grade 3				*Grade 5*				*Grade 6*	
	(n)	*4th*	*6th*	*8th*	*(n)*	*4th*	*6th*	*8th*	*(n)*	*4th*	*6th*	*8th*
% words defined correctly:												
ESL Population												
multiple choice	(19)	76	40	42	(20)	76	52	60	(25)	89	77	71
open-ended (written)	(17)	44	27	11	(20)	60	32	17	(25)	82	58	37
Advantaged Population												
multiple choice	(21)	88	71	67	(19)	93	76	75	(21)	93	85	78
open-ended (written)	(20)	76	60	44	(21)	85	70	46	(20)	87	74	59

Assessing Vocabulary With Context Sentences
Versus Multiple-Choice Pictures (PPVT)

In another study, Boote and I contrasted our context-sentence method with the standard Peabody Picture Vocabulary procedure (Biemiller & Boote, submitted). We were especially interested in Sentence versus Picture testing. Our context-sentence method tends to underestimate vocabulary below Grade 2, and we wished to see if a picture vocabulary test would show knowledge of more words.

In this study, we contrasted a short form (20 items) of Form B of our Root Word Vocabulary with 20 pictured items from the Peabody and 20 context sentence Peabody items. All children encountered both picture test items and context sentence items. However, there were two cohorts of children in each grade so some children were tested on particular words with pictures while others were tested on the same words with context sentences. Vocabulary levels measured all three ways were highly correlated. The correlation between means for word meanings assessed with Peabody Pictures and the same words with assessed with context sentences was $r = .76$, whereas correlations with children's vocabulary assessed with a short form of our Root Word Inventory were $r = .79$ for picture vocabulary and .86 for context sentence vocabulary. Children's scores on all three measures were highly correlated with reading comprehension (Canadian Test of Basic Skills) ranging from $r = .72$ for PPVT and reading comprehension to $r = .81$ for Root Word Inventory and reading comprehension.

Figure 11.2 shows the growth of word knowledge as assessed with different methods. (We included only items between 20% and 80% on the Peabody Picture Vocabulary as there were many "floor" and "ceiling" items which blurred results.) In this Figure, readers can see that in kindergarten and Grade 1, children scored considerably higher using Peabody pictured items than when the same items were presented in sentences. From Grade 2 on, the difference between the two methods is considerably smaller.

Summary: Reliability of Word Order Data.

The information summarized here indicates that findings of a robust order for word acquisition is reliable and not explicable through details of testing. The implications of this order of word-meaning acquisition are examined in the next section.

SEQUENCE OF WORDS ACQUIRED

Words tested in our research were sampled from 17,500 root word meanings reported known by children in Grade 12 or lower in Dale & O'Rourke's

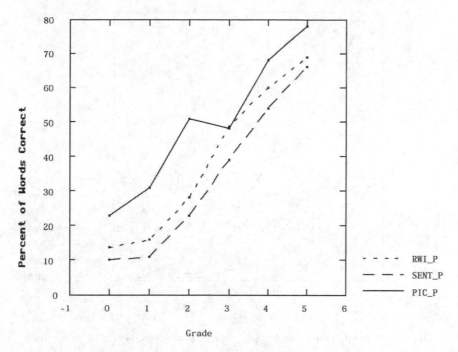

FIG. 11.2.   Knowledge of word meanings assessed with pictures, sentences, and Root Word Inventory. (For this graph, only words known between 20% and 80% on the Peabody Picture Vocabulary Test were used.)

Living Word Vocabulary (1981). Words can be ordered by how well they are known on average by Grade 1 to Grade 5 children. As the order of root word means is highly correlated between each grade, it is possible to consider words in the first decile (1,750 words) as those best known by most children. Conversely, those in the tenth decile are little known (2%) by *any* children in elementary school. We are then able to look at how well children know words from each decile of words. Combining data from our two normative samples, we have 11 or 12 words from each decile.

Achievement groups were based on overall performance on our vocabulary tests: 0% to 10%, 11% to 20%, etc. Children from different grades could be included in the same achievement group. Mean scores for each of these groups of words were calculated for each ability group of children.

Evidence can be seen in Fig. 11.3 that words are learned in a roughly fixed order, and that at any given level of overall word knowledge, there are two or three deciles of root words at the 30% to 70% correct range. The groups of children knowing only 3% to 10% and 11% to 20% of all words in the test mainly knew words from the first two or three sets of words (from the

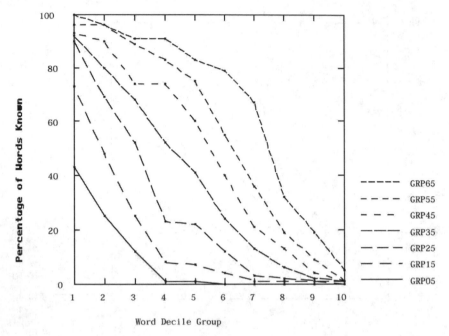

FIG. 11.3.   Words from different difficulty levels by children of different vocabulary size.

best-known decile, the second best known decile, and so on.) The group with knowledge of 45 percent of words overall knew over 70% of words in the first four deciles of words. Those knowing 55% or 65% of word meanings knew over 70% of the first five or six deciles of words respectively. Overall, these descriptive data strongly suggest that children are acquiring vocabulary in a relatively predictable order.

The existence of a strong order in which words are acquired means that "individual differences" are in, fact, mainly "developmental differences." I do not mean that differences between children must be determined by constitutional maturation. However, when children have reached a vocabulary of a given size (whether they are in Grade 2, 4, or 6), they are likely know certain word meanings, be learning other identifiable word meanings, while still other meanings will be unlikely to be learned at this vocabulary level.

The Fallacy of Grade-Level Vocabulary

There is a large difference in the number of words particular children in the same grade have acquired. We tend to talk of words "learned at Grade 1" or words "learned in kindergarten." In fact, although children's vocabulary follows an identifiable sequence, that sequence is defined by children's vocabulary size, rather than by grade. Table 11.5 shows rough spreads of vocabulary among children from different grades. For example, in Grade 2, about 30% of children scored *below* the modal Grade 2 level vocabulary range of 5,000 to 7,000 root word meanings. (This represented 30% to 40% of our corpus of 17,500 words known by Grade 12.) Similarly, about 40% of Grade 2 children achieved *above* the modal Grade 2 level.

Many of these words were also known by *some* children in Grades 1 or younger or Grade 3 or older. Thus it is misleading to refer to them simply as "Grade 2" words. We can better think of them as a group of words to be emphasized in the primary grades, rather than specifically in Grade 2.

Is Sequence Important?

We do not know why words are learned in approximately the same order, whether being learned at age 7 or 10. However, inasmuch as this order holds, it seems likely that children really need to learn words in the observed order. Although some words are doubtless not crucial either to vocabulary order or general understanding of our world (e.g., *oar, canoe*), others are probably necessary for explaining words further up the se-

TABLE 11.5

Normative Population: Percentage of Vocabulary
Achievement Group by Grade (Combined Forms)

Grade	N	Estimated Vocabulary Group[a]							
		0-1750	1751-3500	3501-5250	5250-7000	7001-8750	8751-10500	10501-12250	12251-14000
kind.	43 (100%)	35%	42	21	2	0	0	0	0
gr. 1	37 (100%)	22%	30	43	5	0	0	0	0
gr. 2	49 (100%)	2%	8	18	33	27	10	2	0
gr. 3	29 (100%)	0%	7	21	28	34	10	0	0
gr. 4	41 (100%)	0%	2	15	27	29	22	10	0
gr. 5[b]	24 (100%)	0%	0	0	10	45	20	25	5
gr. 6	20 (100%)	0%	0	0	5	30	25	30	10

Note a.   Categories represent "deciles" of 1,750 root words—sampled from 17,500 total root words reported in Dale & O'Rourke (1981) as words passed by 67% at Grade 12 or at younger levels.

Note b.   Data from Form A omitted because anomalously high levels of vocabulary were seen in this Grade 5 sample.

quence. At any rate, it appears that if we wish to facilitate vocabulary growth, we would be well advised to focus on words from the sequence that contribute to general vocabulary growth.

Note that to date, most studies of vocabulary instruction have *not* demonstrated effects on general vocabulary. Given that children are typically acquiring 800 to 1,000 word meanings per year, brief instructional interventions of 1 to 3 weeks are unlikely to impact general vocabulary assessed with sample words. (Of course, if the sample test words were deliberately taught, large but fallacious vocabulary gains would be recorded.) Until vocabulary interventions succeeding in teaching10 to 15 word meanings per week are sustained over at least half a school year, we should not expect to have much impact on general vocabulary as assessed with the Peabody Picture Vocabulary Test or other standardized assessments of vocabulary.

A STRATEGY TO IDENTIFY WORDS FOR INSTRUCTION

Using Partially Known Words

The best strategy for finding words for instruction would be to introduce words in sequence, or better, drawn from groups of words in the sequence appropriate to children of a specifiable vocabulary size. When identifying words needed by children at the end of the primary grades, my strategy is to focus on words "partially known." Words known between about 30% and 70% tend to be rapidly learned at each vocabulary size group. Thus by the next vocabulary size group, words which were known between 30% and 70% show an increase of 20 percentage points or more, whereas words known better or worse, show much less change going from one vocabulary size group to another. (This phenomenon can be seen in Table 11.6.) To identify such words for instruction in the primary grades, I suggest words meeting this criterion by "average" children in Grade 2. Word meanings that are typically well-learned by Grade 2 need not be instructed during the primary years. Word meanings that are unlikely to be well-learned by Grade 2 probably are of less value to children in the primary grades than word meanings that are learned more rapidly at this age range. Unfortunately, these words are too often selected for primary-grade children. For example, Foorman et al. (in press) report that 80% of words were from "fourth grade level or higher" in four out of six *first-grade* basals .

Word Significance

Our selection of words, although greatly influenced by the observed sequence of acquisition, should also be influenced by the practical significance of a word. We may need to further distinguish between "important

TABLE 11.6

Normative Population: Performance of Vocabulary Achievement Groups on Words of Varying Difficulty (Data Combined From Forms A and B)

Avg. %		Estimated Vocabulary Achievement Group[a]							
Word Decile	Words Gr. 1,2,4,5	0-1750	1751-3500	3501-5250	5250-7000	7001-8750	8751-10500	10501-12250	12251-14000
10	02%	00%	00	01	01	01	02	05	45
9	05	00	01	01	02	04	09	19	50
8	11	00	01	03	07	14	19	32	58
7	20	00	01	03	13	21	36	67	63
6	32	00	05	13	24	40	55	**79**	**88**
5	47	01	07	22	41	60	**76**	**83**	**79**
4	56	01	08	24	52	**74**	**84**	**91**	**88**
3	62	13	25	52	68	**74**	**89**	**91**	**100**
2	71	25	48	**70**	**80**	**90**	**96**	**96**	**100**
1	87	43	**74**	**91**	**92**	**93**	**97**	**100**	**100**

Numbers of Children at Each Grade in Each Vocabulary Achievement Group

Grade	Total	Number of Children at Vocabulary Achievement Level							
kind.	43	15	18	9	1	0	0	0	0
gr. 1	37	8	11	16	2	0	0	0	0
gr. 2	49	1	4	9	16	13	5	1	0
gr. 3	29	0	2	6	8	10	3	0	0
gr. 4	41	0	1	4	11	12	9	4	0
gr. 5	44	0	0	1	3	15	15	9	1
gr. 6	20	0	0	0	1	6	5	6	2
total	263	24	36	45	42	56	37	20	3

Note. Numbers in *italics* were at 30% or lower average word knowledge. Numbers **bolded** were known at 70% or higher word knowledge. Estimated Vocabulary Achievement Group was based on number of words known sampled from Dale and O'Rourke's *Living Word Vocabulary* Grade 2 to 12 words (Biemiller & Slonim, 2001).

words," "words", and "unimportant words" These judgments will have to be made by teachers, curriculum builders, and state curriculum mandates. However, those selecting words for instruction would be well-advised to think several times about emphasizing words and concepts that are rarely found among average children of a particular grade.

In the upper elementary grades, it is possible for children to identify words not understood and seek their meanings. When reading, a reader can pause to deal with unknown words. This is not possible when listening to adults reading—especially in a group situation. Thus with older children, it is possible to place greater responsibility on students for seeking needed vocabulary. For example, Grade 5 and 6 children report that they often ask others for word meanings (Biemiller, AERA 1999). However, preliterate children rarely ask about word meanings during group discourse or lessons. (Beals, 1997).

Selecting Words for the Primary Years.

Of root words "known" by children with 5,250 to 7,000 root words, words from the first 2 deciles (3,500 words) were mainly known. The average child in the 5,250–7,000 word meaning group would know about two thirds of the words from the third decile or about 1,200 of the 1,750 words. By the fourth and fifth deciles, individual children in the 5,250–7,000 word meaning group know about 1,500 of the next 3,500 words. Average Grade 2 children know relatively few of the harder words (deciles 6 and beyond). Thus, across a list of 5,000 words in deciles 3–5, average Grade 2 children at the median level will know a little over half. Different children will know different words at these deciles. We cannot simply specify a list to be learned. We cannot and should not expect every Grade 2 child to know all of these words. (By Grade 5, average children will know most of these words.) On the other hand, it would be really nice to bring low vocabulary children in Grade 2 toward knowledge of half of these 5,000 words.

Samples of words *known, being learned,* and *unlikely to be learned* by Grade 2 are given in Table 11.7. Detailed examples of root words, *Living Word Vocabulary* definitions, and test context sentences are given in Table 11.8.

To get to the point of knowing half of 5,000 decile 3–5 root word meanings, children whose vocabulary progress is well below average will have to be *accelerated* during the primary years. At present, such children enter kindergarten with an estimated vocabulary of 2,000 to 2,500 root word meanings. This compares to an estimated root vocabulary of 3,400 words at kindergarten for average children.[2] In order to reach a total of even 5,000 words by the

---

[2]These estimates are larger than the vocabularies we have actually obtained with children at this age. I believe that our context-sentence method underestimates vocabulary below Grade 2. These estimates are obtained by simply projecting vocabulary size back from Grade 2.

TABLE 11.7

Words Known at Grade 2, Being Learned at Grade 2,
and Not Usually Learned at Grade 2

Known Well	*Being Learned*		*Unlikely to Learn*	
Decile 1	**Decile 3**	**Decile 5**	**Decile 6**	**Decile 9**
fish	done	blab	mammoth	bit
flood	buckle	stock	thigh	franchise
throat	boulder	peeve	because	sequence
Match	secure	shimmer	Tree (shoe)	inquisitive
café	right	straight	astronomy	vain
spread	react	Root	distant	popular
shot	fresh	know	man	(vote)
voice	peep	beat	period	jurisdiction
near	dodo	haul	garble	perpendicular
stab	wad	gull	duplex	empty
		parcel	curious	republic
		Possum		discord
Decile 2	**Decile 4**	transit	**Decile 7**	cow
stuff	cobra	knoll	victim	female
subtract	Tally	envelope	polo	
flown	thud	lash	Guard (v.)	**Decile 10**
fuss	drama		former	etch
sliver	through		alias	question
anchor	matting		robust	problem
space	litter		text	valor
shadow	Vaseline		nation	parch
loop			ominous	destitute
listen			narrow	cognac
drop			writhe	locomotion
swing			lance	
(baseball)			**Decile 8**	abrasive
kept			dibs	reformation
math			induct	oligarchy
justice			vice	
			rotary	
			swoon	
			junction	
			lust	
			character	
			cartilage	
			matron	
			delinquent	
			whittle	

Note. Words taken from Appendices B and C of Biemiller and Slonim (2001).

TABLE 11.8

Sample Test Sentences for Words Known at Grade 2,
Being Learned at Grade 2, and Not Usually Learned at Grade 2

Level & Word	Meaning Tested	LWV Level	Test Sentence
Words known by Grade 2 (70% or better)			
fish	a water animal	2	Johnny caught a fish
flood	unusual flow of water	2	The flood caused a lot of damage to the town.
throat	passage from stomach to mouth	2	He felt a lump in his throat.
match	thing to light fire	2	Where is the box of matches?
cafe	eating place	2	She met him at the cafe.
loop	a circled string	2	He made two loops with his shoe laces.
listen	to try to hear	2	You should listen to your mother.
drop	fall	2	The ball dropped from his hand.
swing	strike at a ball	4	Jamie took his second swing at the ball.
kept	keeps/keep	2	He kept his old hockey trophies.
math	school subject	6	John got his math work done quickly.
Words being learned at Grade 2 (deciles 4 and 5)			
cobra	snake	6	The cobra lived in the house.
tally	count	8	The teacher kept a tally of days missed.
react	act back[a]	10	When the cat saw the mouse, she didn't react.
thud	dull sound	8	There was a thud in the next room.
drama	plays	6	She enjoys watching drama productions.
blab	tell secret	10	He made a promise not to blab.
vaseline	petroleum jelly	6	The jar of Vaseline is on the shelf.
parcel	package	6	The parcel was delivered to the office.
possum	animal	4	He saw a possum.

distant	long ago	6	The year my mother was born seems distant to me.
transit	Public transportation	8	The children took transit to school.
man	humankind	2	Man has always had trouble with the weather.

Words unlikely to be known in Grade 2 (30%; examples from deciles 6–10)

tree	rack for shoes, hats	12	The guests hung their hats on the coat tree.
polo	game played on horseback	4	They were watching polo.
guard	a defense	6	Keep your guard up.
lust	strong desire	10	Their lust for battle was strong.
character	nature of	8	Difficult times in life may show the true character of a person.
cartilage	tough tissue	8	She suffered from torn cartilage
bit	item of computer data	12	There are 8 bits in 1 byte.
franchise	chain of businesses	10	He bought a restaurant franchise.
sequence	connect in series	8	The sequence of events was surprising.
locomotion	ability to move	8	His locomotion was poor.
lance	cut open	8	He lanced the wound.
abrasive	scratch material	12	That material is abrasive.

Note a.   A derived word but probably learned as a basic word.

end of Grade 2, such children would, on average, have to acquire 1,100 words a year or approximately twice the rate of words lower quartile children have demonstrated at present (Biemiller & Slonim, 2001). It is probable that the words they need most will fall into the 4th and 5th deciles of words.

Experience with vocabulary instruction shows that it is typical for some of the words taught to be learned while others are simply not (Biemiller & Boote, submitted). Again, in many cases, we are seeing an increase in the percentage of children knowing a word—not an "all or nothing" result. In many cases, we are teaching words that some children already knew. *Some* of the rest of the children acquire the word as a result of classroom instruction. Thus to some extent, we will need to teach more words than will be learned.

NEED FOR A WORD ACQUISITION SEQUENCE THEORY

Today I have described evidence for a robust sequence of word meaning acquisition, and some implications of that sequence for classroom instruction.

It would be nice to have a theory explaining this order. The evidence that a sequence of words exists is stronger than evidence explaining *why* the sequence is observed. Print word frequency is not a major factor. There is little correlation between print word form frequency and observed word order. This partly because many word forms have many meanings (polysemy) so that print word frequency bears little relationship to specific root word meaning frequency. Furthermore, prior to Grade 3, children are really very little influenced by print word frequency, as they read little or not at all. The frequency of oral root meanings may in fact have a major role in word acquisition. Certainly words which are not experienced cannot be learned. Unfortunately, we do not have good estimates of oral word frequency, much less an estimate of oral word *meaning* frequency.

It is also clear that word meanings that are likely to be learned relatively early are for the most part "not abstract" (i.e., these words refer to objects that can be seen, actions that can be carried out, and modifiers that can be apprehended directly (e.g., color, size, sound, etc.).

My colleagues and I are currently examining some other statistical sources—Rinsland's (1947) count of word use in young children's writing and oral speech (first grade), Hart and Risley's (1999) reports of words used early in life, and other published sources of oral word frequency. The total number of words spoken in homes is correlated with the number of words learned (Hart & Risley, 1995; 1999). However, in addition to the total number of words spoken in families, the number of *different word meanings* parallels the total number of words. I suspect that the number of *different* words, may be more important than the total number of words heard.

Beyond approaches based on oral or print word frequencies, we are attempting to identify empirically words that fall into the "fourth and fifth deciles" of words, by simply testing words likely to be at this level. These are words drawn from *Living Word Vocabulary* levels 4 to 8, using a rating process to eliminate some words and testing to confirm the remainder. We hope to have 5,000 to 6,000 such words identified by 2006. We hope that with a larger corpus of appropriate words, we may be able to identify relevant aspects of these words that may allow us to construct a theory of word meaning order.

CONCLUSIONS

In this chapter, I discussed the importance of vocabulary. As I noted, although the ability to read words in a text is prerequisite to comprehending the text, many children can read words but fail to understand what they read due to vocabulary limitations.

Before describing our approach to identifying words for instruction for use in the primary grades, I reviewed a number of studies which support the conclusion that words are acquired in a predictable order. Of particular importance is the finding that the order of word knowledge in different populations (normative-English speaking, advantaged, and ESL) is remarkably similar. The *correlation* of words in different populations are correlated around $r = .90$ or better.

Given that words are, in fact, acquired in the same order—whether one reaches a vocabulary of a given size at age 6, 8, or 10—the actual word meanings learned will be similar. Thus to accelerate the rate of word acquisition for low-vocabulary children, we should probably fill in the words that have been partially learned by those with larger vocabularies. We have targeted words typically known by some but not all children at a specified grade level. We propose to find words known at 30% to 70% by median children at a target grade. For the primary grades, we believe such a list can be constructed based on target words at the end of Grade 2. Once we have such a list in hand, we can begin to design an effective vocabulary curriculum. In my view, such a curriculum would primarily use repeated reading of narrative and expository adult-read texts, combined with explanations of selected word meanings and reviews of words taught. *Without knowledge of appropriate target words, it will be extremely difficult to run a program that is worth using classroom time.*

REFERENCES

Anglin, J. M. (1993). Vocabulary development: A morphological analysis. *Monographs of the Society for Research in Child Development*, Serial No. 238, *58*, 1–186.

Beals, D. (1997). Sources of support for learning words in conversation: Evidence from mealtimes. *Child Language, 24*, 673–694.

Biemiller, A. (1998). *Oral vocabulary, word identification, and reading comprehension in English second language and English first language elementary school children*. Paper presented at the annual conference of the Society for the Scientific Study of Reading, San Diego, CA.

Biemiller, A. (1999). *Estimating vocabulary growth for ESL children with and without listening comprehension instruction*. Paper presented at the annual conference of the American Educational Research Association, Montreal, Quebec.

Biemiller, A. (2001). *The relationship between vocabulary assessed with picture vocabulary methodology, same words with sentence context method, root word inventory, and reading comprehension*. Paper presented at the Society for the Scientific Study of Reading Conference, Boulder, CO.

Biemiller, A. (2003). *Using stories to promote vocabulary*. Paper presented at a symposium entitled Fostering Early Narrative Competency: Innovations in Instruction, International Reading Association, Orlando, FL.

Biemiller, A. & Boote, C. (submitted). *An effective method for building vocabulary in primary grades*. Manuscript submitted to the *Journal of Educational Psychology*.

Biemiller, A., & Slonim, N. (2001). Estimating root word vocabulary growth in normative and advantaged populations: Evidence for a common sequence of vocabulary acquisition. *Journal of Educational Psychology, 93*, 498–520.

Chall, J. S., Jacobs, V. A., and Baldwin, L. E. (1990). *The reading crisis: Why poor children fall behind*. Cambridge, MA: Harvard University Press.

Cunningham, A. E., & Stanovich, K. E. (1997). Early reading acquisition and its relation to reading experience and ability 10 years later. *Developmental Psychology, 33,* 934–945.

Dale, E., & O'Rourke, J. (1981). *The living word vocabulary*. Chicago, Ill.: World Book/Childcraft International.

Dickinson, D. K., McCabe, A., Anastasopoulos, L., Peisner-Feinberg, E. S., & Poe, M. D. (2003). The comprehensive language approach to early literacy: The interrelationships among vocabulary, phonological sensitivity, and print knowledge among preschool-aged children. *Journal of Educational Psychology, 95,* 465–481.

Elley, W. B. (1989). Vocabulary acquisition from listening to stories. *Reading Research Quarterly, 24,* 174–186.

Foorman, B. R., Seals, L. M., Anthony, J., & Pollard-Durodola (in press). A vocabulary enrichment program for third and fourth grade African-American students: Description, implementation, and impact. In B. Foorman (Ed.) *Preventing and remediating reading difficulties: Bringing science to scale*. Timonium, MD: York Press.

Hart, B., & Risley, T. (1995). *Meaningful differences in the everyday experience of young American children*. Baltimore: Paul H. Brookes.

Hart, B., & Risley, T. (1999). *The social world of children learning to talk*. Baltimore: Paul H. Brookes.

Hazenberg, S., & Hulstijn, J. H. (1996). Defining a minimal receptive second-language vocabulary for non-native university students: An empirical investigation. *Applied Linguistics, 17,* 145–163.

Nagy, W. E., & Anderson, R. (1984). The number of words in printed school English. *Reading Research Quarterly, 19,* 304–330.

Nagy, W. E., & Scott, J. A. (2001). Vocabulary processes In M. L. Kamil, P. B. Mosenthal, P. D. Pearson, & R. Barr (Eds.) *Handbook of reading research* (Vol. 3, pp. 269–284). Mahwah, NJ: Lawrence Erlbaum Associates.

National Reading Panel (2000). *Teaching children to read: An evidence-based assessment of the scientific research literature on reading and its implications for reading instruction: Reports of the subgroups*. Bethesda, MD: National Institute of Child and Human Development.

Rinsland, H. D. (1947). *A basic vocabulary of elementary school children*. New York: Macmillan

Scarborough, H. (2001). Connecting early language and literacy to later reading (dis)abilities): Evidence, theory, and practice. In S. B. Neuman & D. Dickinson (Eds.), *Handbook of early literacy research* (pp. 97–110). New York: Guildford Press.

Senechal, M. (1997). The differential effect of storybook reading on preschoolers' acquisition of expressive and receptive vocabulary. *Child Language, 24,* 123–138.

Senechal, M., Thomas, E., & Monker, J. A. (1995). Individual differences in four-year-olds' ability to learn new vocabulary. *Journal of Educational Psychology, 87,* 218–229.

White, T. G., Power, M. A., & White, S. (1989). Morphological analysis: Implications for teaching and understanding vocabulary growth. *Reading Research Quarterly, 24,* 283–304.

Chapter 12

In Pursuit of an Effective, Efficient Vocabulary Curriculum for Elementary Students

Elfrieda H. Hiebert
University of California, Berkeley

> *She ran and she ran, until the blizzard became a whiteout. Then she could run no more. While Mick and the team took refuge in Galena, seven hours ahead, Akiak burrowed into a snowdrift to wait out the storm.*
>
> *In the morning the mound of snow came alive, and out pushed Akiak.*
>
> —Blake, 1997

This 52-word excerpt contains 3 of the 22 words that are targeted for vocabulary instruction of the text *Akiak* (Blake, 1997) in the teacher's edition that accompanies the fourth-grade textbook of a basal reading program: *refuge, burrowed*, and *whiteout*. All three words appear only once in the story and in the entire fourth-grade program. Not only do these words occur infrequently in the program but also they are unlikely to occur with any frequency in typical instructional texts. According to Zeno, Ivens, Millard, and Duvvuri's (1995) analysis of 17.25 million words of school texts, *burrowed* and *whiteout* would be expected to appear less than once per one-million-word corpus and *refuge* three times. Of the 24 words that are highlighted for vocabulary instruction of this text in the teacher's edition, 11 would be expected to have one or fewer appearances per one-million-word corpus of school texts from kindergarten through college. Furthermore, the number of rare words in this text is not limited to those that have been chosen for instruction. Within this 52-word sample, there are five additional words of this type: *blizzard, Galena, mound, snowdrift,* and the title and name of the protagonist of the story, *Akiak.*

This text illustrates the vocabulary demands that face American students. Nagy and Anderson (1984) estimated the number of distinct words in school texts used in Grades 3 through 9 to be approximately 88,500 different words and, according to Zeno et al. (1995), an additional 70,000 different words are part of the corpus of texts in Grades 10 through college. Which of these words should be taught? Is the choice evident in this teacher's edition to address rare words the appropriate one?

This chapter proposes that vocabulary curricula need to be derived from principles that are grounded in research and theory, if the many American students at or below basic standards on state and national tests (Donahue, Finnegan, Lutkus, Allen, & Campbell, 2001) are to read at acceptable levels. In this chapter, such principles are identified and applied. The current principles are not proposed as the only basis for a vocabulary curriculum. However, the feature of this chapter that is proposed as invariant is the application of a set of theory- and research-based principles to defining vocabulary curricula, especially when the recipients of those curricula are the students of an entire state or, in the case of textbook programs, students across the country.

The principles that are the focus of this chapter are aimed at identifying an "effective and efficient component" of a vocabulary curriculum for Grades 1 through 4. "Effective" in the phrase refers to a vocabulary curriculum that ensures experience for elementary students with words that are unknown to them but that account for a significant portion of texts in Grades 5 and beyond. "Efficient" refers to the emphasis in this curriculum on words that have the widest possible application within texts, such as words that are in semantic families with many members. Finally, "component" is an important part of this goal in that this curriculum is regarded as part of a larger vocabulary curriculum, not the entire vocabulary curriculum, in Grades 1 through 4.

THE UNDERLYING PRINCIPLES OF THE CURRICULUM

An Effective Vocabulary Curriculum

The authors of the textbook program from which the excerpt that introduced this chapter came have chosen to direct teachers' instruction to rare words and fairly common words. In addition to the 11 rare words that were previously mentioned, 8 of the other 13 instructional words have frequencies of 100 or more per one million word corpus. Only a handful of the words are in the in-between range that Beck, McKeown, and Kucan (2002) have described as part of literate, written discourse. The words that Beck et al. have described as part of written discourse are illustrated in the following text that comes from the first unit of a second-grade science text: "Pollen, a powdery material, is made by one part of the flower. Pollen is needed to make seeds form." (Badders, Bethel, Fu, Peck, Sumners, & Valentino, 2000).

If students do not understand words such as *material, form*, and *part*, they may have difficulty understanding words that are likely new to second graders: *pollen, powdery*. The words *material, form*, and *part* occur with substantial frequency in written language: 153, 384, and 694 times per million-word corpus, respectively (Zeno et al., 1995). Young children do not necessarily know the meanings of these three words. According to Dale and O'Rourke (1981), the percentages of fourth graders—the youngest students in their study—who identified the chief meanings of *part* and *form* from several choices were 81% and 77%, respectively. The meaning of *material* was even more difficult, recognized by 91% of sixth graders but less than 67% of fourth graders. In the content areas, the meanings of such words are assumed and so it is not surprising that the teacher's edition of this science text does not direct teachers to attend to the words *material, form*, and *part*. An effective vocabulary curriculum is defined as one where the words that are used most often in literary and content area texts are taught—words such as *form, material,* and *part*.

The current interest was to establish an effective vocabulary through fourth grade. As has frequently been recognized (Chall, Jacobs, & Baldwin, 1990), Grade 4 is a watershed in students' reading. The gap between the students who are reading well and those who are not is evident at this point. In an analysis of the Degrees of Reading Power readability system, Zeno et al. (1995) provided evidence of the demands on fourth graders. If 12th-grade vocabulary is considered as constituting 100% of a word corpus, fourth-grade texts demand that students know about 84% of the vocabulary. From Grades 4 through 10, the increase in the percentage of the total vocabulary is approximately 9% and from Grades 10 to 12 the final 7%. In all likelihood, these increases from Grades 5 through 10 and from Grades 10 to 12 are in the specialized vocabularies of content areas. However, to learn this specialized vocabulary, students need to have acquired the foundational vocabulary by the end of Grade 4. An effective curriculum for the elementary years from Grades 1 through 4 should support students in acquiring the foundational vocabulary that accounts for a substantial portion of academic, written discourse.

An Efficient Vocabulary Curriculum

When analyses of word corpora indicate that approximately 88,500 unique words appear in the texts that students read from Grades 3 to 9 (Carroll, Davies, & Richman, 1971; Nagy & Anderson, 1984) and 150,000 from kindergarten through college (Zeno et al., 1995), it becomes clear that all words cannot be taught. An assumption of the current work is that students' learning of key words from semantic families with numerous members should comprise at least part of a vocabulary program. For example, by learning a group of words that come from the same root—*satisfy*, *satisfaction*, *satisfactory*, *satisfied*, *unsatisfied*—students had exposure to a semantic family almost 50 times per 1 million words. In contrast, when single words are addressed—even words with 10 appearances per million such as *cargo*, *era*, and *linen*—students have considerably less opportunity for exposure or the need to use the words. By addressing words in semantic families with at least two or more members from among the most frequently used words in written language, a curriculum can be more efficient in developing word knowledge in students.

A Component of a Vocabulary Program

Baumann et al. (chapter 9, this volume) have suggested that explicit vocabulary instruction occurs in a 20:80 ratio to reading, discussing, and learning from literature and content texts. Although the amounts of time that are devoted to explicit instruction of vocabulary may vary at different times in students' school careers, the vocabulary curriculum that the current scholarship aims to identify is intended for only part of the vocabulary experiences of elementary students. The manner in which the targeted vocabulary curriculum emanates from the texts that students are reading in reading/language arts is as yet uncertain. In that narrative texts are the almost exclusive fare of elementary reading/language arts programs (Duke, 2000) and that children's literature contains a high percentage of rare words (Hayes, Wolfer, & Wolfe, 1996), it may be difficult to attend to words that occur frequently in content areas with these narrative texts.

The identification of an effective and efficient vocabulary is the aim of this chapter, not addressing either the best materials or instructional procedures by which this vocabulary can best be taught and learned. Although a vocabulary that is effective and efficient needs to be developed in the elementary grades, this vocabulary should not be viewed as the be-all and end-all of vocabulary instruction. Words such as *connect*, *develop*, *form*, and *materials*—although critical—form only part of a vocabulary program. Vocabulary instruction is also needed of specialized vocabularies in science (e.g., *igneous*, *sedimentary*, *metaphoric*) and social studies (*equality*, *democracy*, *federal*). Furthermore, instruction is needed on strategies for figuring out the rare but context-rich words of literature such as *rambunctious* and *forlorn*.

METHOD: IDENTIFYING THE WORDS OF AN EFFECTIVE, EFFICIENT CURRICULAR COMPONENT

The process of identifying words for the proposed vocabulary curriculum occurred in two phases. The first was to identify the overall corpus that would be the focus of the curriculum; the second was to identify words within this overall corpora for inclusion in a vocabulary curriculum for Grades 1 through 4.

Choosing the Overall Corpus

Before designating particular words that might be taught, the overall corpus that underlay the vocabulary curriculum needed to be established. Decisions also needed to be made as to which portions of the corpus would be addressed.

Selecting a Database. With an underlying assumption that an elementary curriculum should address words that occur with frequency in written discourse, a search was conducted of studies that summarize word frequencies in written discourse. Beginning with Thorndike (1921), periodic efforts have been made to establish the words in texts read by children and adults. The most comprehensive and recent list of the frequencies of words in written text is that of Zeno et al. (1995). Zeno et al. established the U function of 150,000 words from a corpus of 17.25 million words that came from texts used in educating kindergarten through college students. The U function indicates the number of times a word appears per one million words of written discourse. Zeno et al. (1995) grouped words by U functions of 30,000, 10,000, 3,000, 1,000, 300, 100, 30, 10, 3, 1, and less than 1. Data on the number of words that share a U function, the proportion of total words for which the group accounts, and the proportion of the total word corpus accounted for by a single word within a group appear in Table 12.1. Inasmuch as Zeno et al.(1995) included college texts with highly specialized vocabularies in their analyses, it is not surprising to find that their list includes a higher percentage of words with frequencies less than 1 than was the case in the Carroll et al. (1971) analysis that had a smaller range of grade-level text (third through ninth grades).

Designating the Scope of a Curriculum From Grades 1 Through 4. Individual texts would not be expected to have profiles such as the one in Table 12.1. That is, a particular text at a particular grade level is unlikely to

TABLE 12.1

Definition of Word Zones

Word zone	Appearances in 1 million words	Words per zone		Proportion of total of 1-million-word corpus	Single word's contribution to total corpus (%)
		New words	Cumulative		
0	30,000	1	1	.07	7
	10,000	7	8	.21	2
	3,000	30	38	.37	.5
	1,000	69	107	.48	.16
1	300	203	310	.57	.04
2	100	620	930	.67	.02
3	30	1676	2606	.74	.004
4	10	2980	5586	.79	.002
5	3	5654	11240	.82	.0005
	1	8228	19468	.87	.0006
6	.99 and fewer	135473	154941	1.0	.0001

have 67% of its words with frequencies of 100 or more, 7% with words with frequencies of 30, and so on. But what words might be expected to be prominent in Grades 1 through 4?

To establish the vocabulary that accounts for a substantial portion of fourth-grade texts, released versions of the standards-based tests of three of the United States' four largest states[1] (Texas, New York, and Florida) and the 2002 National Assessment of Educational Progress (NAEP) were analyzed. The aim was to establish the group of words within these levels or zones that account for 90% of the vocabulary on these tests. Ninety percent was chosen because this level has typically been viewed to be the minimal level required for meaningful reading (Clay, 1985). In the frustration, instruction, and independent levels of Betts (1946), 90% designates the lower end of instructional level. Kuhn & Stahl (2003) have suggested that readers who can recognize 9 out of 10 words in a text automatically should have sufficient resources to use context to figure out the one unknown word in 10.

The results of the analysis of the passages on the fourth-grade assessments are summarized in Table 12.2. The data indicate that the three state tests and the NAEP have remarkably similar characteristics. An average of 92% of the unique words on all three state tests and the NAEP assessment

---

[1]Sample items or passages from the standards-based assessment of America's largest state, California, were not available to researchers at the time this chapter was written.

TABLE 12.2

Percentages of Unique Words in Word Zones:
Three Primary States and NAEP

Word zone	FCAT, 2003		NY State, 2003		TAKS, 2003		NAEP (2002)		Average per zone(s)
		Cumulative		Cumulative		Cumulative		Cumulative	
0–2	67	67	72	72	70	70	80	80	72.3
3	16	83	12	84	10.5	80.5	7	87	11.1
4	8	91	8	92	11	91.5	6	93	8.3
5	8	99	5.5	97.5	6	97.5	6.5	99.5	6.5
6	1	100	2.5	100	2.5	100	.5	100	1.6

was accounted for by words with U functions of 10 appearances or more per one million-word corpus. In light of this consistency across large-state assessments and the NAEP, it could be argued that the most effective curriculum through fourth grade consists of words with frequencies of 10 or more per million words of text.

Within a curriculum that moves fourth graders to proficiency with this corpus of words, words with particular U functions will be referred to as *word zones*. A first choice in establishing word zones was to exclude the first 107 words that have U functions of 1,000 or more from the developmental vocabulary curriculum. These words are ones that serve grammatical functions in written discourse (e.g., *the, of, and, a*) and, although first graders may be able to recognize them, most first graders (as well as proficient adult readers) may be hard-pressed to define these words. However, fluency in recognizing these words automatically is required for the initiation of a vocabulary curriculum. For lack of a better label, this zone will be identified as "0."

Vocabulary instruction would begin with word zone 1—those words that appear 300 times per 1 million words. This word zone is proposed as the target for instruction in Grade 1. Each subsequent frequency group is described as a word zone with the number of its corresponding grade level. By the fourth word zone (corresponding to Grade 4), approximately 80% of the entire word corpus through college (Zeno et al., 1995), 90% through ninth grade (Carroll et al., 1971), and approximately 92% of the words on the standards-based tests of prominent states and on the NAEP are accounted for.

The words with frequencies less than 10 occurrences per 1 million words are not a focus of the Grades 1 through 4 developmental curriculum. The numbers that correspond with these two zones—5 and 6—are not meant to imply a focus for a particular grade. Hopefully, specialized vocabularies that are represented in these word zones would be taught in Grades 5 and above. The current work aims to establish a vocabulary curriculum that will support fourth graders in reading content area and literary texts with sufficient knowledge of frequent words to leave enough cognitive resources for figuring out unknown words.

Identifying the Target Words Within the Word Zones

The analysis of tests supported attention to particular zones of words. The next step was to establish which words within these zones should be the focus at a grade level. Two criteria were applied in establishing the appropriateness of words for instruction: (a) their semantic connections and (b) their known-ness to students at particular grade levels.

Semantic Families.   The 5,586 words from zones 1 through 4 were analyzed for semantic families. To establish these semantic families, Nagy and Anderson's (1984) categorization scheme was used. In their investigation of the number of distinct words in printed English using the Carroll et al. (1971) word list, Nagy and Anderson (1984) developed a set of categories of semantic relatedness. These categories were formed to answer the question, "Assuming that a child knew the meaning of the immediate ancestor, but not the meaning of the target word, to what extent would the child be able to determine the meaning of the target word when encountering it in context while reading?" (Nagy & Anderson, 1984, p. 310).

Target words and their immediate ancestors from the 5,586 words are given in Table 12.3 for each of Nagy and Anderson's six categories. In their first category, a target word's meaning can be established immediately, if the ancestor of the family is known. The sixth and final category on Nagy and Anderson's (1984) semantic relatedness scale is described as having "no discernible semantic connection; the meaning of the immediate answer is of no use in learning or remembering the meaning of the target word" (p. 311). They classify the first three categories as semantically transparent and the last three as semantically opaque. The former refers to relationships where meaning of an unknown target word can be accurately ascertained based on knowing a related word, whereas the latter refers to relationships where the meaning of the unknown word is sufficiently different that the meaning of a known word is not useful or even distracts from the appropriate meaning. The current aim in identifying a first- through fourth-grade curriculum was to stay in the "semantically transparent" set of categories (Nagy and Anderson's first three) rather than semantically opaque (their last three).

The first clustering of words into semantic families was on the basis of inflected endings. Whereas the focus of the semantic relatedness categories is

TABLE 12.3

Examples of Target Word and Immediate Ancestor
for Six Categories of Semantic Relatedness[1]

	Target Word	Immediate Ancestor
0	automatically	automatic
	achievement	achieve
1	Sunshine, sunlight, sunset	sun
	shiny	shine
2	knowledge	know
	everyday	every
3	password	pass
	visualize	visual
4	apartment	apart
	artificial	artifice
5	prefix	fix
	peppermint	pepper

[1]These categories were first identified by Nagy and Anderson (1984).

on suffixation, prefixation, and compounds of root words, inflected endings account for a substantial number of the members of semantic families. To establish semantic relatedness among words with suffixes, prefixes, and compounds of root words, meanings were confirmed with the Merriam-Webster Online Dictionary (2002). Although the aim was to stay with semantic families where connections across members were semantically transparent, the connections across words can become complex. The difficulties are evident in Nagy and Anderson's (1984) acknowledgement that "exact agreement on the 6-point scale was not achieved" (p. 312). Even in sorting between the two general categories of transparent and opaque, Nagy and Anderson (1984) reported an agreement level of 76.6%. Whereas each of the members of a semantic family is tied directly to the root word, connections between pairs of words in families can be less transparent. Take, for example, words related to *vision*. Nagy and Anderson give *visual* (ancestor) and *visualize* (target word) as illustrating semantic category 4—where the meaning of the target item includes semantic features that are not inferable from the meaning of the immediate ancestor without substantial help from the context. Although *visualize* is not among the 5,586 words, *visual, vision, visible,* and *invisible* are. All of these words are defined in relation to *vision* by Merriam-Webster (2002). Consequently, all of these words are clustered into the same semantic family, even though the connection between *visual* and *visible* is not as transparent as that, for example, between *visual* and *vision* or between *vision* and *visible*.

A semantic family was assigned to the zone in which the first member of the family appeared. For example, *continued* appears in zone 2, whereas *continue* appears in zone 3. The latter is the ancestor of the former. However, the semantic family with these words (and others) was assigned to zone 2.

Word Known-ness.   The vocabulary curricula of basal reading programs have been criticized as addressing known words (Beck et al., 2002). To ensure that the current curriculum was the most effective one possible, a measure was needed to establish "known-ness" of words. A chapter on defining a vocabulary curriculum should not be proposing the addition of new words to the lexicon. However, the various words that have been proposed to describe the construct of children's grasp of a word's meaning (e.g., familiarity, knowledge, understanding) do not convey the emphasis on words that students already understand. Consequently, the word *known-ness* is used to describe students' knowledge of word meanings.

To establish the appropriate range of "word known-ness," the key words from semantic families were vetted through two procedures: (a) eliminating words that are known by the overwhelming majority of a grade cohort and (b) moving words from a zone where they may be too difficult for grade-level students to an appropriate zone.

The Dale and O'Rourke (1981) *Living Word Vocabulary* (LWV) and Biemiller and Slocum's (2001) adaptations of it were used as resources for both procedures. The methods whereby the LWV was developed and the time frame within which it was validated make the LWV a less-than-ideal resource for use with students in the early part of the 21st century. At the present time, however, the LWV is the only comprehensive, existing database on students' familiarity with word meanings. It consists of 44,000 word meanings that have been assigned to grade levels based on at least 67% of a grade-level cohort correctly identifying a word's meaning from three choices. Dale and O'Rourke (1981) gathered information on students from grades 4, 6, 8, 10, 12, and young adults. Words that were recognized by more than 80% of an age cohort were given to students at the next lower grade level. As fourth graders were the youngest students tested, the words in the sample—11%—that were known to this group were assigned a Level/Grade 4 rating. Biemiller and Slocum (2001) identified these words as a Level 2. Biemiller and Slocum (2001) examined a small percentage of words from Level 2 with students ranging from kindergarten through sixth grade. Of the 20 Level-2 words that were tested, 80% or more of second graders knew half of the words. Even 80% of the first-grade cohort knew a quarter of the Level 2 words.

In addition to procedures used to establish the LWV, issues of cultural specificity of words for particular age cohorts and economic and linguistic groups leave numerous questions about the LWV. A word that was known by 69% of sixth graders according to Dale and O'Rourke (1981)—*shot,* as in an injection—was known by 83% of first graders and 94% of second graders in the Biemiller and Slocum (2001) sample. Other words may be specific to time periods, such as these words on the Dale-Chall (Chall & Dale, 1995) list: *boxcar* and *tiddlywinks.* Both words achieve Biemiller and Slocum's (2001) Level 2 status by virtue of being known by 80% of fourth graders that were sampled by Dale and O'Rourke (1981) over the two decades that preceded its initial publication in 1976.

Because of shortcomings in the LWV system, an additional resource was used for decisions of inclusion or exclusion on grade-level lists in the present study: The Ginn Word Book for Teachers (GWBT; Johnson & Moe with Baumann, 1983). To develop a listing of 9,000 words in the GWBT, Johnson et al. (1983) developed a composite rating of a word based on (a) word frequency in middle-grade texts (based on the Carroll et al. [1971] list), (b) word frequency in popular trade books for primary grades, and (c) words in the speaking vocabularies of first-grade students. These composite ratings were used to rank words and from these rankings, words were assigned to grade-level groups. For example, whereas the word *form* in zone 1 has a LWV rating of 77% for fourth graders, the GWBT places this word in the first half of Grade 1. As the GWBT is based on word frequencies through ninth grade (Carroll et al., 1971), primary-level trade books, and speaking vocabularies of first graders, this verification indicates that it is a word that has some applicability to first graders.

The percentages on the LWV were assigned numbers on a scale with the same number of points as the GWBT: 23. Category 1 encompassed ratings of 96% and higher at fourth-grade level on the LWV, and each subsequent point represented a span of five percentage points. The final point of 23 represented words that had ratings of 94 or lower at Grade 10 on the LWV.

A summary score was established by dividing the sum of the LWV and GWBT scores. The ranges for the word zones/grade levels were as follows: (a): Zone 0/Primer: 1–3; (b) Zone One/Grade 1: 4–6; (c) Zone Two/Grade 2: 7–11; (d) Zone Three/Grade 3: 12–14; and (e) Zone Four/Grade 4: 15–17. For example, the word *form* had a sum of 4.5 (5 for the 77% Grade 4 LWV rating plus the 4 rating in the GWBT). This meant that the word remained in zone 1, where the first member of the family appeared. Words with scores that were more than one level below a grade-level range (e.g., 5 for words in zone/grade 2) were eliminated, while words with ratings that were more than one level above a grade-level range (i.e., 13 for zone/grade two) were moved to the next word zone. The numbers of words within a particular zone/grade, those that were eliminated, and those that were moved to dif-

ferent word zones appear in Table 12.4. Table 12.5 provides examples of
words from each of the four target word zones.

RESULTS: DESCRIBING THE VOCABULARY CURRICULUM

The summary of numbers of words in Table 12.4 and the illustrated words
in Table 12.5 support several observations about the proposed vocabulary. The first observation pertains to the number of semantic families. Of
the 5,586 words that are likely to appear 10 or more times per one-million-word corpus, approximately 10% represent a cluster of semantic relatedness within the corpus and are sufficiently unknown to a critical
portion of an age cohort to merit instruction. Approximately 550 words
taught over the course of four grades would seem to be a doable task, in
light of previous projects (e.g., Baumann, Edwards, Boland, Olejnik, &
Kame'enui, 2003; Beck, McKeown, & McCaslin, 1983). As the distribution
indicates in Table 12.4, the numbers of words that need to be taught differ
for different grade-level groups. At Grades 1 and 2, when children are developing the fundamental fluency that serves as the foundation for their
reading, the number of words that require direct, varied, and rich instruction is substantially lower than in Grades 3 and 4. In Grades 3 and 4, the
chief reading task changes from fluency building to vocabulary building.
At this point, the number of words that require direct, varied, and rich instruction increases substantially.

A second observation is that each of these semantic groups accounts for,
on average, 3 words in the 5,586 most-frequent words in kindergarten
through college texts. That is, instruction in the 538 words of this designated vocabulary curriculum will address approximately 30% of the 5,586

TABLE 12.4
Curriculum Focus Words and Sources

Word zone & grade	Total words	Semantic families	Semantic families with 2+ members	Unknown semantic families	Carryover	Zone-focus words
1	203	160	124	49	8 to Zone 2; 1 to Zone 3	40
2	620	231	221	76	18 to Zone 3	86
3	1676	840	612	250	20 to Zone 2; 24 to Zone 4	225
4	2980	1233	332	163		187

TABLE 12.5

Illustrations of Words Within the Four Target Zones/Grades

Word Zone/Grade	Words within Zone/Grade
1	body
	important
	form
	believe
	example
2	nature
	scientists
	behavior
	considered
	section
3	defense
	express
	sample
	style
	managed
4	exposed
	minor
	tense
	associated
	merchandise

most-frequent words. Furthermore, these are words that have meanings that at least a core group of students are likely *not* to know.

Third, many of the words have a high level of utility across the texts of several content areas. As part of their database, Zeno et al. (1995) provided a dispersion index that indicates the level to which a word appears across texts from different content areas. Altogether, texts from nine content areas were sampled in their corpus—language arts and literature, social science, science and math, fine arts, home economics and related fields, trade and technical fields, health and safety, business, and popular fiction and nonfiction. A word that appears in numerous content areas, such as *fact*, has a dispersion index of .99. Because of Zeno et al.'s (1995) sampling procedure (a relatively small sample of texts from numerous grade levels across numerous content areas), those words that appeared frequently would be expected to have high dispersion indexes. This pattern was confirmed. Only a few words with frequencies of 10 or more per one-million-word corpus had lower dispersion indexes. These words are important but specific to a particular content area such as *acid*, a zone 3 word, with a dispersion index of .65 and *government*, a zone 1 word, with a dispersion index of .71. On average, however, words with appearances of 10 or more per one-million-word corpus had dispersion indexes of .88. That is, the words in this curriculum have high utility across content areas.

This utility across content areas also means that the majority of words have a range of meanings, often specific to particular content areas. For example, the word *style* in zone 3 is fairly typical of the group. It has 12 meanings, including ones that are part of literary language (distinction; manner; current fashion) and content areas (the part of a carpel between the stigma and ovary in botany; a projection on some insects in zoology; and a particular manner of dealing with spelling, punctuation in printing). Few of these meanings can be learned by a simple association with a known word. To understand these various meanings will not be a simple task.

Additional analyses are being conducted on the characteristics of these words such as parts of speech and imagery value. One characteristic of the words as a group that seems highly promising is the number of words that have a shared cognate with Spanish. Within a group of 50 words from the curricular list that were randomly selected, non-Spanish-speaking adults were asked to write the English equivalent of the word when given exposure to the Spanish word for a second (e.g., *aceptar/accept, horizonte/horizon*). They identified the corresponding English word for 53% of the corpus.

CAUTIONS, IMPLICATIONS, AND CONCLUSIONS

The proposed curriculum requires substantial validation before it can be established that it is, indeed, effective and efficient in increasing the reading comprehension of students in the middle grades. Caveats related to the principles that were chosen for this curriculum need to be addressed. But even with these caveats, the use of principles—the specific ones used in this project as well as others—should be the source of considerable discussion among policymakers and researchers. Furthermore, while the particular curriculum described in this chapter should be one of many, a set of guidelines can be useful to the many classroom teachers across the country who are aware that their students require vocabulary guidance that is substantially more disciplined than that which is currently available.

Cautions

A primary caution about the methodology that was used in establishing the effective, efficient vocabulary curriculum presented in this chapter was the criteria for known-ness. In particular, the systems available for establishing known-ness of words do not reflect the norms of early elementary students at the beginning of the 21st century. Both the Dale and O'Rourke (1981) and the Johnson et al. (1983) systems were developed with students and/or texts in the decades prior to an extensive immigration of speakers of languages other than English to American schools during the 1980s and 1990s. While the Dale and O'Rourke system has been examined with English-language learners to some degree (Biemiller & Slocum, 2001), numerous questions remain about the generalizability of this list to 21st-century students, especially those who speak Spanish as a native language. For example, native Spanish speakers may grasp the meanings of words where the common word in Spanish has a transparent Latin cognate for the English word more quickly than native English speakers.

Implications for Scholars

In choosing vocabulary for the elementary curriculum, a fundamental issue is the role of text in guiding the selection of vocabulary. The text excerpt that introduced this chapter is typical of literature where the number of rare words is high (Hayes et al., 1996). Literary writers, unlike those who write even the informational texts that are sold on the trade rather than textbook market (Duke & Kays, 1998), use many words a single time. When writers of narrative want to communicate a trait or an action of a character, they select words that are specific. This use of words by narrative writers is illustrated in the introductory excerpt from *Akiak* (Blake, 1997) where Akiak burrows into the snowdrift and pushes out of a mound of snow. The same nouns and verbs are not repeated as the writer selects words to communicate nuances of behavior or character traits.

Because an overwhelming portion of the texts of reading instruction consists of narrative literature from trade books (Duke, 2000; Hoffman, Roser, Patterson, Salas, & Pennington, 2001), the number of unique per total words is high in current textbook programs (Foorman, Francis, Davidson, Harm, & Griffin, 2004). As is typical of narrative literature, many of the unique words in the anthologies of first-grade basal programs appear a single time (Foorman et al., 2004).

As the instruction of vocabulary has typically occurred as part of reading lessons and in connection with the reading textbooks, these characteristics of school texts have consequences for the vocabularies students are acquiring. This observation does not mean that a vocabulary curriculum should be disconnected from the texts of instructional lessons. The first criterion for the words in the present effective and efficient vocabulary curriculum was their frequency in text. In that the "dispersion" index of the words was used to confirm the choice of words for the vocabulary curriculum, few words are used in a single content area. This frequency in literate, written discourse is also evident in the literature used in the basal reading programs. When an analysis was done of the texts of the first unit of a fourth-grade basal program, which included *Akiak*, the 5,538 words that were the basis for this curriculum accounted for 82% of the unique words. Although this percentage was lower than that of the texts on the state and national standards-based assessments, the most frequent words of a literate, written word corpus also account for a significant percentage of words in literature. The difficulty of attending to the multiple meanings and derivatives of high-frequency words such as *associated* and *tense* in literature is illustrated by the examples from *Akiak*. The high-frequency words are present, but the percentage of rare words in children's literature is higher than is typical of fourth-grade assessments. Rather than needing to be able to attend to 1 unknown word per 100, the literature—at least of this widely used basal program (Cooper et al., 2003)—requires students to be able to figure out 2 unknown words per 100.

The question is whether the texts of instruction, especially the narrative texts that are now common to basal reading programs, should drive the "explicit" vocabulary curriculum. An alternative is suggested in the report of the National Reading Panel (2000): "A large portion of vocabulary items should be derived from content learning materials" (pp. 4–25). Not only does vocabulary instruction with content text prepare students for the texts that can be challenging for many students (Chall et al., 1990) but, as Duke and Kays (1998) have shown, vocabulary representing critical concepts is repeated in informational text. This repetition is evident in the writing of Gail Gibbons, a well-known author of informational trade books. When the word *cultivated* is first introduced in *The Berry Book* (Gibbons, 2002), Gibbons repeats it several times: "Some berries are grown in gardens. They are called cultivated berries. Cultivated berries also are grown in nurseries and on farms. Cultivated berries are harvested in different ways (pp. 13–14).

Implications for Policymakers and Publishers

The proposed curriculum requires substantial validation with students before it can have widespread dissemination. However, policymakers and publishers can apply this work's aim of using a principled approach to select vocabulary for instruction. The principles of effectiveness and efficacy have a strong foundation in existing theory and research. Other principles may well be applied. One such construct that has a substantial foundation in theory and research is semantic connections (Marzano & Marzano, 1988). Marzano and Marzano (1988) organized 7,230 words that are commonly found in elementary school texts. They grouped these words into 61 superclusters of meaning—tied together by a common theme such as transportation or location/direction.

A thematic construct such as that suggested by the Marzano and Marzano (1988) superclusters is presumably what underlies the selection of literature—and subsequently vocabulary—in the textbook program from which the illustration that introduced the chapter came (Cooper et al., 2003). The story *Akiak* (Blake, 1997) is in a theme entitled "Journeys" with three other texts: *Grandfather's Journey* (Say, 1993), *Finding the Titanic* (Ballard, 1993), and *By the Shores of Silver Lake* (Wilder, 1939). Attempts to organize the 85 words that are highlighted for vocabulary attention in the teacher's manual did not result in discernible semantic categories, either from the Marzano and Marzano (1988) clusters or other groupings. However, when the 1,009 unique words in this unit were reexamined and the 246 words from zones 3 and 4 in the proposed vocabulary (words with probable appearances of 10 and 30 within a one-million-word corpus) became the focus, 35 words were readily sorted into five semantic categories pertaining to journeys. The results of this activity appear in Table 12.6. In examining the categories and words in Table 12.6, the usefulness and potential power of such a scheme for student learning are evident.

TABLE 12.6

Vocabulary From a Fourth-Grade Basal Reading Unit:
Clustered According to Semantic Categories

Subcategory of Journeys	Vocabulary Words
Feelings people might have on journeys	Amazed, anxious, confused, alert, excited, frightened, brave, miserable, satisfied, dangerous
Actions that might be part of journeys	Explored, escaped, disappeared, struggling, rescued, arrived, greet, arrived, fidget
Places that people might travel over/see on journeys	Valley, trail, deserts, harbor, creek, hotel
Descriptions of perilous places that might be encountered on journeys	Rugged, towering, steep, descent, slopes
People who might be encountered on journeys	Conductor, passengers, survivors, crew, pilot

This scheme illustrates that many principles could drive a vocabulary curriculum. The critical perspective, however, is that a vocabulary curriculum has an apparent set of underlying principles based on theory and empirical validation. The principles from scholarship that publishers have used to specify vocabulary in their programs need to be unveiled and examined by users in states and districts. In the same vein, the standards of states that give publishers guidance in choosing vocabulary need to be revisited. Do state standards provide teachers and publishers sufficient guidance to implement a vocabulary curriculum that is effective and efficient? At the current time, the vocabulary standards of most states and published reading programs are vague and nebulous. If students are to read with expertise and interest in the middle grades and beyond, vocabulary curricula must be clear and defined according to a set of principles drawn from scholarship.

Implications for Teachers

Although the responsibility for identifying a core vocabulary should not be placed on the already heavily laden shoulders of classroom teachers, many classroom teachers will recognize the need and usefulness of an effective and efficient vocabulary curriculum. For those who cannot wait until state agencies and committees have identified principles and applied them to a vocabulary curriculum, three questions can guide the amount of time that teachers spend on particular vocabulary. The first question a teacher can ask in examining the critical vocabulary in a text is: Which unknown words might students know by association with known words? Graves (1984) hypothesized that there are many words for which students already have a concept. They simply do not have this particular label for the word. A simple association can be made to the new vocabulary when the known label is elicited. For example, two of the three words that are highlighted for vocabulary instruction from the text excerpt that introduced this chapter—*burrowed* and *whiteout*—can be treated in this manner. Students are familiar with the word *dig*, which defines *burrowed* in this context, while *whiteout* is easily defined in relation to a snowstorm. The word *refuge*, by contrast, could merit a more extended discussion. In the context of this text, *refuge* is used as a protected spot. The word is used in different content areas with sufficiently distinct meanings that this word and the derivative, *refugees*, could support the development of a rich vocabulary among students.

A second question is: Which words in the text have derivatives that are frequent in students' reading and writing? In considering the text that introduced this chapter, consider this sentence: "Six hours after Mick and the team had left, Akiak padded softly, cautiously, into the checkpoint." The word that is singled out for vocabulary instruction in this sentence is *checkpoint*, a word that occurs infrequently and can be identified through association with the roots in this compound word. The word *cautiously*, on the other hand, is part of a family that has members that can be expected to appear frequently and in a range of subject areas: *cautious, caution (-s, -ed, -ing)*, and *cautionary*. Furthermore, the reason for Akiak's cautionary approach merits discussion as part of the story.

Third, with which words might students need support because of the multiple meanings of the word? Again, drawing from the text *Akiak*, consider the following two sentences: "Screaming winds threw bitter cold at the team as they fought their way along the coast." and "'That old dog will never make it!' he laughed at Akiak across the biting wind." Neither *bitter* nor *biting* is targeted for vocabulary attention in the teacher's edition. Both words, however, are within zone 4 families (words that appear with frequencies of 10 to 29 times per one-million-word corpus). These two words are not members of the same semantic family, at least when the criterion is semantic transparency. However, they do have the same historical root and both have multiple meanings and are used across subject areas (their dispersion indices are .8). Both words deserve attention in this context because the author's use differs from their most common definitions. Furthermore, both words are used in numerous metaphors. Not only is *bitter* used to describe the attitude of characters in narratives but things are described as *bitter-sad* and someone waits until *the bitter end*. Similarly, several phrases use the word *bite*, as in *bite the bullet* and *bite off more than can be chewed*. Selecting vocabulary based on answers to these three questions can go a long way to developing a broad and also deep vocabulary.

Conclusions

Among the most pressing questions that empirical investigations of the proposed curriculum need to address is the nature of instruction that best supports learning of these words. The National Reading Panel (2000) summarized the need for both direct instruction and exposure to many, varied texts. The latter has been viewed as the means for incidental learning of vocabulary (Anderson, Fielding, & Wilson, 1988). Anderson et al. (1988) reported that the amount of vocabulary that fourth- and fifth-graders acquired through after-school reading of text was reflected in comprehension scores on school tests. The nature of fluency with complex and abstract words as a result of differing amounts of school reading has not been considered. Although after-school learning cannot be manipulated in school investigations, the amount of in-school reading can be. If the goal of a million words of reading (the amount of out-of-school reading done by Anderson et al.'s [1988] most prolific readers) is applied to school reading from Grades 1 through 4, students would have had exposure to the words on the target curriculum a minimum of 20 times each. This minimum number reflects the manner in which words in the curriculum were chosen: (a) only words with frequencies of 10 or more per million were addressed (through zone 4) and (b) only semantic families with two or more members were included. In that available research indicates that middle graders need to see words in texts from six to 12 times to use them knowledgeably, students will have had sufficient exposure to these words—many of which may require even more exposure because of their abstractness. How differing amounts of extended reading and of direct instruction affect students' understanding of the complex vocabulary that has been identified here should be a focus of future study. Yet, although many questions remain about this particular curriculum, there can be little question that systematic attention is needed to vocabulary curricula on state and national levels. If the trajectories of the substantial portion of American students who are not now reading at designated levels are to change, vocabulary instruction will need to be effective and efficient.

REFERENCES

Anderson, R. C., Fielding, L. G., and Wilson, P. T. (1988). Growth in reading and how children spend time outside of school. *Reading Research Quarterly, 23,* 285–304.

Badders, W., Bethel, L. J., Fu, V., Peck, D., Sumners, C., & Valentino, C. (2000). *Houghton Mifflin Science DiscoveryWorks: California Edition.* Boston, MA: Houghton Mifflin.

Ballard, R. D. (1993). *Finding the Titanic.* New York: Cartwheel Books.

Baumann, J. F., Edwards, E. C., Boland, E. M., Olejnik, S., & Kame'enui, E. J. (2003). Vocabulary tricks: Effects of instruction in morphology and context on fifth-grade students' ability to derive and infer word meanings. *American Educational Research Journal, 40,* 447–494.

Beck, I. L., McKeown, M. G., & Kucan, L. (2002). *Bringing words to life: Robust vocabulary instruction.* New York: The Guilford Press.

Beck, I. L., McKeown, M. G., & McCaslin, E. S. (1983). Vocabulary development: All contexts are not created equal. *The Elementary School Journal, 83,* 177–181.

Betts, E. (1946). *Foundations of reading instruction.* New York: American Book.

Biemiller, A., & Slocum, N. (2001). Estimating root word vocabulary growth in normative and advantaged populations: Evidence for a common sequence of vocabulary acquisition. *Journal of Educational Psychology, 93,* 498–520.

Blake, R. J. (1997). *Akiak.* New York: Philomel Books.

Carroll, J. B., Davies, P., & Richman, B. (1971). *The American Heritage word frequency book.* Boston: Houghton Mifflin.

Chall, J. S., & Dale, E. (1995). *Readability revisited: The new Dale-Chall readability formula.* Cambridge, MA: Brookline Books.

Chall, J. S., Jacobs, V. A., & Baldwin, L. E. (1990). *The reading crisis: Why poor children fall behind.* Cambridge, MA: Harvard University Press.

Clay, M. M. (1985). *The early detection of reading difficulties* (3rd ed.). Portsmouth, NH: Heinemann.

Cooper, J. D., Pikulski, J. J., Ackerman, P. A., Au, K. H., Chard, D. J., Garcia, G. G., Goldenberg, C. N., Lipson, M. Y., Page, S. E., Templeton, S., Valencia, S. W., & Vogt, M. E. (2003). *Houghton Mifflin Reading.* Boston: Houghton Mifflin.

Dale, E., & O'Rourke, J. (1981). *Living word vocabulary*. Chicago: World Book/Childcraft International.

Donahue, P. L., Finnegan, R. J., Lutkus, A. D., Allen, N. L., & Campbell, J. R. (2001). *The nation's report card for reading: Fourth grade*. Washington, DC: National Center for Education Statistics.

Duke, N. K. (2000). 3.6 minutes per day: The scarcity of informational texts in first grade. *Reading Research Quarterly,35*(2), 202–24.

Duke, N. K., & Kays, J. (1998). "Can I say 'Once upon a time'?": Kindergarten children developing knowledge of information book language. *Early Childhood Research Quarterly, 13*, 295–318.

Foorman, B. R., Francis, D. J., Davidson, K. C., Harm, M. W., & Griffin, J. (2004). Variability in text features in six grade 1 basal reading programs. *Scientific Studies of Reading, 8*, 167–197.

Gibbons, G. (2002). *The Berry House*. New York: Holiday House.

Graves, M.F. (1984). Selecting vocabulary to teach in the intermediate and secondary grades. In J. Flood (Ed.), *Promoting reading comprehension* (pp. 245–260). Newark, DE: International Reading Association.

Hayes, D. P., Wolfer, L. T., & Wolfe, M. F. (1996). Schoolbook simplification and its relation to the decline in SAT-verbal scores. *American Educational Research Journal, 33*, 489–508.

Hoffman, J., Roser, N., Patterson, E., Salas, R., & Pennington, J. (2001). Text leveling and little books in first-grade reading. *Journal of Literacy Research, 33*, 507–528.

Johnson, D. D., & Moe, A. J. with Baumann, J. F. (1983). *The Ginn word book for teachers: A basic lexicon*. Boston, MA: Ginn & Company.

Kuhn, M. R., & Stahl, S. A. (2003). Fluency: A review of developmental and remedial practices. *Journal of Educational Psychology, 95*, 3–21.

Marzano, R. J., & Marzano, J. S. (1988). *A cluster approach to elementary vocabulary instruction*. Newark, DE: International Reading Association.

Merriam-Webster (2002). *Merriam-Webster online dictionary*. Boston: Author.

Nagy, W. E., & Anderson, R. C. (1984). How many words are there in printed school English? *Reading Research Quarterly, 19*, 304–330.

National Reading Panel. (2000). *Teaching children to read: An evidence-based assessment of the scientific research literature on reading and its implications for reading instruction*. Washington, DC: NICHD.

Say, A. (1993). *Grandfather's journey*. Boston: Houghton Mifflin Co.

Thorndike, E. L. (1921). *The teacher's word book*. New York: Columbia University Press.

Wilder, L. I. (1939). *By the shores of Silver Lake*. New York: HarperTrophy.

Zeno, S. M., Ivens, S. H., Millard, R. T., & Duvvuri, R. (1995). *The educator's word frequency guide*. New York: Touchstone Applied Science Associates, Inc.

Author Index

Subject Index